Information
Anxiety

Other books authored or co-authored by Richard Saul Wurman

Cities: Comparisons of Form and Scale
Urban Atlas: 20 American Cities
Making the City Observable
Yellow Pages of Learning Resources
Yellow Page Career Library (12 vols.)
What-If, Could-Be
Guidebook to Guidebooks
What Will Be Has Always Been: The Words of Louis I. Kahn
Various Dwellings Described in a Comparative Manner
Our Man Made Environment Book 7
Man Made Philadelphia
The Nature of Recreation
The Notebooks and Drawings of Louis I. Kahn
The ACCESS Guide Series (20 vols.)

Information
Anxiety

WHAT TO DO
WHEN INFORMATION
DOESN'T TELL YOU
WHAT YOU NEED TO KNOW

Richard Saul Wurman

BANTAM BOOKS
NEW YORK · TORONTO · LONDON · SYDNEY · AUCKLAND

This edition contains the complete text
of the original hardcover edition.
NOT ONE WORD HAS BEEN OMITTED.

INFORMATION ANXIETY
A Bantam Book / published by arrangement with
Doubleday

PRINTING HISTORY
Doubleday edition published February 1989

Bantam edition / September 1990

Library of Congress Cataloging-in-Publication Data

Wurman, Richard Saul, 1935–
Information anxiety : what to do when information doesn't tell you what you
need to know / Richard Saul Wurman. —Bantam ed.
p.   cm.
Includes bibliographical references (p. 339).
ISBN 0-553-34856-6
1. Communication.   2. Mass media.   I. Title.
[P90.W8   1988b]   89-18662
302.23′4—dc20   CIP

PRINTED IN THE UNITED STATES OF AMERICA

0 9 8 7 6 5 4 3 2 1

To Gloria Nagy, my wife and my motivation

Books are a major source of information anxiety, and I'd like to ensure that you won't feel anxious about reading this one. So, I've departed from the conventional book format in ways that I think will reduce your book-induced anxieties.

If you are nervous that someone will mention this book and you haven't read the whole volume, just take a look at the twenty-one page table of contents. It has been designed to approximate a class outline, and in it you will find all you need, not only for a good summary but also to help you plot your personal reading path.

This book has been heavily annotated with marginalia, made up of anecdotes, quotes, and references to other publications that illustrate, expand on, and sometimes depart from the text. Often when I read, the text reminds me of ideas I've read about elsewhere. I rack my brains trying to remember where. I've saved you the trouble by including in the margins the kind of material you might be trying to remember when you are reading the text—and you don't have to leave your chair. Material that was paraphrased or summarized from the original for space considerations is marked with a ⊘. Long quotes and conversations with other people are boxed in to separate them from the text.

Unlike many other books, *Information Anxiety* doesn't have to be read sequentially. You can open to any chapter and read forward or backward. The text and the marginalia can be read together or independently. You can read the last chapter first. You can read only the even-numbered chapters.

Introduction
John Naisbitt

1

A weekday edition of The New York Times *contains more information than the average person was likely to come across in a lifetime in seventeenth-century England.*

When I was a child in Philadelphia, my father told me that I didn't need to memorize the contents of the Encyclopaedia Britannica; I just needed to know how to find what is in it.

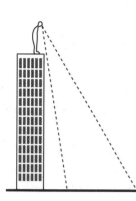

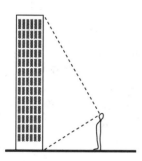

The 5 ways of organizing
information:

Category
Time
Location
Alphabet
Continuum

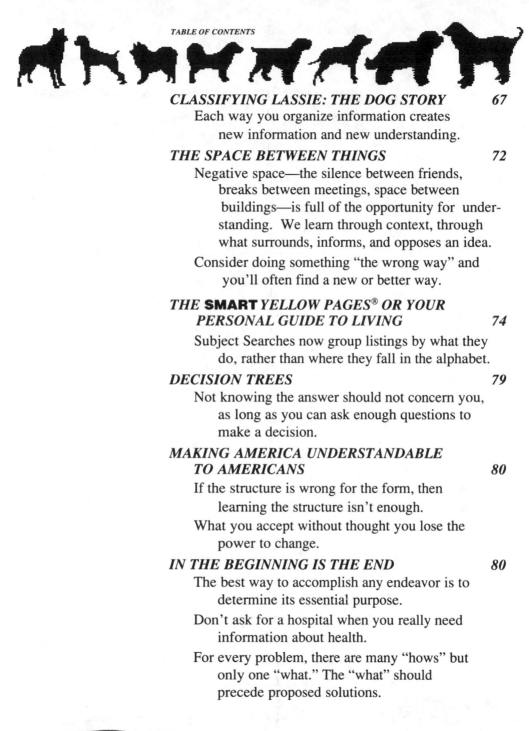

Computers have become a ubiquitous symbol of a new age, mascots of the information era and of a new way of thinking.

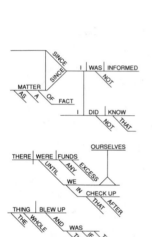

Sentence diagram adapted from *Harper's* magazine, taken from *Roll Call*, a Washington D.C. weekly.

Communication is equivocal. We are limited by a language where words may mean one thing to one person and quite something else to another. There is no ordained right way to communicate. At least in the absolute sense, it is impossible to share our thoughts with someone else, for they will not be understood in exactly the same way.

Since the advent of the industrial age, we have had a terrific word: "more." It really worked for everything. When our roads became crowded, we built more roads. When our cities became unsafe, we hired more police officers, ordered more police cars, and built more prisons.

Learning can be seen as the acquisition of information, but before it can take place, there must be interest; interest permeates all endeavors and precedes learning. In order to acquire and remember new knowledge, it must stimulate your curiosity in some way.

Finally a world-class guide constructed like the city itself! **ACCESS**●PRESS presents the city in geographical order. Brilliantly designed and easy to read, the form of the book follows the form of the city, providing instant orientation and an historical explanation of London's magical streets and squares. Feast at ★, ★★ & ★★★ restaurants, wine bars & pubs. Shop at bountiful boutiques and browse unique galleries. Stay at cozy comfortable or luxurious landmark hotels. View museums through the connoisseur's infallible eyes. A plethora of specially created maps, illustrations & lists of celebrities' personal favorites unveil London's deepest hidden treasures. This guide is as fascinating to read in an armchair before your trip as it is extraordinarily useful to carry in your pocket as you **ACCESS** the exotic theater of London from this unequalled backstage vantage point.

LONDONACCESS© *Cover*

Contrary to Voltaire's Dr. Pangloss, we are not living in the best of all possible worlds. Not only are we overwhelmed by the sheer amount of information, most of us are also hampered by an education that inadequately trains us to process it.

*Follow your own pathways to
learning.*

The origin of the word "Eureka" is attributed to Archimedes on discovering the principle of specific gravity. As the story goes, he was sitting in the bathtub and, as the water ran over him, the idea came to him, and he shouted, "Eureka, I understand!"

Which one of the following descriptions of the size of an acre is more understandable? Which is more accurate?

1   an acre is 43,560 square feet in area.

2   an acre is about the size of a football field without the end zones.

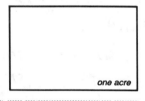
one acre

American football field

The winds of Puget Sound twisted, contorted, and destroyed the Tacoma Narrows Bridge—but also prompted urgent and exacting aerodynamic research that ultimately benefited all forms of steel construction.

We are what we read. In both our professional and personal life, we are judged by the information we peruse. The information we ingest shapes our personalities, contributes to the ideas we formulate, and colors our view of the world.

11

When people were dependent on the town crier for their news of the world, the amount of disturbing and anxiety-producing information they came across was rather limited; there was only one channel, so to speak, and people didn't have to spend much time comparing sources. The boundaries of their world were narrow and manageable.

Every day we see thousands of "events" that take place around us. Inasmuch as an event is "anything that happens or is regarded as happening," everything we see or hear can be regarded as an event, albeit of varying consequence.

Palmanova from *Cities: A Comparison of Form and Scale.*

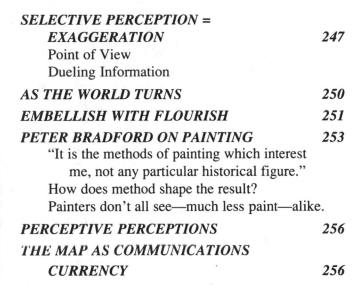

You cannot perceive anything without a map. A map provides people with the means to share in the perceptions of others. It is a pattern made understandable; it is a rigorous, accountable form that follows implicit principles, rules, and measures.

14

The information explosion didn't occur solely because of an increase in information. Advances in the technology of transmitting and storing it are as much a factor. We are affected as much by the flow as by the production of information.

15 ℞

Most people regard information processing as a specific job undertaken by people who wear glasses on chains and sit in vast open offices tinged with the greenish cast of hanging fluorescent light fixtures, caught in the glow of the cathode ray as they stare into computer screens.

INTRODUCTION

Richard Saul Wurman, trained as an architect of buildings, has become America's premier architect of information.

In *Information Anxiety* he relates how his father sent him from the dinner table to find answers to questions about current events. Information has been his obsession ever since, always asking how information can be structured or restructured so that people can find meaning. With the amount of information doubling every four or five years, Richard's obsession has become the task of our age.

As I defined the situation in *Megatrends*: "The life channel of the information age is communication. In simple terms, communication requires a sender, a receiver, and a communication channel. The introduction of increasingly sophisticated information technology has revolutionized that simple process. The net effect is a faster flow of information through the information channel, bringing sender and receiver closer together, or collapsing the information float—the amount of time information spends in the communication channel.

". . . The combined technologies of the telephone, computer and television have merged into an integrated information and communication system that transmits data and permits instantaneous interactions between persons and computers . . . We have for the first time an economy based on a key resource that is not only renewable, but self-generating. Running out of it is not a problem, but drowning in it is."

Richard says he is in the "understanding business." Imagine that. Someone in the business of making things *understandable*: instructions, forms, maps, guidebooks, your body, your country, your world.

At the age of 26 as a new assistant professor of architecture at North Carolina State University he gave himself a choice: he could teach about what he already knew or teach about what he didn't know. Typically, true to his passion, he chose to teach about what he didn't know so that he could learn the structure of new information.

"Access" is the key to Richard's intentionality. His company, which publishes superb guidebooks to cities, to sports, and to medicine, among other things, is named *AccessPress*. Richard wants complicated things to be easily accessible to people. He has done more to make complicated notions easily accessible to people than any other member of today's information society.

One of his most intriguing ideas is the use of conversation–good conversation–as a model for the communications industry. Conversation, as he puts it, with all its "extraordinary complexities, gentle nuances, and ephemeral magic." While a master at structuring information for clarity and accessibility, he is devoted to the notion that information need not be sterile or bland. *Information Anxiety* is clear but rich. It is modeled after "the quirkiness of conversations and associated ideas."

One of my favorite chapters is "Landmines in the Understanding Field." Noting that the process of information transmission is laden with traps, he identifies a long list, including one of my pet peeves—"unnecessary exactitude" (e.g. when someone in a speech says "revenues increased 60.17 percent").

He also identifies the exotic malady of a "Chinese-dinner memory dysfunction": total memory loss one hour after learning something.

Another landmine is "overload amnesia," a function of trying to assimilate information over which you cannot control the flow: "This is why after listening to a particularly ponderous speech, not only can you not remember a thing the speaker said, but you forget where you parked your car, too."

Richard has some very intelligent things to say about education in this age of information anxiety.

"Learning is remembering what you are interested in" is one of his most important formulations. He says that learning "involves nurturing an interest" and is a guide for all his work and living. "I have tried to encourage my own children's interests, even if they departed from my own. My son, Joshua, got half of the family freezer for storing his insect collection."

In *Information Anxiety* Richard deals with many kinds of information in our lives. He explains why "60 Minutes" is so popular. It tells *stories* in a memorable way (in contrast to the clothes lines of facts and fragments of the nightly news). He is wonderful in talking about maps, which he defines as "anything that helps you find your way." He explains why all the charts generated following the October 1987 stock crash were misleading.

In the "Epilogue" you will find some predictions. I hope they all come true. Among them: "The U.S. 1990 Census will be completely transformed into visually understandable and entertaining documents, available in print and electronic form, and will be used regularly by Americans to find out about America." Wishful thinking? Not if Richard were to take on the project. Who could do a better job of explaining us to ourselves?

I very much like this summary statement from the chapter on education: "The fundamental lesson of my travels and travails has been learning that without prior knowledge, without training you can find your way through information by making it personal, by deciding what you want to gain from it, by getting comfortable with your ignorance. Learn to listen to your own voice and to balance your confidence and your terror."

Later, Carlos Fuentes is quoted as saying, "The greatest crisis facing modern civilization is going to be how to transform information into structured knowledge." Richard Saul Wurman shows us how to turn that crisis into an opportunity.

John Naisbitt

THE NON-INFORMATION EXPLOSION

We are creating and using up ideas and images at a faster and faster pace. Knowledge, like people, places, things and organizational forms, is becoming disposable.

Alvin Toffler, *Future Shock*

A weekday edition of The New York Times contains more information than the average person was likely to come across in a lifetime in seventeenth-century England.

For hundreds of years, the production of information increased in sedate increments. Then, in the 1950s, the advent of technology made possible the almost instantaneous pooling of information. This, along with the increase in the number of people involved in data production and processing and the low cost of collecting it, caused the rate at which information was produced to soar. The amount of available information now doubles every five years; soon it will be doubling every four . . .

With new information comes new demands on our faculties. We must learn new concepts and new vocabularies. Today, the English language contains roughly 500,000 usable words, five times more than during the time of Shakespeare. The number of books in top libraries doubles every fourteen years, giving new meaning to the words "keep up with your reading."

To survive in the workplace and even to function in society in general, we are forced to assimilate a body of knowledge that is expanding by the minute. For evidence, think of the ever-higher pile of periodicals, books, brochures, office memos, and annual reports that are probably accumulating in your office waiting to be read.

Information has become the driving force of our lives, and the ominous threat of this ever-increasing pile demanding to be understood has made most of us anxious.

Information is not knowledge. You can mass-produce raw data and incredible quantities of facts and figures. You cannot mass-produce knowledge, which is created by individual minds, drawing on individual experience, separating the significant from the irrelevant, making value judgments.

Theodore Roszak, author of *The Cult of Information,* **quoted in** *This World* **(5/24/87)**

We now mass-produce information the way we used to mass-produce cars.

John Naisbitt, *Megatrends*

ALL THE NEWS THAT'S POSSIBLE TO CARRY

A landmark edition of *The New York Times* (November 13, 1987) was 1,612 pages long, contained about 2,030,000 lines of type (over 12,000,000 words), and weighed a hefty 12 pounds.

The second largest edition came out December 1986. It was 40 pages shorter, had 112,000 fewer lines, and weighed a pound and an ounce less than the record.

In an average edition, approximately 45 percent of the printed space is taken up by news and editorial matter; the rest is advertising.

On a typical Sunday, about 3,900 tons of newsprint are printed and distributed.

Around 580 tons of newsprint are used to print the daily paper.

This rate of production means that about 346,000 tons of newsprint are used for *The New York Times* every year.

If this book weighed a pound (it doesn't weigh exactly a pound, but it's close), then about 692,000,000 could be printed using about the same amount of paper. Every person in the United States could have three copies.

About 3,600 tons of ink are used per year. If this were milk instead of ink, it would be enough to supply every citizen of Wichita, Kansas, with two gallons of milk per week for a year.

Information anxiety is produced by the ever-widening gap between what we understand and what we think we should understand. *Information anxiety* is the black hole between data and knowledge. It happens when information doesn't tell us what we want or need to know.

Our relationship to information isn't the only source of *information anxiety*. We are also made anxious by the fact that our access to information is often controlled by other people. We are dependent on those who design information, on the news editors and producers who decide what news we will receive, and by decision makers in the public and private sector who can restrict the flow of information. We are also made anxious by other people's expectations of what we should know, be they company presidents, peers, or even parents.

My family used to discuss current events around the dinner table. My father would ask us questions. If we answered one incorrectly, we had to leave the table and go find the correct answer. I experienced my first case of *information anxiety*, had my first intimations that information would be a driving force in my life, and swore I'd learn ways to find it—faster.

Information pollution is the nemesis of the information worker . . . Inundated with technical data, some scientists claim it takes less time to do an experiment than to find out whether or not it has been done before.

 **John Naisbitt,**
Megatrends

Approximately 9,600 different periodicals are published in the United States each year.

Almost everyone suffers from *information anxiety* to some degree. We read without comprehending, see without perceiving, hear without listening. It can be experienced as moments of frustration with a manual that refuses to divulge the secret to operating a video recorder or a map that bears no relation to reality. It can happen at a cocktail party when someone mentions the name Allan Bloom and the only person you know by that name is your dentist. It can also be manifested as a chronic malaise, a pervasive fear that we are about to be overwhelmed by the very material we need to master in order to function in this world.

TELLTALE SIGNS

If the "In" basket in your office casts a shadow over your desk like Annapurna and the mere mention of the word "information" makes you cringe and moan, the chances are that you're suffering from *information anxiety*. But if you're not sure, the following behaviors are indications that dealing with information might be a problem in your life.

☐ Chronically talking about not keeping up with what's going on around you.

☐ Feeling guilty about that ever-higher stack of periodicals waiting to be read.

☐ Nodding your head knowingly when someone mentions a book, an artist, or a news story that you have actually never heard of before.

☐ Finding that you are unable to explain something that you thought you understood.

☐ Blaming yourself for not being able to follow the instructions for putting a bike together.

☐ Refusing to buy a new appliance or piece of equipment just because you are afraid you won't be able to operate it.

☐ Feeling depressed because you don't know what all of the buttons are for on your VCR.

☐ Buying high-tech electronics because you feel that through osmosis you'll become more technologically knowledgeable.

☐ Calling *The Society of Mind* "prophetic" even though you couldn't even understand the book review of it, which is all you read.

☐ Looking down at your digital watch to sign in the exact time in an office building logbook even though you know that no one really cares.

☐ Giving time and attention to news that has no cultural, economic, or scientific impact on your life.

More information should presumably present more opportunities for broader vision and understanding. Yet the sheer volume of the data amassed makes almost inevitable the reduction of our focus to what is in the end a very narrow endeavor.

... If we are to retain any kind of perspective on the role of humankind in the future, we must sometimes stand back and view the landscape, not merely a tree.

Erik Sandberg-Diment, "The Executive Computer: How to Avoid Tunnel Vision," *The New York Times* (3/15/87)

More new information has been produced in the last 30 years than in the previous 5,000. About 1,000 books are published internationally every day, and the total of all printed knowledge doubles every eight years.

Peter Large, *The Micro Revolution Revisited*

☐ Filling out a form and feeling compelled to fill in each and every blank.

☐ Reacting emotionally to information that you don't really understand—like not knowing what the Dow Jones really is, but panicking when you hear that it has dropped 500 points.

☐ Thinking that the person next to you understands everything you don't.

☐ Being too afraid or too embarrassed to say "I don't know."

☐ Or worse, calling something information that you don't understand.

We are bombarded with material from the media, from colleagues, from cocktail party conversation, all of which is delivered in the form of what we have been taught to think of as information. We are like a thirsty person who has been condemned to use a thimble to drink from a fire hydrant. The sheer volume of available information and the manner in which it is often delivered render much of it useless to us.

It's disquieting to hear that computers will provide us with more information. Perhaps you feel you're already bombarded with too much information.

But what people really intend when they speak of information is meaning, not facts. Undoubtedly we're bombarded with too many facts—isolated bits of data without a context . . .

To assign meaning always requires more information to organize what we already have, and computers have a talent for this organization. Computers can take large numbers of facts and convert them into comparisons, spreadsheets, graphs. In short, they can help us to assign meanings.

More meaning, and fewer facts. That's the idea, anyway.

Michael Crichton,
Electronic Life: How to Think About Computers

YOU CAN'T BE TOO RICH OR TOO WELL INFORMED

Most of us are growing apprehensive about our seeming inability to deal with, understand, manipulate, or comprehend the epidemic of data that increasingly dominates our lives. Where once, during the age of industry, the world was ruled by natural resources, it is now run on information, and while resources are finite, information seems to be infinite.

Information is power, a world currency upon which fortunes are made and lost. And we are in a frenzy to acquire it, firm in the belief that more information means more power.

But just the opposite is proving to be the case. The glut has begun to obscure the radical distinctions between data and information, between facts and knowledge. Our perception channels are short-circuiting. We have a limited capacity to transmit and process images, which means that our perception of the world is inevitably distorted in that it is selective; we cannot notice everything. And the more images with which we are confronted, the more distorted is our view of the world.

Take the news as an example. Every day the media seek to deliver us larger amounts of news at a faster rate. We are besieged with accounts of the world in amounts that are impossible to process. And as we scramble to keep up with the news race, we are more likely to make errors of perception. Anyone who has ever played the children's game where you are given a few seconds to look at a tray of objects and then must recount all of the items on the tray knows that the less time you have and the more objects on the tray, the more likely you are to see objects that weren't there and forget ones that were.

The amount of news we are expected to ingest every day hampers our ability to perceive in much the same way. Not only are we more likely to make errors of perception, but the more time we spend with reports of separate events, the less time we have to understand the "whys and wherefores" behind them, to see the patterns and relationships between them, and to understand the present in the context of history. Instead, we are lulled by a stream of surface facts, made numb, passive, and unreceptive by a surfeit of data that we lack the time and the resources needed to turn it into valuable information.

A WORD IN SEARCH OF A DEFINITION

The word "information" has always been an ambiguous term, wantonly applied to define a variety of concepts. The *Oxford English Dictionary* describes the word as having its root in the Latin word *informare*,

Professor Tom Stonier of Bradford University in Yorkshire divides the Industrial Revolution into three phases. The first involved machines that extended human muscle; the second used machines that extended the human nervous system, e.g. radio, television, telephones; and the third yielded machines that extended the human brain, e.g. computers.

Peter Large, *The Micro Revolution Revisited*

WHAT'S IN A TYPICAL NEWSPAPER?

Classified Ads 20%

Soft News 24%

National and International News 8%

Local News 5%

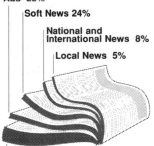

Display Ads 40%

"Hard News" comprises only 13% of the pages whereas ads take up 60% of the typical paper.

Based on a profile of the American newspaper by Bradley Greenberg, *Mass Media in the United States in the 1980s, The Media Revolution in America and in Western Europe*, edited by Everett Rogers and Francis Balle (1985)

> Data are facts; information is the meaning that human beings assign to these facts. Individual elements of data, by themselves, have little meaning; it's only when these facts are in some way put together or processed that the meaning begins to become clear.
>
> **William S. Davis and Allison McCormack,** *The Information Age*

> While we tend to think of boredom as arising from a deficit of stimuli (information underload), it also (and, in fact, more commonly) arises from excessive stimulation (information overload). Information, like energy, tends to degrade into entropy—into noise, redundancy, and banality—as the fast horse of information outstrips the slow horse of meaning.
>
> **Orrin Klapp,** *Overload and Boredom: Essays on the Quality of Life in the Information Society*

INFORM**ATION**

INFORM**ATION**

meaning the action of forming matter, such as stone, wood, leather, etc. It appears to have entered the English language in its present spelling and usage in the sixteenth century. The most common definition is: "the action of informing; formation or molding of the mind or character, training, instruction, teaching; communication of instructive knowledge."

This definition remained fairly constant until the years immediately following World War II, when it came into vogue to use "information" as a technological term to define anything that was sent over an electric or mechanical channel. "Information" became part of the vocabulary of the science of messages. And, suddenly, the appellation could be applied to something that didn't necessarily have to inform. This definition was extrapolated to general usage as something told or communicated, whether or not it made sense to the receiver. Now, the freedom engendered by such an amorphous definition has, as you might expect, encouraged its liberal deployment. It has become the single most important word of our decade, the sustenance of our lives and our work.

Information anxiety has proliferated with the ambiguity of the word "information." This mantra of our culture has been overused to the point of senselessness, in much the same way that a word repeated over and over will lose meaning. The word **inform** has been stripped out of the noun **information**, and the **form** or structure has disappeared from the verb **to inform**. Much of what we assume to be information is actually just data or worse.

Raw data can be, but isn't necessarily, information, and, unless it can be made to inform, it has no inherent value. It must be imbued with form and applied to become meaningful information. Yet, in our information-hungry era, it is often allowed to masquerade as information.

So the great information age is really an explosion of *non-information*; it is an explosion of data. To deal with the increasing onslaught of data, it is imperative to distinguish between data and information. Information must be that which leads to understanding. Everyone needs a personal measure against which to define the word. What constitutes information to one person may be data to another. If it doesn't make sense to you, it doesn't qualify for the appellation.

In their landmark treatise in 1949, *The Mathematical Theory of Communication*, authors Claude Shannon and Warren Weaver define information as that which *reduces uncertainty*.

The differences between data and information become more critical as the world economy moves toward information-dependent economies. Information drives the education field, the media, consulting and service companies, postal services, lawyers, accountants, writers, certain government employees, as well as those in data communications and storage. Many countries already have a majority of their work forces engaged in occupations that are primarily information–processing. The move to an information—based society has been so swift that we have yet to come to terms with the implications.

Understanding lags behind production. "The channel, storage, and retrieval capacities of electronic hardware are rapidly growing, such as in the field of laser optics or microcomputers," said Orrin Klapp in *Overload and Boredom: Essays on the Quality of Life in the Information Society*. ". . . There hasn't been a corresponding gain in human capacity. Better information-processing can speed the flow of data, but is of little help in reading the printout, deciding what to do about it, or finding a higher meaning. Meaning requires time-consuming thought, and the pace of modern life works against affording us the time to think."

Paul Kaufman, an information theorist, claims that "our society has an image of information which, although alluring, is ultimately counterproductive." Kaufman, an executive director of Alvin H. Perlmutter, Inc., a communications company, calls for creating a new image of information that departs from the current view that confuses the capacity to transmit raw signals with the capacity to create meaningful messages:

Social scientist Robert Carkhuff is cited for his belief that it is imperative for corporations to train employees to convert data into information. In a survey of 100 of the fastest-growing companies, this "human processing" was found to be the dominant organizational process, with marketing the dominant component and management the dominant function.

Patricia Galagan, "How to Avoid Datacide," *Training & Development Journal* (10/86)

As technology becomes more sophisticated and complex, so do the problems of controlling it, but ironically as control increases so does the potential to go out of control—evidenced by the mega-disasters in recent times such as the Chernobyl nuclear plant meltdown and the Union Carbide toxic chemical leak in Bhopal, India.

In *The Control Revolution: Technological and Economic Origins of the Information Society*, James R. Beniger analyzes mankind's struggle against entropy, the tendency of all matter to move toward random disorder.

Langdon Winner, "Science & Technology: Keeping Track of All We Know," *The New York Times* **(10/5/86)**

"One reason is that too much attention has been focused on computers and hardware and too little on the people who actually use information in order to make sense of the world and do useful things for each other.

"In our television commercials, information leaps around offices on laser beams of colored light. This is the kind of information that engineers are rightly proud of: pulses and signals zipping along through optical fibers, rather indifferent to the meaning of it all. However, to use information productively, i.e., toward some valued end or purpose, people must know what they are doing and why.

". . . A brief story will, I hope, make my point. I remember watching Larry Bird steal a pass in a Boston Celtics-Houston Rockets game. He dribbles down the court, he slides around one defender, he fakes-out another, and he flips the ball behind his back to Kevin McHale, who dives towards the basket and scores. There is pandemonium in the Boston Garden . . . The coach and former player Tommy Heinsohn is at the mike . . . He shouts: 'The computer mind of Larry Bird! He's three steps ahead . . . He out-thinks you!' The computer mind of Larry Bird? The computer is hailed as the paragon of intelligence. Bird's extraordinary feat of human information processing is so good, ergo: he must have a mind like a computer.

"The problem is not that we think so highly of computers but that we've come to think rather less of humans. We simply don't recognize what Bird is doing from an information-processing point of view. The beauty of Bird's performance on the court derives from his seamless integration of:

● new data (where he is, where other players are and might be going)

● old knowledge (what he knows from playing basketball all those years) and

● clear goals (scoring)

"The result is high-order human information processing: a perfect fusion of memory and potential, ending in productive action.

"This model is appropriate for anyone who works with information. And it is incumbent upon corporate America to recognize the importance of human skills in the use of information. We need a change in the image of information, a change from a static image to a dynamic image which focuses on the individual's creative interpretation of data."

ANXIETY-PROOFING INFORMATION

Understanding the gap between raw data and that which can further understanding and increase knowledge, between information as matter and information as meaning, will make you more competent information processors. The increased proficiency should give you more confidence and more control, enabling you to relax. Feeling more relaxed, having less guilt, will permit understanding.

The premise of this book is that by transcending the anxiety of not knowing, you can begin to understand. This book is about learning how to recognize what is understandable and what is not. It is about realizing that your inability to understand a piccc of information may well be the fault of the information and not you. It is a guide to:

- finding personal pathways to understanding

- laying claim to a feeling of "owning" information

- selecting the pertinent from the superfluous

- transforming data into information

- extracting the full measure of meaning

- improving your powers of information reception

- finding the appropriate organizing principle for different subjects

- reducing *information anxiety*

George Shultz, Secretary of State in the Reagan Administration, defined the information age as one of scientific, economic, and social dimensions. Addressing the Stanford University Alumni Association's first International Conference in Paris in 1986, he said that information has become the international currency upon which fortunes will rise and fall. By 1990, more than half of all households in the United States are expected to be computerized. He lauded the inventors, innovators, and entrepreneurs in the new technology as symbolic of the country's pioneering tradition.

George Shultz, "The Shape, Scope, and Consequences of the Age of Information," *Department of State Bulletin* (5/86)

Futurist Hazel Henderson, an author and economic analyst, sees the potential of the information age to be an "age of light," brought about by the broad dissemination of information, which would enable networks of citizens to "cross-cut old power structures, facilitate learning, and initiate a widespread politics of reconceptualization, transforming our fragmented world view into a new paradigm based on planetary awareness." In an article, "The Age of Light: Beyond the Information Age," in *The Futurist* (July-Aug. 1986), she stated:

"The information age is no longer adequate as an image for the present, let alone as a guide to the future. It still focuses on hardware technologies, mass production, narrow economic models of efficiency, and competition and is more an extension of industrial ideas and methods than a new stage in human development.

"Information itself does not enlighten. We cannot clarify what is mis-information, dis-information, or propaganda in this media-dominated environment. Focusing on mere information has led to overload of ever-less-meaningful billions of bits of fragmented raw data, rather than the search for meaningful new patterns of knowledge."

Too much of communications may finally be no communication at all. Perhaps we should add the Don Juan corollary: Just as the more one seduces the less one loves, so the more one is "informed" the less one knows.

Kingsley Widmer, "Sensibility Under Technocracy," *Human Connection and the New Media*

THE FIVE RINGS

We are all surrounded by information that operates at varying degrees of immediacy to our lives. These degrees can be roughly divided into five rings, although what constitutes information on one level for one person may operate on another level for someone else. The rings radiate out from the most personal information that is essential for our physical survival to the most abstract form of information that encompasses our personal myths, cultural development, and sociological perspective.

The first ring is **internal** information—the messages that run our internal systems and enable our bodies to function. Here, information takes the form of cerebral mes-

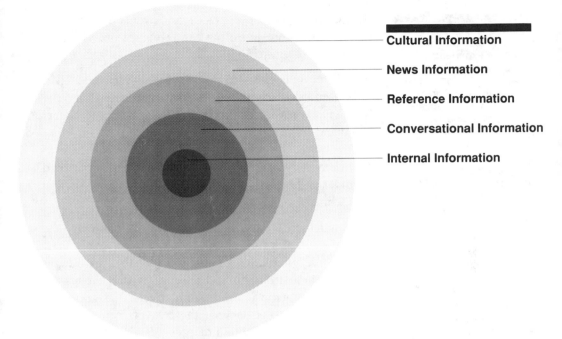

Cultural Information

News Information

Reference Information

Conversational Information

Internal Information

sages. We have perhaps the least control over this level of information, but are the most affected by it.

The second ring is **conversational** information. It is the formal and informal exchanges and conversations that we have with the people around us, be they friends, relatives, coworkers, strangers in checkout lines, or clients in business meetings. Conversation is a prominent source of information, although we tend to play down or ignore its role, perhaps because of the informality of its nature. Yet this is the source of information over which we have the most control, both as givers and receivers of information.

The third ring is **reference** information. This is where we turn for the information that runs the systems of our world—science and technology—and, more immediately, the reference materials to which we turn in our own lives. Reference information can be anything from a textbook on quantum physics to the telephone book or dictionary.

The fourth ring is **news** information. This encompasses current events—the information that is transmitted via

In 1900, the typical industrial worker owned two tailor-made shirts, which lasted for about 10 years. Today, a machine can produce more shirts in a day than a skilled tailor could then produce in a year. But the shirts may not last 10 wearings. The key difference is information—a tailor had to take a dozen measurements for every shirt; today, shirts come in small, medium, and large. More information means more labor and higher cost.

John Barnes, "Riding Shirttails to Productivity: The Information Age Will Create High-quality, Decentralized Industries," *Computerworld* (9/28/87)

The most unpleasant and at the same time the most universal experience, except loneliness, is anxiety . . . Anxiety, as we know, shows in a great variety of ways. Subjectively it may be experienced as a most unpleasant interference with thinking processes and concentration, as a diffuse, vague and frequently objectless feeling of apprehension or as a discomforting feeling of uncertainty and helplessness.

. . . Anxiety arises as a result of overstimulation which cannot be discharged by action.

Frieda Fromm Reichmann, "Psychiatric Aspects of Anxiety," *Identity and Anxiety: Survival of the Person in Mass Society*

the media about people, places, and events that may not directly affect our lives, but can influence our vision of the world.

The fifth ring is **cultural** information, the least quantifiable form. It encompasses history, philosophy, and the arts, any expression that represents an attempt to understand and come to terms with our civilization. Information garnered from other rings is incorporated here to build the body of information that determines our own attitudes and beliefs, as well as the nature of our society as a whole.

Although there are specific characteristics inherent to the transmission of information at each of these levels, their systems are remarkably similar and often they are fraught with the same problems and pitfalls. Within each is the potential for anxiety. And cumulatively, the grappling with information at each of these levels can weigh us down and induce a state of helplessness. It can paralyze thinking and prevent learning.

Information anxiety can afflict us at any level and is as likely to result from too much as too little information.

There are several general situations likely to induce *information anxiety*: not understanding information; feeling overwhelmed by the amount of information to be understood; not knowing if certain information exists; not knowing where to find information; and, perhaps the most frustrating, knowing exactly where to find the information, but not having the key to access it. You are sitting in front of your computer, which contains all of the spread sheets that will justify the money you are spending to develop a new product, but you can't remember the name of the file. The information remains just out of your grasp.

You are trying to describe yourself as a lover of wine, but you have no idea how to spell the word "oenophile." Now dictionaries are quite useful if you know how to spell, but if you can't remember how the word starts, you're in trouble. This is the nightmare of inaccessibility—trying to find something when you don't know what it is listed under. How do you ask for something if you don't know how to spell it or you don't know what it's called? This is *information anxiety.*

We are surrounded by reference materials, but without the ability to use them, they are just another source of anxiety. I think of them as buddhas, sitting on my shelf with all that information and a knowing smile. It's a challenge for me to get access to them and to make them more accessible to others.

ACCESS IS THE ANTIDOTE TO ANXIETY

Access has a range of meanings that are related to making things usable and understandable. If you are in a wheelchair, access represents ramps, elevators, and special toilets. It signifies the ability to do what everybody else can do and to make use of what everybody else can use; access means the liberty to take advantage of resources.

The concept of access is so central to my work that I've named one of my companies **ACCESS**®Press, Ltd. The guidebooks I design open doors of understanding to cities, jobs, sports, medicine. I am an expert on none of these subjects, which makes me the appropriate author. Why? My expertise is my ignorance. I ask the obvious questions, the ones everyone else is embarrassed to ask because they are so obvious.

I've found there is a relationship between creating books that make cities accessible and creating books that make medicine, finances, and sports understandable. In each case, accessibility is made possible by the discovery of a structure—the simplest correct form of organization— unique to a specific subject, one that allows readers to find what interests them and feel no guilt about ignoring what does not.

Accessibility is the breeze through the window of interest.

In somewhat technical terms we say there is a data explosion, not an information explosion. The total number of bytes or bits of stuff being produced or sitting around has increased. The value of it, in terms of what is really there that's of any function or utility, has not increased. There's also a distinction between potential information and realizing information. The British Museum is full of information. I challenge you to go in any reasonable amount of time and find out what color hat Queen Victoria wore on her 63rd birthday. It's not represented in any way that's easy to retrieve.

Dick Venezky, Ph.D., professor of computer and information sciences at the University of Delaware

Where am I?
What's around me?

45

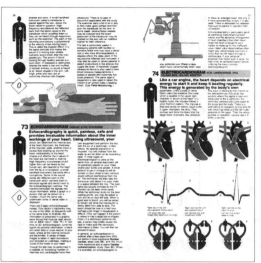

ACCESS® Guides explain *what* things are and *where* things are. They're designed so that you can skip around and follow your own interests without feeling guilty for not reading the whole thing. Information is organized in bite-sized chunks and is always in context— you know where something is or how expensive it is or how interesting it is compared with something else.

MEDICALACCESS
Diagnostic Tests

Being a patient is fraught with enough anxiety without adding *information anxiety.* How much does it hurt? What is the test for? How long does it take? Is it uncomfortable? Can I eat beforehand? Will I need to fill out a permission form?

TOKYOACCESS
Hotels and Shopping

For Westerners, navigating the twisting, turning streets of Tokyo can be quite intimidating. By consistently relating locations to a major landmark (the Imperial Palace, for example), one gains confidence to explore the city.

I am concerned with public access to experience and to information, with giving people new ways to look at their environment, their lives. In fact, I regard myself as a teacher about physical and emotional experience, one who communicates via a printed page that has been stretched to new applications. And as a teacher I want to test my ideas about how people learn to decode experience, especially experience that relies on visual understanding—shape, color, relationships between objects and empty space.

In developing these guides, I've employed some principles that are applicable to the study of information at large and to reducing its anxiety-production factor in particular. Perhaps the three principles closest to my heart—and the most radical—are: (1) learning to accept your ignorance, (2) paying more attention to the question than the answer, and (3) never being afraid to go in an opposite direction to find a solution.

Three principles close to my heart:

accepting ignorance

paying attention to questions

going in the opposite direction

I've applied these principles in this book in its content and in its form. The emphasis is on learning how to ask questions. When I don't know an answer, I ask someone else; thus throughout these pages are conversations I've had with people in various arenas of the information field. The traditional book form has been broken to allow me to insert marginalia, stories, and diagrams inspired directly and indirectly by the text; the book is modeled after the quirkiness of conversations and the association of ideas—the opposite of the sequential, linear way books are supposed to work.

I believe diversions and distractions inspire our thinking. I've tried to apply this to my book. It mirrors the way the mind works; it follows the natural, organic, wandering, informal model of a conversation. As Laurence Sterne claimed in *The Life and Opinions of Tristram Shandy, Gentleman:*

> ". . . When a man sits down to write . . . he knows no more than his heels what lets and confounded hindrances he is to meet with in his way—or what a dance he may be led, by one excursion or another,

before all is over. Could a historiographer drive on his history, as a muleteer drives on his mule—straight forward—for instance, from Rome all the way to Loretto, without ever once turning his head aside either to the right hand or to the left,—he might venture to foretell you to an hour when he should get to his journey's end;—but the thing is, morally speaking, impossible: For, if he is a man of the least spirit, he will have 50 deviations from a straight line to make with this or that party as he goes along, which he can no ways avoid. He will have views and prospects to himself, perpetually soliciting his eye, which he can no more help standing still to look at than he can fly; he will moreover have various; accounts to reconcile: anecdotes to pick up: inscriptions to make out: stories to weave in: traditions to sift: personages to call upon:—All which both the man and his mule are quite exempt from."

ORDER DOESN'T EQUAL UNDERSTANDING

I think there is a debilitating misconception that the shortest way from Point A to Point B is the best way and that order is the solution to all problems—that, if we could just deliver information in a more orderly fashion, we could make it more understandable.

Order is no guarantee of understanding. Sometimes just the opposite is true. The traditional format for guidebooks calls for chapters divided into neat categories—restaurants, museums, hotels, stores, each with its own chapter. In the **ACCESS**® guidebooks, all are jumbled together. They are divided by neighborhoods. This is the way the cities are laid out and experienced. My guidebooks are an attempt to mirror cities, to capture the fabric of urban life. Cities don't come in chapters with restaurants in one section and museums in another; their order is organic, sometimes confusing, never alphabetic. To really experience a city fully, you have to acknowledge confusion.

Cities don't come in chapters with restaurants in one section and museums in another. City descriptions should convey that diversity too.

But confusion is anti-American; it flies in the face of benevolent efficiency, that outstanding puritanical virtue. To admit to anything that suggests chaos is subversive.

But sometimes subversion is the way to understanding, and understanding is the cure for *information anxiety*. To entertain the radical idea that understanding might involve accepting chaos threatens the foundations of our existence. Maybe that's why so many people avoid the subject of understanding altogether.

WHAT'S MISSING FROM THIS PICTURE?

Within the communications industry, there are only three kinds of businesses that have to do with the dissemination of information: businesses of transmission, storage, and understanding.

The **transmission** business is easily recognized. It is television, telegraph, telephone, telex—anything that starts with "tele," can be sent over wires, bounced off a satellite, or printed on a page. The nature and demands of delivering information have made this field almost exclusively the province of Fortune 500 companies, which over the last hundred years have developed a transmission technology that has periodically approached brilliance and, for the most part, has produced extravagant profit.

Three businesses that have to do with the dissemination of information

the transmission business

the storage business

the understanding business

The **storage** business. The storage of information isn't the sole domain of big business, but rather is made up of companies of all sizes; among them are the computer and data-base corporations. This is an area where some of the most exciting breakthroughs are currently taking place. Imagine a laser technology that permits the storage of 250,000 pages of material on a single disk!

What is virtually untapped is the third component: the **understanding** business. Understanding is the bridge between data and knowledge; it's the purpose of information. Although there are people concerned with understanding, there are few businesses devoted to it, yet.

Many people are involved with making things simpler and easier to use. Computer programmers, for example, design software that permits millions of people to use computers, people who would otherwise lack the time and inclination to learn computer languages themselves. But these software programs depend on users memorizing a code that someone else designed. The programs don't encourage users to understand the principles of programming that might help make them less anxious when something goes wrong.

The understanding business would teach people to understand the language of computer principles. It would be the place to go if you wanted to make the U.S. Census intelligible; if you wanted an annual report that gave hard information instead of glitz; if you wanted insurance forms and loan applications in plain English. Networks and newspapers could turn to understanding businesses to make the news of the world understandable to the public. Government agencies could consult them to ensure that public information was really made public. Consumers would have a place to go if they wanted to understand their phone and electric bills.

We need understanding businesses devoted to making information accessible and comprehensible; we need new ways of interpreting the data that increasingly directs our lives and new models for making it usable and understandable, for transforming it into information. We need to re-educate the people who generate information to improve its performance, and we, as consumers, must become more adroit as receivers if we are ever to recover from *information anxiety*.

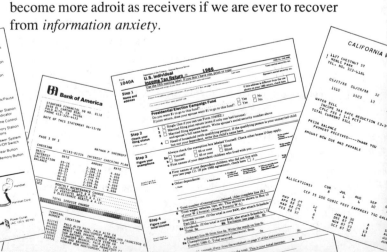

I think the reason why you can say anything in the United States is because there is so much noise, so much informational cacophony that no one is going to hear you, and the political leaders and businessmen know this. The key for making information understandable is to get it through the noise level.

Dick Brass, president of General Information, Inc.

*W*hen I was a child in Philadelphia, my father told me that I didn't need to memorize the contents of the Encyclopaedia Britannica; I just needed to know how to find what is in it.

That was my first lesson in information theory: you don't have to know everything, you just need to know how to find it. This can keep your anxiety in check. It can inspire you to ask questions about the information that determines your life at all levels—from reference materials to world events to cultural phenomena. Knowing how to look for information gives you the freedom to find it.

The refrain has stayed with me throughout my life. It has colored all of my endeavors and led me on the path to helping people access information and making sure that the information they find is understandable. It inspired me to ask questions about how the guides, maps, and reference materials around us could be made more usable and thus less prone to creating perceiver anxiety. I like to think of myself as being in the business of finding things.

The magnitude of information will involve more skill and more people in the finding and processing of information. Concomitantly, the people who determine the form in which much of it is presented to us—the writers and graphic designers—must learn new ways to make the search easier.

The old formulas and systems for data processing are impotent against the complexity of information we must assimilate today. We need to develop new formulas for understanding. We need to treat understanding as a business in itself, not only as a component of all other businesses.

The deeper meaning that we seek from information is, so to speak, always under our feet. We don't always look in the right place. There's an old spiritual tale about two men from different villages. The first man dreams of great treasure buried in the other village. He travels to this village to find the treasure and there he meets the second man who tells him that he too has had a strange dream about a treasure. You can guess where the second man dreamed the treasure was buried.

Paul Kaufman, an information theorist

ODE TO IGNORANCE

To comprehend new information of any kind—be it financial reports, appliance manuals, or a new recipe—you must go through certain processes and meet certain conditions before understanding can take place. You must have some interest in receiving the information; you must uncover the structure or framework by which it is or should be organized; you must relate the information to ideas that you already understand; and you must test the information against those ideas and examine it from different vantage points in order to "possess" or know it.

But the most essential prerequisite to understanding is to be able to admit when you don't understand something. Being able to admit that you don't know is liberating. Giving yourself permission not to know everything will make you relax, which is the ideal frame of mind to receive new information. You must be comfortable to really listen, to really hear new information.

When you can admit to ignorance, you will realize that if ignorance isn't exactly bliss, it is an ideal state from which to learn. The fewer preconceptions you have about the material, and the more relaxed you feel about not knowing, the more you will increase your ability to understand and learn.

At the age of twenty-six, I began teaching as an assistant professor of architecture at the University of North Carolina in Raleigh. I realized immediately that there was a binary choice. I could teach about what I already knew or teach about what I would like to learn. I was more motivated by what I didn't know and was comfortable with admitting my ignorance, so I chose the latter. As a teacher, I directed my subjects of inquiry to that which I wanted to know and ran my mind parallel to the mind of a student, rather than acting as a director of traffic.

My expertise has always been my ignorance, my admission and acceptance of not knowing. **My work comes from questions, not from answers.**

"My thoughts," said the wanderer to his shadow, "should show me where I stand; but they should not betray to me where I am going. I love my ignorance of the future and do not wish to perish of impatience and of tasting promised things ahead of time."

Friedrich Nietzsche,
The Gay Science

If a little knowledge is dangerous, where is the man who has so much as to be out of danger?

T. H. Huxley

A learned blockhead is a greater blockhead than an ignorant one.

Benjamin Franklin

When you can admit that you don't know, you are more likely to ask the questions that will enable you to learn. When you don't have to filter your inquisitiveness through a smoke screen of intellectual posturing, you can genuinely receive or listen to new information. If you are always trying to disguise your ignorance of a subject, you will be distracted from understanding it.

By giving yourself permission not to know, you can overcome the fear that your ignorance will be discovered. The inquisitiveness essential to learning thrives on transcending this fear.

Yet this essential prerequisite to learning is a radical concept in our society. As there are few rewards and abundant punishments for admitting ignorance on a personal or professional level in our culture, we go to great lengths to mask a lack of understanding.

And the energy expended diminishes our ability to learn. The classic progression of conversations—especially those in the workplace—illustrates how destructive this process is.

Let's say two people are talking about a project they are both working on, and Person A introduces new material. This will most likely set off a warning bell in Person B, who will start to worry: "Should I have known this? How did he find this out? What's wrong with me? How can I pretend that I knew this too?" While Person B is berating himself with these questions, he or she is likely to miss the chance to make the new material his own, to ask the questions born of a genuine desire to learn. The same people who would delight in confessing to sexual indiscretions or income tax evasion blanch at the idea of saying, "I don't know." Instead, we practice the "Uh-huh, ah, yes" defense. One of the things we all learn in school is how to respond with a look of thoughtful intelligence to even the most incomprehensible information. I could probably elicit this look from most Americans if I suddenly started speaking Swahili. The focus on bravado and competition in our society has helped breed into us the idea that it is impolitic, or at least impolite, to say, "I don't understand."

We have gained in terms of reality and lost in terms of the dream. We no longer lie under a tree, gazing up at the sky between our big toe and second toe; we are too busy getting on with our jobs . . . It is exactly as if that old-time inefficient mankind had gone to sleep on an ant-hill, and when the new one woke up the ants had crept into its blood; and ever since then it has had to fling itself about with the greatest of violence, without ever being able to shake off this beastly sensation of ant-like industry.

Robert Musil, *The Man Without Qualities*

American students ranked last on seven different test scores when compared to students of other industrialized countries; average SAT scores dropped about 90 points between 1967 and 1982; and the Navy reported that one-quarter of its recent recruits could not read at the ninth-grade level necessary to understand written safety instructions.

John Naisbitt, Patricia Aburdene, *Re-inventing the Corporation*

Most of us have been taught since childhood, at least implicitly, never to admit ignorance. We've all heard the parental admonition: "If you keep your mouth shut, the world can only suspect that you are a fool. If you open it, they will know for sure."

This plays on an almost universal insecurity that we are somehow lesser human beings if we don't understand something. We live in fear of our ignorance being discovered and spend our lives trying to put one over on the world. If we instead could delight in our ignorance, use it as an inspiration to learn instead of an embarrassment to conceal, there would be no *information anxiety.*

The refusal to admit to ignorance hampers us every day in our personal relationships and professional development. Collectively, it bears primary responsibility for the anxiety and frustration of staying informed. It also partly explains why the subject is often neglected by those most directly involved in the delivery of information—the communications industry.

The issues related to ignorance and understanding are so highly charged, ephemeral, and subjective that, human nature being what it is, we are all easily distracted from the intangible toward more imminently solvable, corporeal concerns. It simply is easier to conceive of building a new corporate headquarters than creating a new corporate philosophy.

AESTHETIC SEDUCTIONS

While numerous fields are involved with the storage and transmission of information, virtually none is devoted to translating it into understandable forms for the general public. As the only means we have of comprehending information are through words, numbers, and pictures, the two professions that primarily determine how we receive it are writing and graphic design. Yet the orientation and training in both fields are more preoccupied with stylistic and aesthetic concerns.

A physical system contains information if it exhibits organization. The information content is affected inversely with probability and entropy. Information and energy are readily interconvertible. A quantum of light has both energy and information . . . Therefore, information is not only an intrinsic property of the universe, but, like matter and energy, may appear in particulate form.

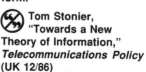 Tom Stonier, "Towards a New Theory of Information," *Telecommunications Policy* (UK 12/86)

He has the facts, but not the phosphorescence of learning.

Emily Dickinson

Despite the critical role that graphic designers play in the delivery of information, most of the curriculum in design schools is concerned with teaching students how to make things look good. This is later reinforced by the profession, which bestows awards primarily for appearance rather than for understandability or even accuracy. There aren't any Oscars, Emmys, or Tonys for making graphics comprehensible.

If you remember this, perhaps you won't feel so inadequate the next time a chart or graph doesn't make sense to you even though you have an urge to hang it on your wall.

JUST THE FACTS, PLEASE

Writers also serve the golden calf of style and are easily seduced into sounding literary rather than writing clearly. Iris Murdoch once said that to be a good writer, you have to kill your babies. Cross out something you might think approaches brilliance because it doesn't belong or doesn't move your point along.

Writers are usually held somewhat in check by considerations of accuracy. Even writers of fiction strive to convey accurately their own inner vision of the world. However, serving the god of accuracy doesn't always translate into understanding. Facts can do just as much to cloud meaning as to clarify it. I believe there is a god of understanding out there and the god of understanding is not served by just the facts. Facts in themselves make no sense without a frame of reference. They can be understood only when they relate to an idea.

To use a simple, Platonic example, we are able to recognize all of the diverse furniture types that fall into the category of chairs only because we hold some idea of the concept of chair in our minds. This is how we make the connection that a folding chair is in the same group as a lounge chair. Without this recognition, we wouldn't be

When asked what single event was most helpful in developing the theory of relativity, Albert Einstein is reported to have answered, "Figuring out how to think about the problem."

Wilbur Schramm & William Porter, *Men, Women, Messages and Media: Understanding Human Communication*

able to distinguish what a chair is, and the world would be an even more confusing place than it already is.

Ideas precede our understanding of facts, although the overabundance of facts tends to obscure this. A fact can be comprehended only within the context of an idea. And ideas are irrevocably subjective, which makes facts just as subjective. This is why if you serve the exact same meal to fifteen people and ask them to describe what they ate, no two descriptions would be alike. Some descriptions will emphasize taste, others smell or texture. There is a tendency to forget that facts are subjective, especially within the news industry which worships objectivity with the zeal of Shiite Muslims. But send fifteen reporters out to cover the same fire and see what happens. Based on their own understanding of the world and the influences under which they operate, each reporter will recognize certain details and miss others. They will report on the event through the context of their own understanding, which will determine what they choose to emphasize or omit. The pitfalls and seductions of writing and graphic design apply to anyone trying to understand or communicate information.

Accuracy, in itself, is not the means to making things understandable. Once you realize that absolute accuracy is impossible, you can be more relaxed and comfortable with your own choices as to the level of detail and to the point of view. The key to understanding is to accept that any account of an event is bound to be subjective, no matter how committed the recounter is to being accurate and objective. Once you accept that all information comes to you filtered through the point of view or bias of someone else, somehow it will be less threatening and you can begin to understand it in perspective and to personalize it, which is what enables possession.

A chair is a chair, right? Actually, chairs can be quite different from each other. It's only our frame of reference—our mental map—that makes identifying something as a chair seem to be such a straightforward and natural event.

From the book *Chair* by Peter Bradford and Barbara Prete. The photos above are of one-quarter scale model entries in an International Chair Design Competition sponsored by the San Diego chapter of the American Institute of Architects. Photography by Michael Pateman.

PERSONAL TABLE OF CONTENTS

After you can admit what you don't know, you can focus on uncovering the table of contents that acts as a road map to understanding. This is what gives you a sense of the whole. Sometimes it is explicit, but too often it is implicit and requires attention. Trying to wade through information without a sense of its structure is like going to the Library of Congress and aimlessly combing the shelves for a particular book. Once you have a sense of how the whole is organized, you will reduce the frustration of searching for a needle in a haystack. Even if the needle is all that you need, it will behoove you to know how the hay is organized.

THE FIVE ULTIMATE HATRACKS

The ways of organizing information are finite. It can only be organized by (1) **category**, (2) **time**, (3) **location**, (4) **alphabet**, or (5) **continuum**. These modes are applicable to almost any endeavor—from your personal file cabinets to multinational corporations. They are the framework upon which annual reports, books, conversations, exhibitions, directories, conventions, and even warehouses are arranged.

While information may be infinite, the ways of structuring it are not. And once you have a place in which the information can be plugged, it becomes that much more useful. Your choice will be determined by the story you want to tell. Each way will permit a different understanding of the information. Within each are many variations, but recognizing that the main choices are finite and limited makes the process less intimidating.

If you were preparing a report on the automobile industry, you could organize cars by model (category), year (time), place of manufacture (location), or *Consumer Reports* rating (continuum). Within each, you might list them alphabetically. Your choice would depend on what

---

The five ways of organizing information:

Category
Time
Location
Alphabet
Continuum

One of the most striking examples of organization by time is the book *10:56:20 PM EDT*, which is about the moments surrounding the landing on the moon. It describes a way of seeing by looking at the time leading up to this event. That focus is the framework that supports, sustains, and propels the book.

The book, put together by Frank Stanton, president emeritus of CBS, Inc., and Lou Dorfsman, senior vice president of CBS, Inc., leads up to a singular event, a particular second in our lives when a foot touches the surface of the moon. It slows the moment down—excruciatingly— so you can appreciate the complexity of the accomplishment.

you wanted to study or convey about the industry. If you wanted to describe the different types of cars, your primary organization would probably be by category, e.g. convertibles, sedans, four-wheel drive, etc. Then, you might want to organize by continuum, from the least expensive to the most. If you wanted to examine car dealerships, you would probably organize first by location, and then by the number or continuum of cars sold.

Once the categories are established, the information about the cars is easily retrievable. Each way of organizing will permit a different understanding; each lends itself to different kinds of information; and each has certain reassuring limitations that will help make the choices of how the information is presented easier.

Category. Category pertains to the organization of goods. Retail stores are usually organized in this way by different types of merchandise, e.g. kitchenware in one department, clothing in another. Category can mean different models, different types, or even different questions to be answered, such as in a brochure that is divided into questions about a company. This mode lends itself well to organizing items of similar importance. Category is well reinforced by color as opposed to numbers, which have inherent value.

Time. Time works best as an organizing principle for events that happen over fixed durations, such as conventions. Time has also been used creatively to organize a place, such as in the Day in the Life book series. It works with exhibitions, museums, and histories, be they of countries or companies. The designer Charles Eames created an exhibit on Thomas Jefferson and Benjamin Franklin that was done as a time line, where the viewers could see who was doing what when. Time is an easily understandable framework from which changes can be observed and comparisons made.

Location. Location is the natural form to choose when you are trying to examine and compare information that comes from diverse sources or locales. If you were examining an industry, for example, you might want to know

We are, I know not how, double in ourselves, so that what we believe, we disbelieve, and cannot rid ourselves of what we condemn.

Montaigne

. . . Don't be too certain of learning the past from the lips of the present. Beware of the most honest broker. Remember that what you are told is really threefold: shaped by the teller, reshaped by the listener, concealed from both by the dead man of the tale.

Vladimir Nabokov, *The Real Life of Sebastian Knight*

how it is distributed around the world. Doctors use the different locations in the body as groupings to study medicine. (In China, doctors use mannequins in their offices so that patients can point to the particular location of their pain or problem.)

Alphabet. This method lends itself to organizing extraordinarily large bodies of information, such as words in a dictionary or names in a telephone directory. As most of us have already memorized the twenty-six letters of the alphabet, the organization of information by alphabet works when the audience or readership encompasses a broad spectrum of society that might not understand classification by another form such as category or location.

The ABCs are drummed into schoolchildren so early and in such a rigorous way that this system of organization sometimes seems as if it's God-given. But it isn't: only a cultural consensus puts L before M instead of the other way around.

Continuum. This mode organizes items by magnitude from small to large, least expensive to most expensive, by order of importance, etc. It is the mode to use when you want to assign value or weight to the information, when you want to use it to study something like an industry or company. Which department had the highest rate of absenteeism; which had the least? What is the smallest company engaged in a certain business? What is the largest? Unlike category, magnitude can be illustrated with numbers or units.

We already employ these modes almost subconsciously in many ways. Most of us organize our checkbooks first by time, then by category when we figure our taxes. We organize our record collections, libraries, and even our laundry according to certain principles whether or not we are aware of them. But it is only the conscious awareness of these methods that will reduce the frustration of searching through information—especially new information. Uncovering the organizing principles is like having the ultimate hatrack. It is as essential when working with already existing bodies of information as it is in developing your own information programs. The time spent in comprehending someone else's method of organization will reduce the search time spent looking for individual components. When you arrange information, the structure you create will save you the frustration of

Almost anything can be classified in terms of the way it's organized. Things that seem to be unfamiliar or confusing on the surface almost always share a simple organizational scheme with something that is more familiar and simpler. Knowing this is a key to alleviating anxiety—even if something seems overwhelming at first, you can have confidence that there does exist an organizational "handle" that can help you come to grips with the subject.

What follows are some informal snapshots of the organizational forms of some books, processes, things and ideas.

Yellow Pages Directories	These directories are organized by category and arranged alphabetically, with alphabetical listings within categories, e.g. *Attorneys* are listed alphabetically together under the heading "Attorneys" in the A's.
Pacific Bell SMART Yellow Pages ®	Special nonalphabetical index of Yellow Pages directory category headings, organized by broad subject category like "Automobile" with alphabetical listings underneath.
Dictionary	Words, in alphabetical order. Definitions are organized by category of meaning; etymologies are organized by time.
Goode's World Atlas	The overall organization is by category, according to type of map (thematic, city, or regional). The information within these sections is then organized by location.
World Almanac	Organized by subjects (categories) and within these by all five ways as listed in the key, to varying levels of organization (some as many as three levels deep).
***Books in Print* Series**	Each multi-volume set is organized alphabetically within a category (e.g., there is a three book set on authors, in which authors are listed alphabetically).
Sears Catalog	This catalog is organized by category, and within these, by continuum of either price or sophistication. The index is then organized alphabetically.
***SPY* Magazine**	Most magazines are organized by category; features are secondarily organized by time, like a story. The features in *SPY* are in many cases organized in innovative ways—by location, continuum, time, or category.
USA TODAY	Like most newspapers and magazines, *USA TODAY* is grouped into categories and then organized along a continuum of importance as seen by the editors of the paper. Television news is grouped the same way, although the categories are very often the shows themselves (local news, evening news, 11:00 news, etc.).

EPCOT Center	The organization of a place can be in any of the five ways—not just by location as is EPCOT Center but by national cultures, historical eras, etc.
Powers of Ten	Information and photographic plates range in scope from gigantic to microscopic.
Information Anxiety	Information arranged by topics (chapters).
State of the World Atlas	Pages arranged by topic with maps (location) and charts (continuum) related to specific topics.
A Conversation	A conversation has no determined flow or pattern and moves sequentially through different topics.
Romeo and Juliet	Like most stories, novels, and jokes, this book is organized by time. Most television shows and commercials are organized in the same way.
Disneyland	Unlike EPCOT Center, Disneyland is organized by category (Adventureland, Frontierland, etc.). These are categories and not locations because they are not based on real places, but on combinations of real places.
Roget's Thesaurus	Words are organized alphabetically, but the synonyms under each word are organized along a continuum based on proximity to the meaning of the base word.
TV Guide	Usually, television schedules are organized by time, and television movies are organized alphabetically. There are also indexes for children's programming and for sports events.
Sears Tablesaw Owner's Manual	The manual is broken into categories. Some of these are organized by time (the assembly and operation sections), some by location (the parts map), and others by still more categories.
Richard Scarry's Children's Books	Instead of being arranged by time, as a story is, many of these books are arranged by category, continuum, location, and alphabet.
A Hospital Emergency Room	Emergency rooms are usually organized along a continuum of importance or likelihood of need. Items most often needed are closer to doctor and patient.

ACCESS® City Guides	These are divided into regions. Entries are organized by location and color-coded by category. Ratings are organized by continua (price, quality, etc.).
DOGACCESS	Dogs are arranged in a continuum from smallest to largest. Each dog is further identified by category.
MEDICALACCESS	Diagnostic medical tests are listed alphabetically, then secondarily by category. A surgical procedures section is arranged by location (head to toe) and then by category.
MoMACCESS	Exhibit space is organized by curatorial department (category); each department is then organized along a continuum of time (a timeline).
Governments	Organized by location of authority and power, and then further by degree of authority and power.
Families	Also organized by degree of authority and power.
The Human Body	Organized by functional category (blood system, nervous system, etc.). Although location is important, location is not the fundamental basis by which humans as biological entities are organized.
A Living Cell	Cell organization is based on functional categories. In fact, most organelles and cell components move around freely within the cell without affecting the overall identity or activities of the cell at all.
DNA	With only four possible amino acids, it is the elaborate sequence of locations of these acids that creates the complex organization on which life as we know it is based.
A Factory or Assembly Plant	Factories that do not use assembly lines extensively can be organized by category, by time, or by continuum. Factories with assembly lines are organized by time. The assembly line itself is usually organized by time, beginning with the first things to be assembled.
A Product	Products with moving parts are organized by location because the parts need to associate with other parts based on where they are. Electronic products do not necessarily have this need and so the arrangement of these parts can be based on other attributes, such as size (continuum), need for access (continuum), assembly sequence (continuum), subassemblies (continuum or category), etc.

juggling unconnected parts. Many people get into trouble when they mix the different methods of organization, trying to describe something simultaneously in terms of size, geography, and category without a clear understanding that these are all valid but separate means of structuring information. Understanding the structure and organization of information permits you to extract value and significance from it.

VANTAGE POINTS

Once you have a sense of organization, however casual, you can relax with that knowledge and begin to examine the information from different vantage points, which will enable you to understand the relationship between bodies of information. Ask yourself: How can I look at this information? Can I move back from it? Can it be made to look smaller? Can I see it in context? Can I get closer to it so it is not recognizable based on my previous image of the subject? Can I look at the detail?

Whatever problems you have in life—personal relationships, putting together a business deal, designing a house—can be illuminated by asking these questions. How can I pull myself out of the situation? How do I see it by changing scale? How can I look at the problem from different vantage points? How do I divide it into smaller pieces? How can I arrange and rearrange these pieces to shed new light on the problem?

In Holland telephone directories were recently reorganized to reflect different geographical areas. The country, which has a population of about ten million people, used to have twenty-nine directories; the number was then raised to forty. Now, the number is being reduced to ten. Essentially, this rewrites the "chapters of the country," for that is what a phone book is. The restructuring will change the way advertising dollars are spent throughout the country. Where it was once feasible for a shoe repair store

Mozart was once criticized by his patron, the Emperor of Austria, who told him that his music contained too many notes. The Emperor suggested that a few of them could be cut. Mozart responded by asking which few did he have in mind . . .

THE GREAT DIVIDE

As far as many statistical series related to activities of mankind are concerned, the date that divides human history into two equal parts is well within living memory. The world of today . . . is as different from the world in which I was born as that world was from Julius Caesar's. I was born in the middle of human history, to date, roughly. Almost as much has happened since I was born as happened before.

Economist Kenneth Boulding, quoted by Alvin Toffler in *Future Shock*

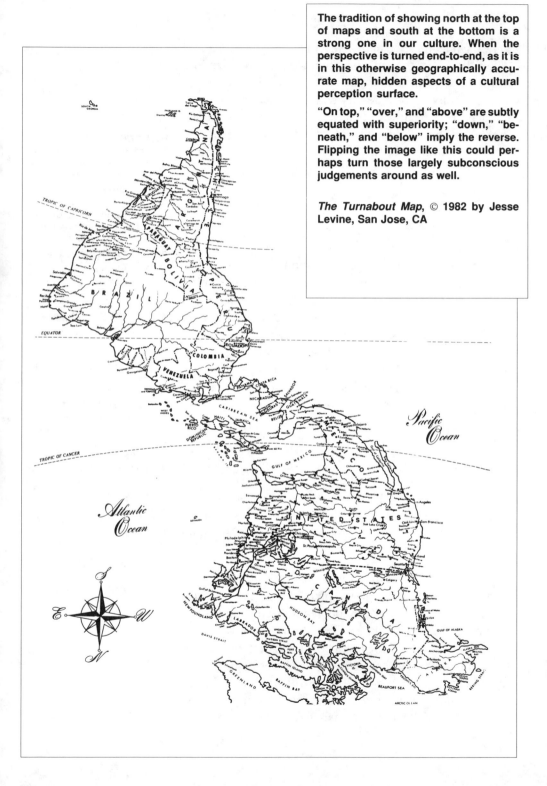

The tradition of showing north at the top of maps and south at the bottom is a strong one in our culture. When the perspective is turned end-to-end, as it is in this otherwise geographically accurate map, hidden aspects of a cultural perception surface.

"On top," "over," and "above" are subtly equated with superiority; "down," "beneath," and "below" imply the reverse. Flipping the image like this could perhaps turn those largely subconscious judgements around as well.

The Turnabout Map, © 1982 by Jesse Levine, San Jose, CA

to advertise in a directory that covered only one city, it becomes impractical in a directory that covers several cities.

In Portugal, where the postal and phone systems are run as one entity, there is both a conventional yellow pages directory organized by subject headings and one organized by postal codes, where you can look up a particular street and find out all the businesses on it. This gives you a new way to look at cities and provides invaluable information to anyone contemplating the new location of a company or residence.

Each vantage point, each mode of organization will create a new structure. And each new structure will enable you to see a different manner of meaning, acting as a new method of classification from which the whole can be grasped and understood.

In New York there is store called Think Big, where all of the merchandise is oversized. While most of us never stop to consider the grace and form of commonplace objects, here we can look at them from a different vantage point. A 6-foot pencil, a 4-foot toothbrush, a 1.5-foot paperclip take on new meaning. We can appreciate their grace and form.

CLASSIFYING LASSIE: THE DOG STORY

I could contact Avanti, an Italian company that makes stuffed animals, and ask them to make me a set of 260 life–sized dogs representing a male and female of each of the 130 breeds recognized by the American Kennel Club. Now I want to make the dogs understandable to people. I would put this extraordinary bevy of stuffed dogs on a gymnasium floor and organize and reorganize them. I would put flags on them denoting their country of origin and tie ribbons around their necks, colored according to which of the six different major groups they belonged: sporting dogs, hounds, work dogs, terriers, toys, and nonsporting dogs.

Then I would arrange them from the smallest to the largest, from the shortest to the tallest, from the lightest to the heaviest, from the shortest-haired to the longest-haired, by their level of viciousness, popularity in the United States, population, price, and the number of championships they have won.

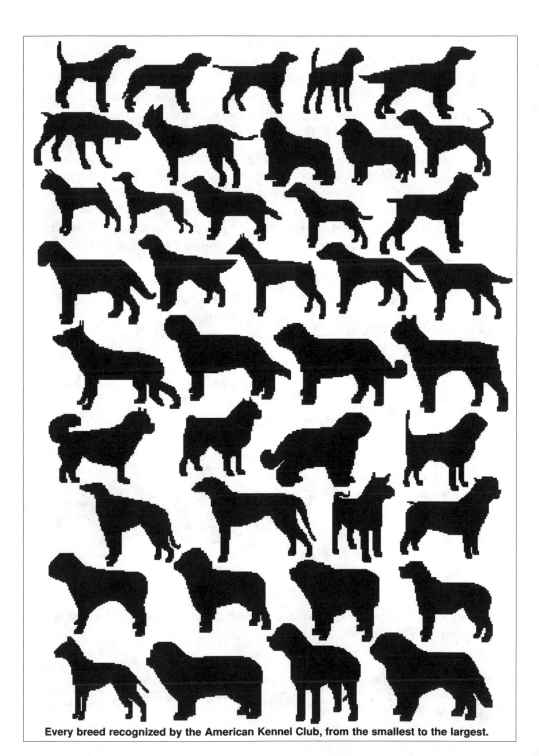

Every breed recognized by the American Kennel Club, from the smallest to the largest.

Every time the dogs are arranged in a different way, you can start seeing new information about the relationships. You might see that the most popular dogs are the shorter-haired ones, or that the most expensive dogs are the small dogs, or that in certain breeds the females are bigger than the males, etc.

Each way I arrange these dogs tells you something different about them; each mode of organization provides additional information. The creative organization of information creates new information. The dogs don't change, but the information about them does. And it takes no prior knowledge or understanding to comprehend.

I could organize these dogs alphabetically . . .

Afghan Hound   Chihuahua   Komondor   Labrador Retriever   Pomeranian   Poodle   St. Bernard   Standard Schnauser   Wirehaired Fox Terrier

or by category (country of origin, for example)

Egypt   England   Germany   Hungary   Switzerland   Newfoundland

Poland

Mexico

or by time (for instance, according to the year in which the breed was officially recognized by the American Kennel Club).

1885   1887   1888   1898   1904   1904   1917   1926   1937

Then again, I might arrange them by weight in pounds,

4 11 18 19 40 60 70 90 175

by height in inches (other kinds of continua),

5" 10" 15.5" 17" 19" 23.5" 25.5" 27" 27.5"

or by breeds as categorized by the American Kennel Club.

Hounds Toy Dogs Nonsporting Dogs Sporting Dogs Terriers Working Dogs

Real learning about the dogs comes from comparing organizations. For example, you can see that the Afghan hound is taller than both the Labrador retriever and the komondor, but is outweighed by both. Most likely they are stockier, which makes sense when you see that they are both in the working dogs category while the Afghan is a hound.

You can do this with many things; it makes your mind work differently because it shows the importance of relaxing and thinking about the arrangement of information before you make it complex. It's a process of simplification, not complication. And you realize that by simplifying, by taking one point of view, one slice, you can make something terribly clear. Whereas if you tried to say this dog is the most popular in Wisconsin, and is of medium height, and said all these things at once, you

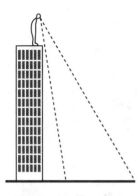

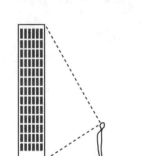

would never get the mental map in your head, nor would you retain the memory of the information. Each way that you organize information creates new information and new understanding.

THE SPACE BETWEEN THINGS

Part of the concept of looking at things from different vantage points is the idea of opposites. I see things in terms of opposites. I rather worship the space between things, the silence between good friends, the time between the notes of music, the break time during a conference, the space between buildings, negative space. I love the space on my desk better than the objects themselves. It makes me see clearer. That is yin/yang. The opposites of things are just so much more fascinating than the things themselves. It's the way I approach everything. I look for a solution which has a valid oppositeness. Not a "different way" of looking at things, but an opposite way.

At dinner parties, I always look at the table with the place settings as the focal points; then I blink a couple of times and look at them as the backdrop for the table, which becomes the foreground. I try to look at cities the same way. In Venice, I look at the buildings as the space between the canals. Artists do these kinds of figure/field exercises all the time; we are all familiar with the drawing of the vase that becomes the profiles of two people facing each other. To see the opposite is illuminating.

Barry Diller, chairman and CEO of Twentieth Century Fox, once asked a junior executive why a certain assignment wasn't finished. The young man said, "It's taking so long because I'm trying to do it the right way." Diller replied, "Did you ever consider doing it the wrong way?"

Opposites embrace the unexpected—what you look at everyday but never really see or what you expect will never happen but does. With the advent of computers came the prediction of the paperless office. But just the opposite has proven to be the case. We have developed desktop computer publishing capabilities. The VCR was predicted to supplant the movie theater, just as television was supposed to take the place of radio. The people who profited most from these new developments were the ones who could look at opposites. One looks at radical alternatives to discover new possibilities and solutions, whether in architecture, writing, book publishing, graphic design, business, surgery, science. It's a way of testing what has already been done, a way of finding solutions via the Hegelian formula of thesis versus antithesis yields synthesis.

Typewriters were historically designed with carriages that moved from left to right to accommodate keys that were always struck in the same place. Then IBM asked the question, why couldn't the paper stay in the same place and the printing mechanism move across the page? That question revolutionized office machines. Volvo designed its production process from an opposite. Instead of using the traditional industrial assembly line process, which calls for one person to perform one task, Volvos are built by small groups of people who each perform different tasks on the same car.

Numerous scientists were researching the possibility of developing a vaccine for polio, believing that it must be developed from a live virus. The Salk vaccine was developed from a dead virus.

The mastering of many subjects demands an acceptance of the counter-intuitive, or the opposite of what you would expect. To become a competent snow skier, for example, you must learn to lean forward, when it seems more natural to lean back.

THE PICKET FENCE

One time there was a picket fence
with space to gaze from
hence to thence.

An architect who
saw this sight
approached it suddenly
one night,

removed the spaces from the fence
and built of them a
residence.

The picket fence stood
there dumbfounded,
with pickets wholly
unsurrounded.

Christian Morgenstern

Opposites inspire most scientific discoveries and business developments. Looking at opposites is a way of testing an idea to see if it works. It is a way of seeing, listening, and testing.

We recognize all things by the existence of their opposite—day as distinguished from night, peace from war, failure from success.

This should be the approach to interpreting information. You should ask yourself, "How can I look at this from different or opposite vantage points?" and "How would reorganizing the information change its meaning?" Instead of being bound by the accepted way of organization, what happens if you mix everything up?

THE **SMART** YELLOW PAGES® OR YOUR PERSONAL GUIDE TO LIVING

These were the questions I asked myself when I was asked to redesign the Yellow Pages in California. A friend, Warren Bennis (a business professor at USC and the co-author of *Leaders*), suggested that I contact one of his friends, John Gaulding, on my next trip to San Francisco. It turned out he was president of Pacific Bell Directory. He asked me if I would help him transform his books and his company, of which he had recently become president.

The Yellow Pages are one of the ubiquitous reference materials that we accept without a thought. They are our path to the commercial environment, to our culture. Yet they are often confusing to use.

Companies are listed under one set of subheadings. If you don't happen to categorize information in the same way the phone company does, they can be pretty inscrutable. For example, pencils are listed under the heading of "Pens & Pencils—Retail," which is fine, but I would have never found them.

If you have an automobile and look up the word, you will find that fewer than ten percent of the total listings that have to do with automobiles begin with AUTO.

DON'T THROW AWAY THE WASTEBASKETS YET

In 1985, 2.8 million tons of computer paper were used in offices in the United States—twice the amount used in 1975. The manager of The Paperless Office, a Washington, D.C. consulting firm, admits that fewer than one percent of the offices in this country are fully electronic and paper is still the primary way that information travels. Among the obstacles to the paperless office are the lack of linkage between computers, mistrust of electronics, and the ease with which computers and printers can generate paper.

USA TODAY

I understand, therefore, I can act.

Where would you look in the Yellow Pages if you were thinking about what you were going to do over a free weekend? S for Sports? C for Concerts? G for Golf Courses? P for Party Supplies?

With a normal, strictly alphabetical arrangement of headings you have to be very specific about what you want. You have to know beforehand what things are called, how they're spelled, and even how the directory company goes about classifying the businesses.

Now, in a special section up front, it's possible to find every heading in the book that has generally to do with Entertainment and Leisure, for example. Or Automobiles. Or Home Improvement, Travel, Food, or other areas of interest in everyone's life.

It's fun just reading the titles on the Entertainment and Leisure Subject Search shown to the right. The pages remind me of a department store catalog, where you more often than not stumble across things that you never would have thought of otherwise.

Community Access Pages © 1988 Pacific Bell Directory. Reprinted with permission.

Knowing the locations of businesses is helpful for anyone who uses the Yellow Pages. It's important to know if a business is in your neighborhood, if it's within a reasonable travelling distance, or if it's clear across town.

I developed a series of maps that organize Yellow Pages information by location. Major shopping areas, parks and recreation facilities, airports, and landmarks are listed along with map locator squares that correspond to the grid on the map as shown below.

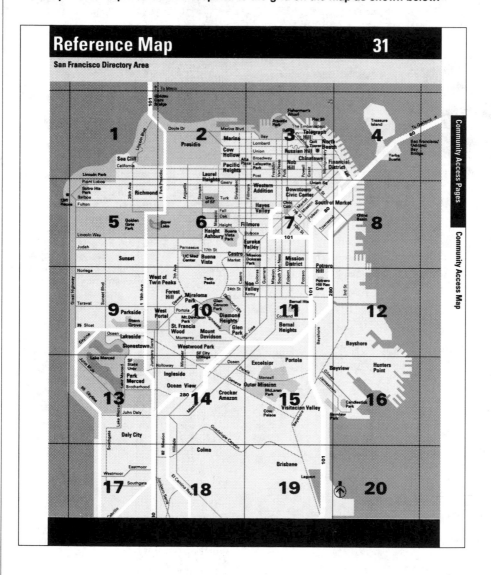

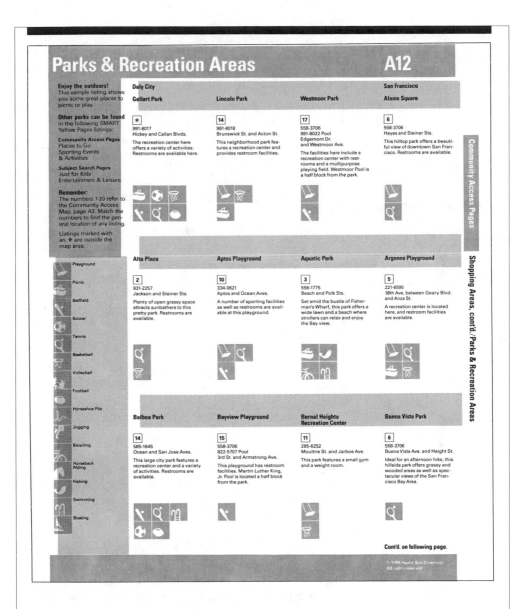

Parks & Recreation Areas — A12

Enjoy the outdoors!
This sample listing shows you some great places to picnic or play.

Other parks can be found in the following SMART Yellow Pages listings:

Community Access Pages
Places to Go
Sporting Events & Activities

Subject Search Pages
Just for Kids
Entertainment & Leisure

Remember:
The numbers 1-20 refer to the Community Access Map, page A3. Match the numbers to find the general location of any listing.

Listings marked with an * are outside the map area.

Playground
Picnic
Ballfield
Soccer
Tennis
Basketball
Volleyball
Football
Horseshoe Pits
Jogging
Bicycling
Horseback Riding
Fishing
Swimming
Boating

Daly City

Gellert Park
[*] 991-8017
Hickey and Callan Blvds.
The recreation center here offers a variety of activities. Restrooms are available here.

Lincoln Park
[14] 991-8018
Brunswick St. and Acton St.
This neighborhood park features a recreation center and provides restroom facilities.

Westmoor Park
[17] 558-3706
991-8022 Pool
Edgemont Dr. and Westmoor Ave.
The facilities here include a recreation center with restrooms and a multipurpose playing field. Westmoor Pool is a half block from the park.

San Francisco

Alamo Square
[6] 558-3706
Hayes and Steiner Sts.
This hilltop park offers a beautiful view of downtown San Francisco. Restrooms are available.

Alta Plaza
[2] 931-2257
Jackson and Steiner Sts.
Plenty of open grassy space attracts sunbathers to this pretty park. Restrooms are available.

Aptos Playground
[10] 334-0621
Aptos and Ocean Aves.
A number of sporting facilities as well as restrooms are available at this playground.

Aquatic Park
[3] 556-1775
Beach and Polk Sts.
Set amid the bustle of Fisherman's Wharf, this park offers a wide lawn and a beach where strollers can relax and enjoy the Bay view.

Argonne Playground
[5] 221-6595
18th Ave. between Geary Blvd. and Anza St.
A recreation center is located here, and restroom facilities are available.

Balboa Park
[14] 585-1645
Ocean and San Jose Aves.
This large city park features a recreation center and a variety of activities. Restrooms are available.

Bayview Playground
[15] 558-3706
822-5707 Pool
3rd St. and Armstrong Ave.
This playground has restroom facilities. Martin Luther King, Jr. Pool is located a half block from the park.

Bernal Heights Recreation Center
[11] 285-6252
Moultrie St. and Jarboe Ave.
This park features a small gym and a weight room.

Buena Vista Park
[6] 558-3706
Buena Vista Ave. and Haight St.
Ideal for an afternoon hike, this hillside park offers grassy and wooded areas as well as spectacular views of the San Francisco Bay Area.

Cont'd. on following page.

(side tab) Community Access Pages

(side tab) Shopping Areas; cont'd./Parks & Recreation Areas

Some new Yellow Pages sections combine organizational plans. Parks and Recreation Areas, for example, are described primarily by category (what kinds of facilities they have), but also by location (the numbers in boxes correspond to a map grid system on another page).

Community Access Pages © 1988 Pacific Bell Directory. Reprinted with permission.

So I asked myself, how could you look at the books from a different vantage point? How could you offer alternative ways of searching for information that would increase the chances that users could find it?

First, I decided that if the 2,300-plus headings could be grouped under larger categories, users would have a more manageable way to start their search. Also, they would be more likely to see categories that they might never have thought to look for. Home improvement, for example, would embrace the headings Carpentry, Building Supplies, Contractors, Hardware Stores. I realized it was logistically possible to assign the specific headings into general groups, such as Health-Care Services, Automobiles, Entertainment, etc.

So I developed Subject Search Pages for each of the general groups. All of the specific headings were listed here followed by the page numbers of where they appear in the book.

With the new books, you can skim a few pages and see things you might not think have to do with your car or home. You can use the Subject Search Pages like open stacks at a library, where in browsing through the shelves you might come across books you didn't at all anticipate finding.

This new product permits you to follow your own thought process instead of the phone company's because it offers you alternative searching mechanisms.

Enabling the user to look at the information from different vantage points also suggested other ways to present or organize. Entries could be organized by their hours of operation or their location. For instance, I would like to know all the automobile places or car rentals, pharmacies, or restaurants that are open twenty-four hours a day in my neighborhood. You can access things by interest, then access them by task, and then by time in much the same way.

Our history is made up of the fact that every time we fulfill just a little of an idea, in our delight we leave the greater part of it undone. Magnificent institutions are usually bungled drafts of ideas.

Robert Musil, *The Man Without Qualities*

Each way of organizing the book provides new information. The listings stay the same, but the means of searching for them have been varied and expanded.

The product and service listings already exist; what I am doing is offering a variety of ways to access the same information, without barriers.

DECISION TREES

One barrier to finding something is not knowing what you want. Decision trees are to be included this year in each of the directories to help people determine what they want. What kinds of questions should you ask to get the information that will help you feel confident of your own decisions and reduce your anxiety? The decision trees give you alternative routes to confirm a decision by making sure that you have asked the appropriate questions. We don't want to make decisions antiseptic, but to actually give you the freedom and confidence to make a decision on what you want by understanding what things impinge on what you want and what you have to go through to make a decision. How do you make a choice of doctors, schools, cars, homes, activities? The process of choice is a wonderful thinking tool.

The most impersonal of books can now be personalized. The changes made to the Pacific Bell Yellow Pages have increased usage. People now use the **SMART** Yellow Pages® 3.5 million times a day. Pacific Bell Directory sells usage, not paper; the book is given away free. From some simple reorganizing principles came 33 million copies of 108 different directories, 41 billion pages that offer the user easier access to the environment. All the changes were based on providing a more natural way to find things.

To formulate hypotheses on the relationship between information media, information choice, and the decision outcome, a study was performed on the use of the computer versus printed information in a policy decision-making environment. Information processing resources and computer literacy significantly affected the selection of information media, which also significantly affected the commitment to a decision.

Ralph F. Shangraw, Jr., "How Public Managers Use Information: An Experiment Examining Choices of Computer and Printed Information," *Public Administration Review* (11/86)

MAKING AMERICA UNDERSTANDABLE TO AMERICANS

The principles of reorganizing the Yellow Pages could be applied to census data, bus, train, and plane schedules, atlases, appliance instructions, and even the dictionary. In addition to word definitions, the average page in a dictionary contains roughly three kinds of information: historical, geographical, and biographical. Approximately 15 percent of each page is devoted to this kind of material. Dictionaries provide a wealth of reference information, yet we use them almost solely for word spellings and definitions. Wouldn't it be useful to skim down the page and find that nondefinitional 15 percent? Something which could easily be done by color-coding the type or changing the typefaces? I think it would make the page come alive and would tell you the structure of information listed.

The whole world is running on communication, perception, and synthesis of information. Often the structure is inappropriate to the form. Yet we take the forms for granted; we are intimidated by the forms and blame ourselves for not being able to understand them. My motto is not to accept, not to be afraid to ask why something couldn't be done in a completely different or opposite way, a way that might make it more accessible, more understandable, and less intimidating. My pet project is "Making America Understandable to Americans" by restructuring the reference materials that are fundamental to our lives. I think this is the challenge, the gauntlet, of the information age.

IN THE BEGINNING IS THE END

Before any solutions to any undertaking can be developed, a movement must begin to discover its beginning. Understanding the vein of the problem is the course to solving it. The best way to accomplish any endeavor is to determine its essential purpose, its most basic mission. What is the endeavor supposed to accomplish? What is the reason for embarking upon it? This is where the solution lies.

Originality is in the origins.

Let's say your community is thinking about building a hospital. On the surface, the purpose of a new hospital is to provide better medical services. But the purpose of medical services is really to improve health care, which in turn is to improve health. And the most essential purpose of all is to improve the quality of life in the community. Maybe the best way to do this is not to build a hospital; maybe the community needs only emergency medical services and more programs that emphasize preventive medicine.

There are two parts to solving any problem: what you want to accomplish and how you want to do it. Even the most creative people attack issues by leaping over what they want to do and going on to how they will do it. There are many hows but only one what. What drives the hows. You must always ask the question "What is?" before you ask the question "How to?"

Here is a story about what is and how to. I'm in a desert. I'm dying of thirst. I see a trickle of water. It is not a mirage. *I want that liquid in my mouth.* **Getting the water into my mouth** is the **what.** How am I going to get it? First I make a container out of my hands and scoop up the water.

I think, *Ah! I can design a cup.* So I make a cup, and it works, but it is too large for me to hold, so I make a smaller cup and put a handle on it, and I realize I have designed a spoon. I spoon that water to my mouth. I see some reeds growing; it occurs to me that I could put that reed in the water, draw the air out, suck up the water. I have designed a straw. I get the water to my lips. These things all have to do with *how to.* Design is about *how to.* But first you have to understand the *what is.*

Only one what, but many hows. Each how has its moment in the sun.

VOLUME ZERO

It is my desire to sense Volume Zero. Volume Minus One. A search for the sense of beginning, because I know that the beginning is an eternal confirmation. I say eternal because I distinguish it from universal. Universal deals with the laws of nature and eternal deals with the nature of man. So beginning is a revelation which reveals what is natural to man . . . The beginning reveals the nature of the human, right?

Louis Kahn, *What Will Be Has Always Been*

The new source of power is not money in the hands of a few but information in the hands of many.

. . . Knowledge has already become the primary industry, the industry that supplies the economy the essential and central resources of production.

The pace of change will accelerate even more as communications technology collapses the information float. The life channel of the information age is communications.

John Naisbitt, *Megatrends*

People want to buy lights before they understand lighting, which is what they really need. People go on diets before they understand nutrition, which would enable them to evaluate the relationship between their health and their food intake.

If you neglect to ask *what is the purpose of the project?* your choices of how to solve it become arbitrary and you will suffer the nagging feeling of that arbitrariness. You will experience the anxiety of wondering *would another solution have been more successful?*

Many of us move too quickly into the how to before we fully understand what we want to do. Uncovering the essential purpose of any endeavor requires asking something what it wants to be and discovering how that relates to what you want or need it to be. In fact, I believe the design of your life evolves from asking these questions.

This practice can be employed on global issues, as well as on the mundane. It can mean asking questions about the national debt or on the design of your kitchen. Should your kitchen be a space for elaborate culinary undertakings or just an excuse for a microwave oven and an ice machine? Should your desk be just a surface or a place for storage?

I believe all information is out there and the trick is allowing it to talk to you.

We don't invent information; we allow it to reveal itself as it marches past. The parade must be encouraged, so that we can develop marvelous new organizational patterns that spark new understandings.

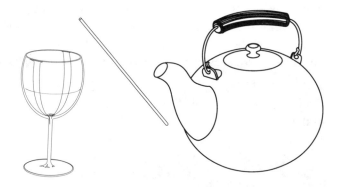

THE CONVERSATION

3

It takes two to speak the truth—one to speak and another to hear.

Henry David Thoreau

*C*omputers have become a ubiquitous symbol of a new age, mascots of the information era and of a new way of thinking.

Unlike a computer, the brain is highly fallible when it comes to storing voluminous amounts of information, but it is without parallel in grasping the total meaning of the information with which it is presented.

Jeremy Campbell, Grammatical Man: Information, Entropy, Language, and Life

However, computers are not, nor should they be, a model of the mind. While you would be hard-pressed to find someone who would argue with this statement, the reverence, adulation, and cult worship accorded to them would suggest that we have come to believe not only that they are modeled after the human mind, but that we would all be much better off if we modeled our human minds after them.

But as yet they cannot rival the magic of the mind for understanding. A case in point: Mr. Smith hates artichokes, but sometimes he mixes up words and calls an artichoke "asparagus," which he happens to love. His wife is quite familiar with his penchant for mixing up words. She knows that when he says he'd love artichokes for dinner, it means he wants asparagus. Until computers can do that, we are cheating ourselves by regarding them as paragons of thinking.

The easy linking of machine to mind is partially due to the easy parallels between computers and cerebral processes. Computers have a "memory"; they are storehouses of information; they can make calculations and predictions. They are extremely sophisticated keypunch machines, which by virtue of miniaturization can perform a myriad of calculations in a minutiae of time within a microscopic amount of space. But as yet they cannot think or reason or imagine. Until very recently all computer processes could be traced and plotted and were bound by a binary on-off system of operation. This is still the case in most computers—this is hardly true of the mind.

"But thanks to the cultlike mystique that has come to surround the computer, the line that divides mind from machine is being blurred," said Theodore Roszak in his book *The Cult of Information: The Folklore of Computers and the True Art of Thinking.* "That is the great mischief done by the data merchants, the futurologists, and those in the schools who believe that computer literacy is the educational wave of the future: they lose sight of the paramount truth that the mind thinks with ideas, not with information."

He suggests that in the art of thinking, the master ideas that are the foundation of our culture are not based on information. He cites as an example the idea that all men are created equal, an idea that has significantly shaped our culture, yet was hardly founded on facts or existing information.

"So it is with all master ideas. They are born, not from data, but from absolute conviction that catches fire in the mind of one, of a few, then of many as the ideas spread to other lives where enough of the same experience can be found waiting to be ignited," continues Roszak.

There is only one method for transmitting thought, for communicating information in a manner that somewhat captures the spirit of the mind: the medium of the conversation. Conversation can be a mirror of the mind, a petri dish for ideas. It enables us to communicate our thoughts in a manner that most closely models the way they occur in our minds.

Unlike writing, conversations are not bound by principles of logic, transition, and clarity. The spontaneity of conversations prevents them from being edited to a sterile purity. The lapses, nonsequiturs, and quirky associations that characterize the best conversations would be unacceptable in written material. Nor are we as likely in conversations to succumb to scholarly posturing, although every once in a while we encounter a stubborn pedant who has managed to accomplish this.

. . . This inability of the mind to capture its own nature is precisely what makes it impossible to invent a machine that will be the mind's equal, let alone its successor. The computer can only be one more idea in the imagination of its creator.

Theodore Roszak, *The Cult of Information: The Folklore of Computers and the True Art of Thinking*

We should all try to listen with the same intensity we have when we are talking.

The information society, with its emphasis on electronic communication and the computer, has turned human relationships into a commodity. According to W. H. Stoddard, "The translation of society into a form that can be represented electronically, and the abandonment of whatever cannot be so translated, represents a new variety of totalitarianism and a great dividing point in human history."

Anthony Smith, "Technology, Identity, and the Information Machine," *Daedalus* (Summer 1986)

THE ART OF LISTENING

Good communications skills are among the most valuable assets you can bring to your job. That means not only being able to speak eloquently and express your thoughts clearly but also registering what others tell you. Since most people remember a mere 15 percent of what they hear, good listeners are at a premium. Here's how you can master the art of listening.

● You have two ears and one mouth. Remember to use them more or less in that proportion.

● Don't plan your reply while the other person is speaking.

● Be aware of your personal prejudices (everyone has them), and make a conscious effort to maintain your objectivity.

● Show that you are listening by keeping eye contact, even if you must take notes during the conversation.

● Don't interrupt or try to finish the speaker's sentences for him or her.

● Allow a pause after the person has finished speaking before leaping with your response. Don't be afraid of silence; people often reveal the essence of what they're trying to say after a pause.

● Use you intuition to read between the lines and pick up body language. Consider what is not being said.

Paula Bern, Ph.D., a syndicated columnist and author of *How to Work for a Woman Boss (Even if You'd Rather Not)* from an article in *New Woman (5/88)*

The implicit and explicit goal of all conversations is understanding. Whether they occur between lovers, friends, relatives, or business associates, conversations have as their express goal to get one's point across, to make a connection between one's thoughts and another person, i.e. the outside world; they are an understanding model, a forum for the exchange of information.

Within conversations are a myriad of self-adjusting systems. As we speak with another person, we constantly readjust our language based on the cues we get from the listener. Do they look baffled or excited, bored or angry?

Unlike almost all machinery, conversations can tune themselves. We make adjustments, simplify, repeat, and move between various levels of complexity based on continuous feedback—a quarter-inch nod of a chin, the lowering or raising of eyes, strange guttural noises that say "uh-huh, uh-huh," blinks, shrugs, turns of the head, loss of eye contact, the making of eye contact. A symphony of signals occurs during even the briefest of conversations.

There is nothing we do better than when we do conversation well.

There is no other communication device that provides such subtle and instantaneous feedback, or permits such a range of evaluation and correctability.

Words are strung together seemingly without hesitation in phenomenally complex sequences and thoughts. Words work with each other to form new meaning. By their existence conversation allows for the development of new ideas. Ideas are created in conversation. E. M. Forster said that "speak before you think is creation's motto." Although spoken language is learned, it becomes natural and seemingly becomes instinctive. It is our pipeline to understanding. We have more skills to put thoughts together by language than we do by pictures.

A conversation forms a two-way communication link; there is a measure of symmetry between the parties, and messages pass to and fro. There is a continual stimulus-response, cyclic action; remarks call up other remarks, and the behavior of the two individuals becomes concerted, co-operative, and directed toward some goal.

Colin Cherry, *On Human Communication*

TALK IS DEEP

There are so few things we do in our life in which the absolute goal is to make things understandable. We have conversations all around us, yet we neither appreciate them as channels for the transmission of information, nor do we exploit their positive principles in other endeavors. No one seems to trust them. The favorite end to most business conversations is "Why don't you put that in writing?"

While the informality and amorphous structure of conversation cannot replace the written word, nor should it, it could be used much more as a model for the exchange of information.

Executives consistently rate communications among themselves as their principal area of difficulty, according to Robert Lefton, president of Psychological Associates Inc. in St. Louis.

● **Planning meetings.** Agendas of meetings should be arranged so that they allow for everyone present to contribute. They should have built-in mechanisms for explaining new ideas, for adjusting the complexity of information based on the responses of those present. They should be flexible enough to permit diversions and changes in course. And ideas should be offered in such a way as to spark others to think and not as though they were handed down from Mount Sinai. I think there ought to be a five-minute new idea rule, where no one could say anything negative about a new idea for at least five minutes after it has been suggested. I think we could save the many wonderful, creative ideas that get squashed this way. They are too fragile and ill-defined to endure criticism, but may nonetheless be valuable seeds.

● **Employee training and education.** Any program should involve new employees in their own training. They should be allowed to tailor their own programs, to learn at their own pace. They should be given the opportunity to ask questions, to stop and test their learning en route. Their training should be plotted like an extended conversation.

● **Social exchanges.** Conversations play an increasingly insignificant role in our lives, contributing to feelings of alienation and isolation from society. Everyone has the opportunity to use conversation as a model for communication. While this seems absurdly simple, and most people would reply that they do this every day, what we are really doing most of the time is lecturing. Conversation in its purest form means listening, responding to new stimuli, exchanging ideas. It requires thought, attention, and a patience of which few of us have enough.

THE LOST ART OF CONVERSATION

The art of conversation has been preempted by technology in almost every area of our lives. The idea that humans are more fallible than machines has caused us to turn toward technology for entertainment, information, and problem-solving. Our ability to communicate through the medium of conversation has atrophied as a result of our idol worship of the machine.

Once our parlors were laboratories where we exercised our verbal skills, testing our wits in active information exchanges with friends and relatives. Now they are entertainment warehouses that demand nothing more of us than button-pushing.

TEACHING THE PRESIDENT TO TALK

Nowhere is this more apparent than in the business community. Studies have shown that poor communications is one of the main problems facing businesses today. Employees are losing the ability to communicate clearly with their coworkers and clients. However, the most perilous problem arises when management loses the ability to speak effectively to employees. This causes management to lose touch with the work force and, consequently, with the company itself.

Independent of an individual's problems of self-expression, there are several external factors that cause the communication breakdowns cutting off the flow of information between management and the work force. It is a basic fact of life that bosses tend to hire people who agree with them; disagreeing with superiors will rarely propel an employee up the corporate ladder. This creates a situation where executives are often surrounded by "yes" people, which prevents the executives from knowing what their staff really thinks or feels. By fostering an atmosphere of subservience and by discouraging dissension, they are depriving themselves of hearing their staff's suggestions and ideas and from benefiting from their honest counsel.

> Your fair discourse hath been as sugar, making the hard way sweet and delectable.
>
> **William Shakespeare**

> Sweet discourse, the banquet of the mind.
>
> **John Dryden**

> Good communication is as stimulating as black coffee, and just as hard to sleep after.
>
> **Anne Morrow Lindbergh**

Employees are often the last to know. A survey done by the Opinion Research Corporation found that fewer than half of employees favorably rated their companies when it came to letting them know what was going on in the company. Employees are kept in the dark under a cloud of buzzword goals that call for them to be in search of "excellence," their work rewarded based on "performance-based coefficients" in a "market-driven economy" so that the company stays on "the cutting edge."

"That this nonsense proliferates during the so-called information explosion would be ironic—if it didn't have such ominous overtones for a U.S. business community already being clobbered by foreign competition," said Robert Bové, in an article, "Is This the Dawn of the Non-Information Age?" in *Training and Development Journal*, April 1986.

An unclear sense of purpose and vague corporate goals undermine employee productivity. By being kept in the dark, they are unable to see how their work benefits the company as a whole.

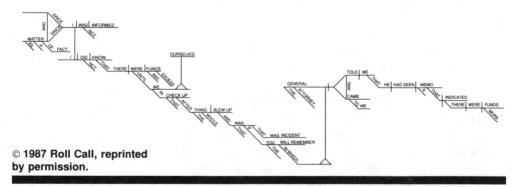

The Capitol Hill Weekly diagrammed an explanation by President Reagan concerning knowledge about certain details of the Iran-Contra affair. The President said, "Since I was not informed—as a matter of fact, since I did not know that there were any excess funds until we, ourselves, in that checkup after the whole thing blew up, and that was, if you'll remember, that was the incident in which the Attorney General came to me and told me that he had seen a memo that indicated there were more funds."

The wave of takeovers and mergers compound the problem by creating larger and larger companies where the management is farther and farther removed from the work force, which may be in another town or even country. In a report on executive self-development, "High Hurdles," published by the Center for Creative Leadership in Greensboro, N.C., we read that "the structure of the hierarchy tends to bring executives in contact with fewer and fewer people inside the organization. Only through extraordinary effort can top executives make contact with a significant portion of the rest of the organization, and then the act is usually more symbolic than substantive. Isolation restricts criticism that an executive could use in an effort to develop and to perform his role even more effectively."

In 1946, Charles Luckman, now an architect, became president of Lever Brothers Company when, less than a month after he joined the firm, its president suffered a stroke. He described how conversations helped him rise to the occasion in an article, "Just Plain Scared," in *The New York Times* (3/27/88):

"I felt as though I was sitting on a powder keg, taking over direction of a huge corporation without the promised six months' education. All I had to do was keep a $140 million company, about which I knew nothing, respectably in the black. Was I frightened? Of course not—just plain scared to death."

To prevent any discovery of this, he followed his regular practice of "getting out of the Ivory Tower and into the stores to talk to the men who sold our products. Then I would go into several neighborhoods to talk to the women who used our products."

At one of his house calls, a woman invited him in for a demonstration of just how "good" his product was. She

---

The best of life is conversation, and the greatest success is confidence, or perfect understanding between sincere people.

Ralph Waldo Emerson

Reading makes a full man, meditation a profound man, discourse a clear man.

Benjamin Franklin

We do not talk—we bludgeon one another with facts and theories gleaned from cursory readings of newspapers, magazines and digests.

Henry Miller

Precision of communication is important, more important than ever, in our era of hair-trigger balances, when a false, or misunderstood word may create as much disaster as a sudden thoughtless act.

James Thurber

ordered him to roll up his sleeves and wash a few dishes. The result was not good. Her parting comment was "Young man, you have a lot to learn about the soap business."

Said Luckman, "She had no idea how terrifyingly right she was."

Management bears the responsibility to set the communications policy and create an environment where employees are encouraged to speak their minds. The CCL report suggested that executives take the following steps to encourage productive dialogue with their employees:

- De-emphasize power differences. The size and position of executive offices can be arranged to keep employee and executive in closer contact.

- Create mechanisms that generate constructive criticism. Employees should get to appraise executives as readily as they are critiqued by their superiors.

- Serious, loyal, outspoken employees should be encouraged. If your organization contains an individual or two who meet this description, consider yourself lucky; courage has never been rampant in organizations.

When people ask me what I do, I tell them that my occupation is giving good instructions.

- Network. Executives, too, can set up the kinds of communication lines their employees have likely been doing for years.

Every week, I spend at least an hour answering the phone at my company. There's no better way to learn how a company is or isn't running. I find out what kind of information people are seeking, where our books are out of stock, what kind of people our customers are, and what is or isn't getting done by the staff. I think all company presidents should be required to spend a little time answering the phone. They might be surprised at what they can learn. At least they would exercise their ability to communicate with their clientele.

Conversation is a viable, appropriate model for the communications industry, but it is largely untapped. It is a simple-minded principle imbued with extraordinary complexities, gentle nuances, and ephemeral magic.

There are boundless applications for conversations and thus there is great value in finding out how conversation works. I'd like to uncover the structure of a good conversation that could be used to develop maps and charts. How could they be designed so they would talk to the user, allow the user to say, "Wait, what I want to know here is this."

Many instruction manuals don't work because they don't talk to the consumer. They don't tell you, "If the red light doesn't go on when you flip this switch, you've made a mistake," or "This should take about ten minutes."

When I am trying to operate a new piece of equipment, the instruction manuals could just as well be in Mandarin Chinese, but if someone can spend five minutes explaining it to me, I can put most things together.

A conversation goes from story to joke to incidence to fact to story to issue, all in a natural, organic way. Yet if you diagrammed a conversation, it would be amazingly complex. If we were to analyze it, it would be more complex than any writing, yet it is often more likely to lead to understanding. The whole apprenticeship system of education, sadly nearing extinction today, is based on the beauty of conversation, of the wise and experienced imparting wisdom to the young through the medium of an extended conversation that unfolds in the workplace.

I think we don't use conversation as a model because it is so obvious and so natural that we don't see its perfection of form. It doesn't seem pure, or elegant, since it is always adjusting; it is changing its emphasis, its level of detail. It is not consistent, it is not the way you are taught to write, but it is exactly the way you think. I'm able to have a con-

Conversation is our account of ourselves . . . Conversation is the vent of character as well as of thoughts . . . It is the laboratory of the student.

Ralph Waldo Emerson

He that converses not knows nothing.

John Ray

Conversation is the beginning and end of knowledge . . . the full perfection of learning.

Gauzzo

Education begins a gentleman. Conversation completes him.

Thomas Fuller

Studying in the solitude of the mountains is not equal to sitting at the cross-roads and listening to the talk of men.

S. G. Champion

Aircraft safety instruction cards in general don't work well as examples of instruction. Why couldn't the environment itself be used to convey more information about what to do in case of an accident? A color coding scheme—green, for example—could be used to mark exits and emergency equipment, so that when real problems arise, making decisions about what to do and where to go will be simpler.

versation, break into a joke, and come back. You couldn't write like that because it wouldn't flow properly. Yet in a conversation the digressions are permissible; nothing has more flow than a good conversation.

THE ARCHITECTURE OF INSTRUCTIONS

Often, in conversation, the *sub rosa* agenda is to give instructions, in that we are instructing others as to our thoughts. Examining the giving of instructions will produce lessons in all aspects of the exchange of information. Built into the program for giving instructions is a natural test of their suitability.

When we communicate, we usually have some idea of what we are trying to share, but we don't always know if that corresponds with the picture we have in fact planted in someone else's mind. When we give instructions, we test our ability to communicate information, and we can gauge how well we really know a process or place by how well our instructions are followed. When people ask me what I do, sometimes I tell them that I give good instructions.

The building blocks of good instructions are the bricks of description. Your ability to describe the existing situation or environment will determine how well your instructions for reacting to it are followed—whether you are telling a dinner guest how to get to your house or telling an advertising agency what you expect from a campaign.

There are only three means of description available to us—words, pictures, and numbers. The palette is limited. Generally, the best instructions rely on all three, but in any instance one should predominate, while the other two serve and extend. The key to giving good instructions is to choose the appropriate means.

If I were going to describe my office, I could tell you in words, but it would take forever. I could tell you in numbers, but you would be left without a sense of the texture

Inasmuch as the words we use disclose the true nature of things, as truth is to each one of us, the various words relating to personal communication are most revealing.

The very word "communicate" means "share," and inasmuch as you and I are communicating at this moment, we are one. Not so much a union as a unity . . .

The theory of communication is partly concerned with the measurement of information content of signals, as their essential property in the establishment of communication links . . .

Colin Cherry, *On Human Communication*

of the environment; you would have statistics without context. Clearly, the most appropriate way to describe my office would be in pictures, with a few dimensions and words of explanation.

If I were going to describe a person, a picture could never convey the complexities of personality. Only words might possibly do this, with a picture to enhance the description.

If I were going to describe the tangible assets of a company, I would probably rely on numbers, i.e. gross sales, profitability, market share, because these would be the easiest to compare, and would help you understand a company in terms relative to others of its kind.

The choices are not always so clear. Often the situation requires asking yourself: "How can I most faithfully describe the thing?" "Which means would be the most economical in terms of time and money?" And "Which means would enable my audience to relate my description to something they might already understand?"

In the business community, descriptions are critical to the successful operation of a company. How clearly the management depicts the company goals will determine how effectively the staff can work toward realizing them; in other words, how well they can follow instructions.

Yet few CEOs know how to give effective descriptions, or see the art of description as essential to giving good instructions. The skill of giving orders bears no relationship to giving instructions—one requires tact and diplomacy, the other the ability to communicate, to give directions within a frame of reference that the directee can understand.

As corporations become more complex, the architecture of instructions plays a larger role as the chain of command lengthens.

Most things today are not produced by a single person, but rather by a combined effort. If it is something of worth, information has to be passed from the person with vision to the people that help develop the pieces of that vision. The pieces of that vision have to do with instructions. Successful instructions have about them a sense of anticipation, aspiration, ownership, and even failure.

I like as a paradigm for giving instructions the directions you give somebody to find a restaurant in the country. How do you give instructions to find someplace? The essential components of good directions are:

- **Time.** Directions should include the estimated time that the entire drive should take as well as points within the drive; "If you are driving in moderate traffic, you should be there in thirty minutes."

- **Anticipation.** The sights you can expect to see along the way are reassuring checkpoints that you are on the right path: "Drive until you see the red brick church, then take a right."

- **Failure.** This is often missing from directions, yet is probably the most essential component. All directions should have in them the indications that you have gone too far, the warning lights to turn back: "If you see a second Mobil station, you have gone too far."

Directions should tell you only what you need to know. For instance, if I am telling you how to drive from New York to Chicago, it is not really important to tell you the three hundred towns you will go through. What gets to be important are the five towns you go through just before Chicago.

Bill Lacy, former president of Cooper Union, was living in a rented summer vacation cottage in a small town without street numbers. He called Federal Express to arrange delivery of a package to his house. He said, "Go down Main Street until you get to Clove Street, turn right at the Clove Deli, and go to the seventh house on the left; it's cranberry-colored with a white mail box with a red ribbon hanging from it." And the package arrived promptly at nine the next morning.

The example of getting someplace is appropriate because of it's commonness. We have a visceral way of measur-

WRESTLING WITH INSTRUCTIONS

One computer manufacturer, Vendex, decided to hire the wrestler King Kong Bundy to promote its new "Headstart" PC. Appearing in a TV ad, Kong leans on a computer and says, "I got a Headstart by Vendex and learned to use it in 23 minutes."

To back up his claim, the company offers intelligent packaging and a set of instructions that literally take users step by step through the setup process, from removing the packing material to connecting the cable.

ing the quality of the instructions without labeling it with preconceptions about the product itself or the intellectual value of what you are doing. How do you measure the path of reality? How do you measure the path of instruction, so it is in tune with your vision but takes advantage of the receiver's sense of ownership and desire to make it better? Better than even you could do?

GIVING GOOD INSTRUCTIONS

Giving good instructions is an art that recognizes the complex, ephemeral, unpredictable nature of communication. Yet few realize the complexity of giving good instructions. Companies spend billions of dollars on research and development of new products with so phisticated features, then write instructions for them as an afterthought.

Consequently, most of us are surrounded with the latest in technology which we are unable to fully use, and, in some cases, even turn on.

The VCR is a prime example. I'd guess that probably few people can use more than 10 percent of any given machine's capabilities. Few use the capability to record things at different times, of playing back, of taping two or three different segments, of taping while you are watching another program, all because it is all too complicated and the instructions are not clear.

Apple's instructions for the Macintosh® are for the most part very friendly, but they are not very informative. I don't remember how many pages I had to go through before I found by accident where the manual told how to get a disk out of the computer. The reason is, of course, that Apple assumed I knew how to do *that*. The person who wrote the instructions can't even imagine a person so ignorant that he couldn't get the disk out.

I don't know how to use the twenty special features on my telephone. And I suspect by my phone conversations with other businesspeople that I am not alone. A business reporter friend of mine claimed that she'd trade her salary for earning ten dollars every time a CEO told her, "I'm going to transfer you to someone who can give you the figures, but you'll have to pardon me if I cut you off. We've got this new phone system and I'm not sure how it works."

The instructions that have been developed by Xerox for their copying machines, on the other hand, have been excellent. They really walk you through errors and problems. If you can figure out how to use your VCR, a videotape is now available to explain desktop publishing. Produced by Ocean Communications in San Jose, the tape allows you to see various software programs being used and includes a discussion of support services for users. The new Polaroid Spectra instructions are also excellent. They take you along and show you errors. They engender a sense of ownership and accomplishment.

I think putting together a hatrack or bicycle is no different. What do you want to get out of putting it together? You want to feel ownership of the construction and without the anxiety of having it not work. It is the same anxiety that children experience in a classroom when they are given an assignment that they don't understand, because they will be prevented from possessing the knowledge.

We spend most of our lives as givers and followers of instructions, whether following the orders of a superior in the workplace or teaching children to tie their shoes. And we have all felt the burden of trying to give instructions to someone else and the frustration of following someone else's instructions. Yet we offer and follow them so unconsciously most of the time. Instead, we should stop and plan our instructions with more thought—ask ourselves: "What are the essentials of this explanation?" "How can I build in reassurance so that the followers will know that they are on the right track?" "What is the language that would enable them to understand?"

LANGUAGE: BABEL, SEDUCTION, CONTENT

Language is a cracked kettle on which we tap out crude rhythms for bears to dance to while we long to make music that will melt the stars.

Gustave Flaubert, *Madame Bovary*

*C*ommunication is equivocal. We are limited by a language where words may mean one thing to one person and quite something else to another. There is no ordained right way to communicate. At least in the absolute sense, it is impossible to share our thoughts with someone else, for they will not be understood in exactly the same way.

Whether or not we are aware of it, we each attach private or special significance to certain words. The best we can hope for is to be partly understood. To acknowledge this is to acknowledge a certain amount of futility and loneliness. So many like to believe this is not the case.

An eighty-four-year-old woman living in Maine has never had a complete medical exam. Her kids insist that she go to the doctor, and although she's never been sick, she goes. She's not a very sophisticated woman, and the young doctor is amazed she's in such good shape.

After the exam he tells her, "Everything seems to be in good order, but there are additional tests I'd like to run. Come back next week and bring along a specimen."

The old woman doesn't know what he's talking about.

He says, "What I need is a urinary sample. Would you bring that in and we'll run some additional tests." She still doesn't understand.

The doctor says, "Before you come in, void in a jar." The woman responds quizzically, "What?"

. . .There is no such thing as a primitive language. All are highly complex.

Jeremy Campbell,
Grammatical Man: Information, Entropy, Language, and Life

Language is a virus from outer space.

William S. Burroughs

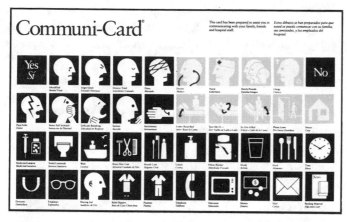

Communi-Card°

This card has been prepared to assist you in communicating with your family, friends and hospital staff.

Estos dibujos se han preparados para que usted se pueda comunicar con su familia, sus amistades, y los empleados del hospital.

Yes / Sí   No

The design firm of de Harak & Poulin Associates kept in mind the special needs of hospital patients who can't communicate verbally when it developed the Communi-Card for Mount Sinai Medical Center (*above*). Patients (or hospital personnel) can point at pictograms that describe symptoms and at figures to indicate the part of the body involved. Those with speech or language problems, or those who lack the knowledge to describe their ailments, can thus communicate their basic needs in a situation already loaded with anxiety.

A woman seeking a divorce went to visit her attorney. The first question he asked her was "Do you have grounds?"

She replied, "Yes, about two acres."

"Perhaps I'm not making myself clear," he said, "Do you have a grudge?"

"No, but we have a carport," she responded.

"Let me try again. Does your husband beat you up?" he said impatiently.

"No, generally I get up before he does," she said.

At this point, the attorney decided to try a different tack. "Ma'am, are you sure you really want a divorce?"

"I don't want one at all, but my husband does. He claims we have difficulty communicating."

U.S. Representative Pat Swindall (Georgia), illustrating that Congress was not listening to the public on the issue of the federal deficit

The doctor finally gets exasperated and says, "Look, lady, go piss in a pot." She gets red in the face, smacks him over the head with her pocketbook, and replies, "You go shit in your hat," and promptly walks out.

In this story the young doctor always tells the truth and uses accurate and increasingly simple nomenclature, yet winds up insulting her. The message is that accuracy or your own truth doesn't necessarily equal communication.

Responsibility for communication does not end by doing the correct thing or finding the presumed optimum way. The observation of etiquette won't guarantee that information is understandable. There is no right way; there may be many ways. In attempting to communicate an idea, you might try several different approaches instead of making the pointless and frustrating search for the one right way.

Even a word is a work of art . . . Usable languages are only made so that expressions can lead to art. The art of saying things, not just little pebbles which form words.

Louis Kahn

ITSY-BITSY BOMBS

Cookie Cutters, Christmas Tree Farms, and *Slick 'ems* are all part of the vocabulary of nuclear weaponry.

Respectively, they name nuclear attacks against a military target, submarine-launched missiles lined up in their tubes, and submarine-launched cruise missiles.

Words have the power to incite or to diffuse. Using language that is perversely cute can intentionally obscure and sugarcoat a deadly reality.

Sarah Boxer, "Patting the Missile: Making Nuclear War Less Threatening" *Discover* (8/87)

A code can be unlocked with one key or another. A language cannot. It has its own logic, grammar, and means of "putting thoughts together with words that span various spectra of meaning. There is no key you can plug in to unlock the exact meaning. At best you can get a close approximation."

Samuel R. Delany, *Babel-17*

When it comes to language, redundancy isn't a crime. Certain combinations of letters and of words appear naturally over and over; they act as checkpoints that enable us to measure whether we are understanding the message. When we don't hear the repetitions, the familiar order of words, we know that something is wrong with the message. So goes dancing. In partner dancing, the one who is leading will repeat a series of motions that enable his/her partner to follow more gracefully. This saves misunderstood clues and fragile toes.

There are good ways to communicate, and there are ways which will probably be well received. That is as good as it gets. There aren't any scientific, pure, ultimate ways. This makes the search for the ways less threatening.

WHICH CAME FIRST, LANGUAGE OR THOUGHT?

Linguists disagree as to the relationship between language and thought, and thus understanding. Some feel that language determines thought, that thought can occur only within the rules and bounds of a language. Others believe just the opposite, that thought determines the form of language. I believe the relationship between thought and language is a combination of these two ideas. Language is used for organizing and communicating thought. It is partly a reflection of how we think, partly an influence, and, sometimes, a limitation on how we think.

As an example, Japanese society is considered to be rigid, but also very precise and efficient. Everything from the tatami mats that form the basis of their architecture, to their command of high technology, to the rules of behavior within their society reflect this. So does their language. Japanese grammar is extremely modular, each word carrying with it another word called a relational that lets everyone know how that word is meant to function in a sentence, (e.g. as a noun, an adjective, etc.) and the main verb is put at the end. This means that you can change the order of words in a sentence without changing the meaning. Try doing that with English. To think in Japanese is to think in a language that is inherently easier and less limiting to combining the process of words, thoughts, and ultimately ideas into new forms. Whether this is a result of the language form, or the language form is a result of the thought process is not important here. The fact is that the language form allows you to put thoughts together in certain ways, and this can affect how you view the world. It is no wonder that the Japanese have taken to building and developing small, efficient, modular electronics; it is a very natural way of thinking for them.

German grammar is similarly constructed in that the main verb is at the end of the sentence. German also has the ability to combine chains of thoughts into one word. Instead of stringing adjectives and modifiers next to nouns, they can be incorporated to form one word. This word is the whole concept and vice versa. It takes a language like German or Japanese, which possesses very modular abilities and flexibilities, to be able to link different concepts together into one whole, new concept so easily and effectively. To think in German is to make use of this aspect, and curiously the Germans are also known for their excellence in engineering and science. This is not to say that those who speak a language without these attributes cannot hope to excel at engineering, but you can begin to appreciate the effect language can have on making certain types of thinking and certain types of understanding easier.

Every language has its peculiarities. Speakers of English can find French difficult when it comes to articles such as "the," "a," and "some." A door is feminine; a pen is masculine. This seems silly to English speakers. Inanimate objects take on an animate character in this language, and to think in French is to accept that character.

Many people around the world talk to their cars, computers, or other things as if they were alive, or speak fondly of the moon or stars, especially in poetry, and it is less awkward to do so in a language that already assigns animate characteristics to inanimate objects.

The American Indian language Hopi offers an interesting example of the relationship between thought and language and the understanding of the things around us. In Hopi, events are always referenced to space and time by two tenses (objective and subjective) and, thus, function without the need for our tenses (past, present, future, etc.) or, for that matter, any reference to time. To think or speak in Hopi (or any language) is to accept the structure of thinking inherent in that language. How you think affects how you deal with information and how you use it.

Benjamin Whorf,
Language, Thought and Reality

"Mine is a long and sad tale!" said the Mouse, turning to Alice, and sighing.

"It is a long tail, certainly," said Alice, looking down with wonder at the Mouse's tail, "but why do you call it sad?"

Lewis Carroll, *Alice's Adventures in Wonderland*

THE DISPARITY BETWEEN LANGUAGE AND THOUGHT

We do not think in a linear, sequential way, yet every body of information that is given to use is given to us in a linear manner. Even language structure is basically linear. We communicate in a linear way; we do not communicate the way we think. The point is we are taught to communicate in a way that is actually constricting our ability to think, because we think in an associative way. When we read a sentence we do not limit our intake of information to what we see in that sentence. We actually make innumerable associations with our own experience. We read in ways we do not write.

Peter Bradford

This leads to a fantastical environment that promotes a certain type of creative language usage in writing, movies, poetry, etc. It supports the formation of new and different—even wild—ideas, for, after all, what is wild once you've already accepted that your table is feminine?

All of these differences can have subtle effects on how we think and communicate. If we can explore the idiosyncrasies of our language, we can use them to our advantage.

American English is extremely inconsistent as to usage, pronunciation, and spelling. There are almost as many exceptions as rules. But it offers a flexibility that most languages and cultures don't have—the acceptance of foreign and/or new words. We can introduce a new word or phrase, and thus a new concept, simply by importing it, without translation, and defining it. These terms quickly get established in the American language, e.g. *faux pas, au courant, en route*, etc. This allows for the spontaneous addition of new ideas and new ways of doing things to our language and our thoughts. Technology has also contributed a significant body of new words to our verbal pool.

Does this shed any light on why the term *American ingenuity* exists? When some language critics scream and complain that these new words are not "real" words, they are missing the chance to make them their own, and, along with the word, the concept that it embodies. We shortchange ourselves by not taking advantage of the full range of language available to us. Despite the fact that more and more words enter our language, we don't make use of them.

When you learn a new language, you are not just learning a new vocabulary and grammar, but a new, or at least slightly different, way of thinking.

There are things we can do to our language and to our thinking process that can help us overcome *information anxiety*, aid us in understanding the information available to us, and transform data into information.

Old words can be given new meanings. The easiest way to accomplish this is to look for words in the vocabulary of one discipline or subject and try to apply them to another. Louis Kahn used to describe the streets of a city as "rivers" and the parking lots as "harbors." It gave his students a heightened perspective on the city. Using words from one frame of reference to another sheds new light and meanings. It's like rain washing the pollen out of the air.

Also, new words can be formed from the combination of existing words, which remain visible in the new words, e.g. newspaper, automobile, motorcycle. Many of these types of words are related to technology because of the constant emergence of new products and systems demanding names. When these new words and the ideas they suggest are named from combinations of already known and accepted words and ideas, the meaning of these new words is fairly obvious to the reader even when seen for the first time. The same can be somewhat true for new words based on Latin or Greek prefixes and suffixes (once you know that *geo-* means "earth" and *-ology* means "the study of," you can quickly understand the word *geology* even if you've never come across it before.

Sometimes, understanding is heavily related to vocabulary. If you don't have the proper word, it becomes difficult to communicate a concept (and sometimes just to think about it). The more concepts you understand, the more powerful your thinking can be, the more combinations you can make, and the more creative you can be.

The computer has introduced most of us to a new vocabulary. Words like *interface*, *modem*, *on-line*, *access*, *hardware*, and *software* have become entrenched in our vocabulary and our thinking. But in a perverse way, the computer has also exposed us to an older language—that of printing. Words like *font, point size, pica, sans-serif,* and *leading,* which were once jargon comprehensible only to a printer, have become mainstream. And those who have learned these words also understand something more of the constraints and possibilities of the printing field. Desktop publishing has made us more creative by this introduction.

New types of logic may help us to understand why certain phenomena, e.g. electrons and the velocity of light, appear to behave illogically and contrary to common sense upon which our civilization is built. Intellectuals have long admitted that our mechanistic way of thinking breaks down before the great frontier problems of science. To surmount these barriers, we need a linguistic foundation that will permit a new way of thinking.

Benjamin Whorf,
Language, Thought, and Reality

I'm very sensitive to the freshness of words, and also to their wearing out—thus, my taste for neologisms: I live constantly in a restless relation to language, and I very quickly take the measure of my taste or distaste for certain words. In fact, I spend my time taking up certain words and getting rid of others. So I don't always live with the same ones, which allows for those periodically necessary, and very useful, deflations of language.

Roland Barthes,
The Grain of the Voice: Interviews 1962-1980

Serif is the name for the little flared-out tops and bases of some typefaces. If the letter is squared off at the ends, it's called *sans-serif*.

a serif S   a sans-serif S

Font is a term for a group of letters, numbers and symbols drawn in a similar style.

The vertical spacing between lines of type is called *leading*. The more leading, the farther apart the lines are.

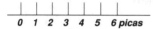

0   1   2   3   4   5   6 picas

A *pica* is a unit of measure, equal to approximately one sixth of an inch. Each pica is divided into twelve points.

The proper metaphor for the life process may not be a pair of rolling dice or a spinning roulette wheel, but the sentences of a language, conveying information that is partly predictable and partly unpredictable. These sentences are generated by rules which make much out of little, producing a boundless wealth of meaning from a finite store of words; they enable language to be familiar yet surprising, constrained yet unpredictable within its constraints.

Jeremy Campbell, *Grammatical Man: Information, Entropy, Language, and Life*

This is not to say that the more words you know the better off you will be. It is not the word itself that is important, but the concept it represents. You must choose and develop your own vocabulary; filled with the words/concepts that have meaning for you. The raw materials are out there, but only you can make the decisions as to what is and is not appropriate.

Understanding concepts is much more difficult than teaching names, dates, and events, but is also incredibly more important. The concept of balance seems simple enough when applied to weight and gravity, but truly understanding the concept allows you to apply it to everything from nutrition, movement, and economics, to philosophy, politics, and design. What would balance mean in the context of the brain? The ecology? A dictionary? A car? Understanding the meaning of this word/concept gives you another brick with which to build.

MIND YOUR MOUTH

Increasing your understanding of language doesn't demand a study of linguistics or etymology. It can be as simple as listening to yourself speak. What words do you rely on inordinately? Does the word really express what you feel? Are there other words that might express your feeling more accurately? Do you fall back on buzzwords and clichés?

You should take control over your language.

●When someone uses a word that you don't understand, ask them to explain it. The chances are you will both learn something.

●Another way to increase your facility with language is simply to listen to others speak and be aware of how they use words differently.

●Feel free to invent words when you need to—especially when you have a new idea. (The Stanford University admissions form asks you to invent and explain a new word.) If your words communicate an idea well, don't let people tell you that they aren't real words. Tell them Shakespeare made up one in ten words that he used in his writing. Children—especially teenagers—invent new words and new meanings for old words all the time. They begin to sort words in new ways, using words in new places and modifying their meanings. They almost develop their own language. Words and phrases like *awesome*, *cool*, *geek*, *chill-out*, and more recently, *gooey* (meaning "romantic" or "mushy") take on new life as they are applied to new situations.

● Weed out the words that mean little or nothing to you and learn new nouns, verbs, and adjectives that will allow you to describe and communicate your ideas effectively.

FILLER PHRASES

Instead of enjoying the delight of creating new words, we laden our speech and our writing with worn-out and/or meaningless phrases that diminish clarity and do little to move our speech along. They are substitutes for expressions that might communicate. They take up communication room and cramp meaning. The following is only a minute sampling of filler phrases, and if they were banished from our language, our communication wouldn't be affected the slightest amount. How many times a day do you use the following expressions?

Another day, another dollar.	Cute as the dickens.
To make a long story short.	Thank God it's Friday.
Needless to say.	I'm on a roll.
Just thought I'd touch base.	I'm talking to you as a person.
Don't mind me.	Where did the day go?
That's life.	What goes around comes around.
I've only got two hands.	As a matter of fact.

VERBAL POLLUTION ON THE RISE

Doublespeak is one of the biggest problems in the English language, according to a National Council of Teachers state-of-the-language report. They cited the following examples:

One stockbroker called the October 1987 stock market crash a "fourth-quarter equity retreat."

The Pacific Gas & Electric Company referred to its bills as "energy documents."

The shutdown at the General Motors plant in Framingham, Massachusetts was labelled by the company a "volume-related production-schedule adjustment."

A recent publication claimed that jumping off a building could lead to "sudden deceleration trauma."

Mark Patinkin, "Double Speak", *The Providence Journal-Bulletin* (6/30/88)

In a manner of speaking.

It's in the bag.

I was scared to death.

Dressed to kill.

How about that?

What's the story?

Can I just say something?

Can I be frank?

I'll be straight with you.

Say what's on your mind.

Something tells me.

Can I ask you a question?

Run that by me again.

It's on the tip of my tongue.

Are you home now?

A fact of life.

I've had it up to here.

I'm not myself today.

Back to the drawing board.

Right on the button.

In any event.

What's the bottom line?

He's a good people person.

I hear where you're coming from.

To be perfectly honest.

Needless to say.

Hold your horses.

Kids say the darnedest things.

Enough is enough.

You're kidding.

That ought to hold me.

I don't want to hear a peep out of you.

Time sure flies.

To tell the truth.

You took the words right out of my mouth.

Raining cats and dogs.

Knock on wood.

Paint the town red.

Get with it.

The way the world turns.

The way the cookie crumbles.

That goes without saying.

Sky's the limit.

Down in the dumps.

Beat around the bush.

Out of this world.

It's never happened to me before.

Tell it like it is.

I was just about to call you.

I'll never live that down.

If these expressions seem to take up an inordinate amount of your speech or writing, pick a few expressions a week and try to exorcise them from your language. Replace them with more meaningful words and phrases. A language that is too static becomes too dull.

Our language gets stifled from laziness, thoughtlessness, and well-meaning criticism from linguistic police, i.e., parents, critics, and teachers, who are trying to teach us a uniform language and may be themselves threatened by its flexibility. But the refusal to resort to worn-out expressions and the commitment to explore new words are the means to expand our language, communication skills, and creativity. No matter what endeavor you are involved in, communication probably plays a role, and the more you can enrich your language, the better your chances are at communicating your ideas. The more you learn about the language you use, the less anxious you will be about communicating with others.

LANGUAGE IS A LAUGHING MATTER

Strangely enough, jokes can be a way to learn about language. The construction of a joke has a lot in common with design. They have in them a balance of surprise, anticipation, and failure. They have in them opposites and radical alternatives; that is why we find humor in them.

George Carlin did a routine in which he talked about words like *farfetched*—is there a word called *nearfetched?* And *nonchalant*—what he wanted to do was get some *chalant*. And on and on, all the words that are composed of parts that should have, but often don't have, obvious opposites. Words suggest an image and they suggest the image that isn't there, the opposite of themselves.

Word play and oxymorons, like *jumbo shrimp* or *military intelligence*, are mirthful ways to question the absurd ways we use language. They cut through our occasional inability to hear duplicities and our reluctance to examine the range of meanings possible in a given word. They are challenges to us to think about what we are saying, what we mean to say, and what the difference is between the two.

> Told to write like Mr. Everyman [Sebastian] would have written like none. I cannot even copy his manner because the manner of his prose was the manner of his thinking and that was a dazzling succession of gaps; and you cannot ape a gap because you are bound to fill it in somehow or other—and blot it out in the process.
>
> **Vladimir Nabokov,**
> *The Real Life of Sebastian Knight*

RENAMING THE WHEEL

I love the cartoon strip "B.C." I remember one where B.C. is in his cave, and he's chopping away at an enormous piece of stone. The shape gives way to a rough circle. He rolls this thing out, puts a hole in the middle of it, and stands there beaming. As his friend comes walking by, he spreads his arms and announces proudly, "I call it fire."

What we call things is what someone else decided to call them. But what we call them now evokes in our minds this enormous system of connections of things to words and words to things. We could have called the wheel *fire*, and we could have called the fire *wheel*. It shows both the importance of words and their whimsy.

Another example is the apocryphal story of the English professor at Amherst College who taught English 101. He always made sure that his classroom was on the ground floor. On the first day of class each semester, he would climb into the classroom through the window, take his hat off, and throw it into the wastebasket. He called the window a door and the wastebasket a hat rack, and the students learned that words aren't absolutes; words are how they perform.

Humor by and large gives you the opposite of what you anticipate. The humor comes from that flash of expectation not met. That is what we find funny. Jokes have in them this element of surprise. One aspect of a joke is as a mind-training exercise. The craft and art of the humorist fascinate me.

My favorite contemporary comedians are Steve Wright, Emo Philips, and Robin Williams. Steve Wright has a series of arcane, droll one-liners symmetrically delivered in an arcane, droll manner. He says, "One day I was walking in a forest and a tree fell and it made no sound." Or "Everything is within walking distance if you have enough time." These stories are pure stories of the anticipation vernacular; they are almost stories without punch lines; they are complete. They are to comedy what haiku is to poetry. They take you to a different vantage point.

Your mind is looking one way through the door, and Wright's humor takes you the other way. Consider the doorway as a metaphor for information; humor is a passageway to understanding.

Emo Philips also encourages you to see things in different contexts, using his peculiar delivery and flexible mind. "I was about seven years old, and I saw the cellar door open just a crack," he says. "Now, my folks had always warned me, 'Emo, whatever you do, don't go near the cellar door.' So of course I was determined to see what was on the other side. So I went to the cellar door, pushed it, and walked through. And I saw strange, wonderful things, things I had never seen before like trees and grass, flowers, the sun. My folks were really protective of me. I couldn't even cross the street without them getting all excited. And placing bets. My dad had very strict rules for me because he loved me. I couldn't be home before a certain hour and that kind of thing," continues Philips.

According to Frank Buxton, comedy is about being led down the garden path, then getting yanked into the bushes. Buxton, a producer/director who did the Emo Philips special for HBO, said that the structure of Philips's material is based on the surprise. His jokes are based on the surprise of connecting one idea to another in an unexpected way. Through the medium of humor, Philips finds different ways of sorting. Sorting is a fundamental idea of organization, of seeking, finding, and understanding.

VERBAL GEOMETRY

The lessons of humor are applicable to other endeavors—to organizing an office, to designing a building, to writing a report. They all involve creating a formidable way of structuring information. You are creating a maplike web of components—in the case of humor with words, ideas, and images—that can be followed or understood by someone else. You are twisting, tweaking, and prodding the accepted, orthodox way of looking at the world to expose possible new interpretations.

The suggestion that words are symbols for things, action, qualities, relationships, et cetera, is naive, a gross simplification. Words are slippery customers. The full meaning of a word does not appear until it is placed in its context, and the context may serve an extremely subtle function—as with puns or double entendre. And even then the "meaning" will depend upon the listener, upon the speaker, upon their entire experience of the language, upon their knowledge of one another, and upon the whole situation. Words do not "mean things" in a one-to-one relation like a code.

Colin Cherry, *On Human Communication*

HUMOR ISN'T A LAUGHING MATTER

At a five-day International Humor Convention at Arizona State University in Tempe, the nature and applications of humor were examined. Everyone from anthropologists to linguists is taking the subject more seriously; hospitals are using laughter therapy groups for patients with chronic pain, and humor has come to be regarded as an essential component in human relationships.

Olive Evans, "Relationships: The Bond of Shared Laughter," *The New York Times*

One of the things I do is look at the morphology or structure of any piece of information and try to find the natural form that will bind together that information, in much the same way that a comedian binds together a routine. Like Philips, I am trying to connect interests and ideas in ways that allow the material to determine the form, instead of imposing on it an arbitrary form.

Comedians like Emo, Jonathan Winters, and Robin Williams are models for the artful connection of information. And I believe the mindset, training, and discipline required to do what they do is very similiar to what is required to do many other creative acts. In each case, you are working with what already exists, with the familiar, and are trying to find a fresh way of representing it, of seeing the things you have always seen, but never really seen, and of planting that vision in someone else's mind.

Buxton says that you have to start with communication as the beginning of your joke. I think that making somebody laugh is the most intimate kind of communication you can ever have. It plays with the problems and pitfalls of communicating and gives you ways to overcome them. You don't have to be on stage or in an audience to benefit from the communication lessons of humor.

WHAT'S IN A NAME

Between 1845 and 1850 a meticulous triangulation of the Himalayas was undertaken by the British colonial administration. Surveyors were instructed to log any peak visible from their stations. Some peaks were given names; others were given symbols, i.e. K-2, K-4, etc. Among them was Peak XV, in Nepal, which, in 1852, was calculated to be 29,002 feet (later adjusted to 29,028 feet), higher than any other summit. In 1865, when efforts to find a local name were exhausted, Peak XV was given the name of *Mount Everest* in honor of Sir George Everest, head of the Indian Measurement Service between 1823 and 1843.

Destinations, a catalog produced by Inner Asia Expeditions, Inc.

SIGN LANGUAGE

Some of the most glaring examples of the problems in communication can be found in the myriad of instruction-bearing signs that attempt to direct our lives. We are bombarded with them; they are rich evidence of just how hard it can be to get a simple message across. Take the simple sign that almost all grocers in New York City feel compelled to put in their window, "We sell kosher and nonkosher food." Why do they bother? What else is there? What the merchants are trying to convey is that they sell kosher food, *too* or *also*. But in trying to be accurate, they become meaningless.

"Unnecessary noise prohibited" is another example. A writer friend of mine who moved to New York from the Midwest was really disconcerted by this. She thought that banal conversation was illegal in New York and suspected she might be guilty. She started saying to herself, "What is unnecessary noise? How much of what I say is really necessary? (Probably, not very much.) Should I take a vow of silence? Should I move to a city that permits unnecessary noise?" As soon as she realized that the sign really meant you can't honk your car horn except to avoid an accident, she came across "Curb your dog."

We are surrounded by absurd instructions. In an attempt to inform us, the sign makers distract us with unnecessary information because they don't take the time to ask, "Just what is it that we are trying to communicate? How might the listener possibly interpret or misinterpret our message?"

Continental Airlines advertises low fares to various cities. Underneath the destination is the phrase "significant restrictions apply." Does this mean you are strapped to a wing or can fly only on the third Tuesday of the month? Unless the advertisements are going to elaborate what constitutes a "significant restriction," it's pointless to include such a phrase.

We labor under the misconception that it is better to have too much information than too little, that it is better to inundate clients with information than risk having them feel cheated because they weren't provided with enough paper.

Our first consideration is usually "How can I cover my ass, make it look as if I have prepared for all outcomes?" Instead, you should ask yourself, "How can I best meet the requirements of communication?"

One effective means of communication is the use of visual clues, such as icons, symbols, pictographs. They can carry a great deal of information in them and can be immediately understandable to speakers of different languages. This is one of the reasons that the Apple Macintosh is so

An excess of messages sent to convey information diminishes the unexpectedness or surprise effect of the information, and, in turn, the information itself. "This extra ration of predictability is called redundancy, and it is one of the most important concepts in information theory. Redundancy is essentially a constraint."

Jeremy Campbell, from *Grammatical Man: Information, Entropy, Language, and Life*

easy to use. It is also why you can tell the men's rest room from the women's without words on the door.

Of course, there are plenty of examples of bad icons and of pictograms that serve only as stylistic decoration or that actually prohibit understanding, but if designed thoughtfully and used properly, visual communication can be very helpful.

I maintain that one clear chart or graph is worth ten pounds of unnecessary paper. Sometimes extraneous information raises more questions than it answers. There is a sign around New York designed to call attention to the problem of violence against women. It reads: "A woman is beaten in her home every 18 seconds." Does this mean that only women who own homes are at risk or that women who stay on the streets are safer? Does this refer to wife beating or does it take into account attacks by strangers? Is this rate for New York, for the country, or for the world? The impact of the message is lost while the reader becomes distracted by the information that isn't there.

LITTLE MS. MUFFET SAT ON HER SOFA EATING HER YOGURT AND GRANOLA

A former elementary school teacher, Susan Ohanian, feels that basal readers (texts that have been adapted and simplified for children) are often stripped of their literary magic in an attempt to make them understandable to young readers.

In the end, it is the ruffles and flourishes that children savor and that will keep them reading.

Susan Ohanian, "Ruffles and Flourishes," *The Atlantic* (9/87)

. . . Do manufacturers know how many people spend about half the year adding or subtracting an hour when they look at their clocks? Why? Because the clocks are a part of radios, stoves, or videocassette recorders, and when daylight saving time rolls around, it seems simpler to live with clocks an hour fast or slow than to read the instructions and adjust each appliance.

Enid Nemy, "New Yorkers, Etc.," *The New York Times*

WILLIAM ZINSSER ON WRITING

The following is excerpted from a talk given by William Zinsser to the American Institute of Graphic Arts national conference in San Francisco in 1987. Zinsser, a writer, editor, and teacher, is a dean of clarity. *On Writing Well,* one of the twelve books he has written, is a seminal text in its field. Although his points are about writing, his suggestions are applicable to a variety of endeavors, and if more of us followed them, we could drastically reduce *information anxiety.*

A clear sentence is no accident. Very few sentences come out right the first time, or even the third time. Meaning is remarkably elusive. I'm always surprised that people think professional writers get everything right on the first try. Just the opposite is true; nobody rewrites more often than the true professional. I rewrite at least five or six times. E. B. White and James Thurber rewrote their pieces eight or nine times.

Remember, you are up against two very powerful adversaries. One is the tendency of almost every sentence to come out just a little wrong. The other is the minuscule attention span of the average reader. So you must constantly put yourself in the reader's position and ask: "Is it absolutely clear?" If a sentence in a piece you're designing doesn't make sense to you, it's not going to make sense to other people. Or if something is missing, some piece of information that the reader needs, speak up. Be a nudge. Clarity must be the god of all of us in the meaning business.

You must also learn to be writers. Writing is how we define ourselves for someone we don't get to meet. Think of all the places where you define yourself in writing for someone whose business you need: the brochure, the sales letter, the proposal, the call report, the strategic recommendation, the press release, the by-lined article, the speech that will give your firm the recognition, the prestige, the business that it doesn't yet have quite enough of. Good writing is integral to the success of every design firm (and of many other businesses as well).

Most people, however, are terrified of writing. Yet writing is not a special language that is owned by the English teacher. Writing is nothing more mysterious than the logical arrangement of thought. Writing is thinking on paper. Anybody who thinks clearly should be able to write clearly and vice versa.

Your style is you; it's who you are. Your style is your personality as you express it on paper. Therefore, always be sure that the person you are claiming to be in your writing is really you and not some pretentious boob that nobody would want to work with. If what you write is pompous and ornate, as most people's writing is, that's how you will be perceived by someone whose business you want. That person has no other choice; he doesn't get a chance to have a beer with you and see what a swell person you really are . . .

Good writing is specific and concrete. Good writing requires the courage of your beliefs. So does good leadership and good management to the extent that you, in your writing, unavoidably reflect the character and the personality of your firm.

A few years ago, I was shanghaied on to an advisory panel at Time Inc., and at our first meeting someone asked the chairman what our committee had been formed to do. He said, "It's an umbrella group that interacts synergistically to platform and leverage cultural human resources strategies companywide." That pretty much ended my interest in the committee. And when it later "experienced viability depravation" (went down the tubes), I was overjoyed.

To inflict that kind of dehumanizing language on your fellow workers, or on anyone you have any contact with, is a little short of criminal. Yet this is the routine language of American business corporations and of American institutional speech.

So if you are in a position of authority, if you are the head of your firm, don't write like the head of your firm. Write like who you are.

The new second edition of the *Random House Dictionary of the English Language* contains more than 315,000 words, 2,500 pages, weighs 13¹/₂ pounds, and costs $79.95. That's about $5.90 a pound.

Part of that weight comes from 50,000 new entries, among which are "tofu," "chocoholic," and "postmodernism."

Definitions, too, have changed; the second definition of "poison pill" is now "any of various business devices created to prevent a company from being taken over by another, as issuing a new class of stock or stock warrants that would become costly to the buyer in the event of a takeover." The dictionary refers to it as "financial slang."

Richard F. Shepard, "New, Unabridged and Heavy," *The New York Times* (9/10/87)

THE WRITE STUFF

Many people are threatened by writing, regarding it with fear or suspicion as the arcane province of someone else, a poet, novelist, or journalist. Anyone who communicates with another on paper is a writer. Anyone who has ever left a note on the kitchen table or written an office memo is a writer, facing on a small scale the same problems as the professional writer.

The discipline of employing language to communicate an idea is one of the most basic, essential activities in which we can participate. Most of the information in our lives comes to us via language.

You shortchange yourself if you think that writing is "someone else's problem." Most of us are frustrated in some way every day by the problems of communication, when it seems as though we cannot make the simplest idea clear to someone else. Even if your job description says nothing about writing, by regarding yourself as a writer even privately, you can take advantage of the discipline of the craft at whatever level you want to practice.

We could all benefit by honing our communications skills. If you can become a better memo writer, you will increase the likelihood that your ideas will be put into action. If you can become a better order giver, your order takers can operate with more precision.

Any effort that we make to improve our knowledge of the language and how to use it will concomitantly improve our ability to understand and manage information.

The chairman of the Chrysler Corporation, Lee Iacocca, agrees. One of his eight commandments of good management is to "Say it in English and keep it short. Write the way you talk. If you don't talk that way, don't write that way."

USA TODAY

LANDMINES IN THE UNDERSTANDING FIELD

When I think of the present dissentions, I read into them not disorder, not insult to the status quo. I see in them an advance in the minds of men who can throw to the wind the convenient avenues of getting ahead and show an inner dissatisfaction with the way things are.

Louis Kahn

*S*ince the advent of the industrial age, we have had a terrific word: "more." It really worked for everything. When our roads became crowded, we built more roads. When our cities became unsafe, we hired more police officers, ordered more police cars, and built more prisons.

We built more schools for our children when we found they couldn't read. We solved our problems by producing endless products in greater numbers.

Imagination is more important than knowledge.

Attributed to Albert Einstein

Now, however, the word that worked so well for a hundred years is creating the problems it once solved. More police officers don't necessarily mean less crime. More hospitals don't mean better health care. More schools don't mean a higher quality of education.

As with new superhighways to relieve the overload of old superhighways, which were to relieve the overload of highways, which were to relieve the overload of roads and streets, the labyrinth may become an infinite regress. This is technocracy.

Kingsley Widmer, "Sensibility Under Technocracy" from *Human Connection and the New Media*

In fact, the opposite has become the case. In our desire to educate, we've penalized imagination and rewarded conformity. In our desire for revenues, we've encouraged deterioration by taxing owners for building improvements instead of penalizing them for letting buildings dilapidate. In our desire for mobility, we've scarred the landscape with highways that are always too narrow for the increase in traffic they generate. In our search for simplicity, we've created overly complex and expensive products that few can operate, let alone fix.

We have attempted to solve all problems with "more" solutions. We have asked ourselves only questions that produce "more" answers.

There is an often-told story about Gertrude Stein that describes the moments before her death. People are huddled around her bed. Suddenly her face lights up. Her friends hover over her and say, "Gertrude, Gertrude, what is the answer?" Her eyes flutter and she says, "What is the question?" and dies.

People either don't know how to ask the right questions or they don't understand the value of asking them.

A clear case where more doesn't mean better is the freeway system in Los Angeles. A recent study estimated that the average speed on a Los Angeles freeway during rush hour will be about the same as that of a horse and carriage by 1990. Instead of solving the transportation problem there, more roads seem to bring about nothing but even more cars.

Source Unknown

POLKA DOTS ON AN EDSEL

Social, economic, and cultural progress has historically been measured in terms of "more" or "better" or "improved."

We attempt to solve problems with solutions that are only improved versions of what didn't work in the first place. We doggedly try to postpone that day of the grim reaper when we have to discount or throw away an idea. And a better version of what doesn't work is like putting polka dots on an Edsel.

We have a spackling-compound mindset that is geared toward products and product improvement. What we are missing is a language of solutions, a language that recognizes the concept of performance over product.

Performance is the art to which function can aspire.

We need a language that can express performance—not merely product.

"More" answers don't describe the performance we need from a person or a product to solve the problem. The issue is learning, not schools; safety, not the number of police officers; mobility, not highways; communication, not signs. The issue is performance, not products.

FUNCTION IS TO PERFORMANCE AS A MODEL T FORD IS TO A FERRARI

Let's talk about performance. What's the difference between function and performance? A Model T Ford is a car that functions as transportation; a Ferrari Testarossa is performance.

In architecture, many buildings function in that they keep occupants safe from the elements; far fewer perform. A building that performs is one where all spaces can be used efficiently, with neither too much nor too little allotted for different activities; where the building systems are designed to accommodate the needs of the occupants; where the design is such that users feel comfortable in the interior environment. Performance is how well the building works. These concerns can be more important than construction costs. In the long run, an inefficient building will cost more.

Performance matters.

What we need is a language that would allow us the power and ability to demand learning, safety, mobility, and communication. What we have is a vocabulary that encourages makeshift solutions that distract us from real problems.

We need the vocabulary that will enable us to understand the essential problems and to ask the questions that will produce answers that perform.

The emphasis on function produces more technology without clear manuals that would enable people to operate it. The emphasis on function produces sophisticated information technology without clear manuals that would enable people to operate it. The emphasis on function will produce *information anxiety*.

> **Be patient toward all that is unsolved in your heart. Try to love the questions, themselves. Do not now seek the answers which cannot be given because you would not be able to live them. And the point is to live everything. Live the questions now. Perhaps you will then gradually, without noticing it, live along some distant day into the answers.**
>
> **Rainer Maria Rilke,** *Letters to a Young Poet*

TRAPS, DISEASES, AND MALAISES

The language of information transmission is laden with traps that lead us away from the concerns of performance and toward anxiety, confusion, and misunderstandings. By merely being wary of them, you can relax and learn. Keep them in mind as you dive into new information, as you peruse a newspaper, listen to the news, embark on a new endeavor, or take a new toaster out of a box. Understanding the pitfalls of communicating information will give you a defense against being intimidated or overwhelmed by it.

The following are misnomers, myths, and diseases that litter the information field, and unless you are aware of them, they will sabotage understanding. They afflict our ability to see the things we have always seen but have never really seen. They obscure our path to learning, and by just recognizing them, we can disarm their potential to mislead us.

● **The disease of familiarity.** Familiarity breeds confusion. Those afflicted are the experts in the world who, so bogged down by their own knowledge, regularly miss the key points as they try to explain what they know. You ask them the time, and they will tell you how to build a clock. We have all had teachers who we have said are extraordinarily bright, yet we cannot understand what they are saying. They fail to provide the doorknob or the threshold into each thought so you can grapple with the learning connections along the journey.

● **Looking good is being good.** The disease of looking good is confusing aesthetics with performance. A piece of information performs when it successfully communicates an idea, not when it is delivered in a pleasing manner. Information without communication is no information at all. It is an extremely common, insidious malady among graphic designers and architects to confuse looking good with being good. The cure obviously is to ask how something performs.

● **The uh-huh syndrome.** This occurs when our fear of looking stupid outweighs our desire to understand. The manifestations are involuntary head nodding and repeating uh-huh, uh-huh, pretending to a knowledge that we do not have. Rather than admit we don't understand the principle of quantum mechanics, we nod our heads as if we were intimately familiar with the subject, desperately trying to give the impression that we understand terms or

According to Jonathan Kozol, author of *Illiterate America*, "statistical narcotics" are responsible for a vicious cycle of false euphoria followed by exaggerated anguish that has confused the illiteracy problem in this country. A study conducted by a Princeton group, proudly released by the Educational Testing Service, reported that the illiteracy rate is better than in the past and better than Third World countries, but 70 million (American) adults could not read as well as eleventh graders. "Lost in a thicket of statistical verbosity and graphs that only the bold or hyperactive dared penetrate were truly disturbing disclosures," said Kozol, who cited that 40 percent of adults cannot use a road map, 80 percent can't figure out a restaurant tip or a bus schedule.

Jonathan Kozol, "Illiteracy Statistics: A Numbers Game," *The New York Times* (10/30/86)

allusions that are in reality incomprehensible to us. This only prevents us from learning and exacerbates our suspicion that everyone else knows more than we do.

● **Unhealthy comparisons.** Comparing unknowns or intangibles is uninformative; so is comparing things that have nothing in common. People warn of the dangers of comparing apples to oranges, when this is a perfectly reasonable comparison. They share many common characteristics—both are globular fruit that grows on trees. An unhealthy comparison would be to compare the cost of a loaf of bread or a movie fifty years ago to the cost today. The dollar had a completely different value then. The informative value of this comparison is very little. Whereas healthy comparison is one of the most powerful information tools—for example, comparing the cost of a loaf of bread relative to a movie fifty years ago and today.

● **If it's accurate, it's informative.** One doesn't necessarily follow the other. The cure is learning to get beyond the facts to meaning and to recognize the nature of the receiver. Accuracy or facts do not necessarily make things understandable. Quoting a price in pounds won't help someone who understands only dollars and cents. Barometric pressure is another example. I would say there is one person in a thousand who knows how the barometric pressure is derived or what it means; yet weather commentators slavishly offer it up in every forecast.

● **Unnecessary exactitude.** Rounding off is not a sin. Not only is extreme accuracy not always information, it is often not necessary. For pilots, knowing the exact altitude of the plane is important. But whether the plane is flying at 32,000 feet or 32,112 doesn't add to their experience of flying. In the business community, an accountant needs exact figures, but someone making a presentation on sales projections might just as well say that projected sales will be $90,000, rather than $91,653. Just because the technology exists to provide accuracy to the nth degree doesn't mean that we have to take advantage of it. Sometimes

One would think, in the wake both of the recent stock market crash and new legislation eliminating the need for companies to file more than summaries of activity, that many companies would scale back on the lavish annual reports of yesteryear. Not so. In lean years, annual reports are as lavish as ever.

The effect of graphic splash on credibility remains questionable. "Most investors believe they get better investment advice from a relative than from the [annual] reports," according to a recent study by Hill & Knowlton, the public relations firm.

An earlier study by the Chicago investment firm of Duff & Phelps "found that the average investor spends about six minutes reading an annual report and then files it—typically in the trash bin."

^{66/99} Eric N. Berg, "Reports Thrive in a Frugal Age," *The New York Times* (4/13/88)

From *What If , Could Be*, a fable for our time, by Richard Saul Wurman. Illustrations by R. O. Bleckman.

extreme detail prohibits you from seeing the bigger picture. Even the federal government permits rounding dollar amounts on tax forms.

● **Rainbow worship or adjectivitis.** This is an epidemic belief that more color and more colorful language will in itself increase understanding. An area where this is particularly insidious is in sports reporting, which has adapted the dramatic language of war. Teams are "annihilated, destroyed, massacred."

● **Chinese-dinner memory dysfunction.** This is characterized by total memory loss one hour after learning something. This has been caused by the educational system's emphasis on short-term memory. The cramming of unnecessary information about unnecessary subjects for unnecessary examinations to get unnecessary grades. The cure is very simple; the key to learning is remembering what you are interested in and that through interest comes understanding.

● **Overload amnesia.** This is a permutation of the Chinese-dinner memory dysfunction that occurs more specifically as a response to overloading yourself with data. When overtaxed, your memory will not only release the data that you were trying to retain, but may arbitrarily download other files as well. This is often experienced when trying to assimilate data over which you cannot control the flow—such as in a classroom, conference, or lecture. This is why after listening to a particularly ponderous speech, not only can you not remember a thing the speaker said, but you forget where you parked your car, too.

● **User-friendly intimidation.** "User friendly" has got to be one of the most absurd terms in the language of technology. Like many other words in techno-talk, this usually means the opposite of itself. Any piece of hardware or software that has to be described as user-friendly is probably not. Often, the appearance of friendship with silly graphics is only a camouflage of incoherent instructions. Besides, why should a computer be friendly? We have the right to expect technology and equipment to

Hermann Ebbinghaus, the nineteenth-century founder of scientific memory research, who used nonsense syllables in his memory tests to ensure that the pure act of recall was not tainted by meaning, found that people forget up to 80 percent of what they learn within twenty-four hours. After that the loss is less rapid. This swift loss of information from the conscious mind became known as "the curve of forgetting."

Jeremy Campbell, *Grammatical Man: Information, Entropy, Language and Life*

perform for us, to save us time, and make our lives easier, but if we expect friendship from it, we are bound to be disappointed.

● **Some-assembly-required gambit.** I have no doubt that somewhere in the instructions for building a Saturn rocket are the words "Some assembly required." This is instant intimidation, a phrase lightly tossed off, designed to make the user feel that any boob could put this machine together during a network station break. I suspect it's sheer business chicanery, a trick so that the manufacturer can collect on a house call and a repair bill after you have failed miserably at the some-assembly-required test.

● **The expert-opinion syndrome.** There is a tendency to believe that the more "expert opinions" we get—be they legal, medical, automotive, or otherwise—the more informed we will be. But we tend to forget that "expert opinion" is by no means synonymous with "objective opinion." Unfortunately, most experts come with a professional bias that makes obtaining truly objective information almost impossible. Take the second-opinion movement in medicine that is even being promoted by health-insurance programs, where patients are encouraged to consult more than one doctor before undergoing nonemergency surgery. Surgeons are trained to respond to problems by performing surgery, so it is likely that they will see surgery as the solution to a patient's problem.

● **Don't tell me how it ends.** The popularity of the suspense genre in books and movies has encouraged people to extrapolate this to maintaining interest when conveying new information, e.g. a salesman unveiling a new product. I think not knowing how something ends makes us apprehensive; it prohibits us from understanding how something was done while we frantically try to guess how it might end. People love Shakespeare because they know the endings; an opera is more pleasurable when you know the whole story before the curtain rise. The Brandenburg Concertos are like old friends because you know them. While suspense has its place, it does tend to induce anxiety, which is probably not an optimum state to receive new information. If you know the ending, you can relax and enjoy the manner in which something is being presented. I've seen more new ideas squelched in committee meetings when the person trying to sell them got bogged down in introductions. An audience will be more receptive to new information if they aren't kept in suspense, made anxious trying to guess where someone is going. Many people can't really listen to an idea until key questions about it have been answered in their minds.

● **Information imposters.** This is nonsense that masquerades as information because it is postured in the form of information. We automatically give a certain weight to data based on the form in which it is delivered to us. Because we don't take the time to question this, we assume that we have received some information. My favorite example of this is in cookbook recipes that call for you to "season to taste" or "cook until done." This doesn't tell very much. Why bother? Information imposters are the fodder for administrativitis.

● **Administrativitis.** This is a disease manifest in schools, institutions, and in big business, where the individuals think that they are running the system, but in operation just the opposite is the case. It is characterized by a preoccupation with the details of operation—administrative issues, salaries, square footage of office space, and supplies—and a neglect of the purposes for operation. It has reached global proportions and is the fundamental curse of our society.

A STAMP FOR ALL REASONS

This amusing evidence of administrativitis was received by an employee in my San Francisco office last year. The U.S. Postal Service has a rubber stamp or plastic package to explain every mistake and a system that makes lots of them.

● **Edifitis.** This is a condition characterized by the belief that a better building or a more lavish office or a flashier annual report will solve all problems. Many a business has crumbled trying to improve its corporate headquarters instead of its corporation.

COMMUNICATION EQUALS REMEMBERING WHAT IT'S LIKE NOT TO KNOW

Information is the fodder that feeds all communication in that the motivation behind all communication is to transfer information from one mind into another that will receive it as new information. Thus perhaps the most universal information trap is the one that inevitably occurs when attempting to communicate information. It is the trap of forgetting what it's like not to know. The minute we know something, we forget what it was like not to know it.

We can't remember what it was like not to be able to read, to walk, to know the names of objects. To some extent, we all fall victim to this when we explain something to another, for the simple reason that once we know something, we can't remember what it was like not to know it.

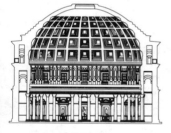

For many years, I had an idea in my mind of what the Pantheon in Rome looked like. Then, the instant I saw it, I forgot the picture of it that existed only in my imagination. It's as if there was a file in my mind under the heading "Pantheon." Once I saw the real thing, the image ran over or erased the original. Once you see or understand something, you cannot conceive of what it was like not to have seen or understood it. You lose the ability to identify with those who don't know.

In the business community, millions of dollars are lost in hours and errors in the training of new employees because the trainers or seasoned employees can't remember what it was like not to know. If you could remember what it was like not to know, you could begin to communicate in terms that might be understood more readily by someone who doesn't know.

We may not be able to completely transcend this trap, but by at least trying to put ourselves in the place of someone who knows nothing about what we are talking about, we can anticipate some of their questions and become better information transmitters. If we can simulate what it is like to be blind by covering our eyes, we can try to remember what it is like not to know when communicating new information to others.

DRAWING THE LINE

Red Sox legend Ted Williams was the last person to hit .400 and probably the greatest hitter of all time. He disliked the press vehemently. In one rare interview, a reporter brought up the subject of Williams's vision, which was 20/10. Yes, he said, his eyes were better than normal, and he had a lot of walks because he really understood exactly where the strike zone was. The reporter said that Williams could get more hits if he swung at some balls just slightly out of the strike zone. Yes, Williams replied, he could get more hits; however, he never swung at pitches outside of the strike zone. Well, the reporter asked, why if you could get more hits, don't you try to do that? Williams said, "Because then there is no place to draw the line." And that was the interview. (Another way of looking at this: even at the height of his career, Ted Williams didn't even get on base 60 percent of the time.)

That story has stayed with me since I first read it when I was twelve, and it became a talisman for me in my uncompromising and rebellious days. In many ways, I carry it with me today—trying to understand where the strike zone is, and the seduction of things right outside the strike zone, and how that seduction always reduces the clarity of your ideas.

I compiled a book on the architect Louis Kahn called *What Will Be Has Always Been.* The cover was a page from one of his notebooks—a messy scrawl with words inserted and scratched out. The publishers of the book, Rizzoli International, didn't like the cover. They wanted a photograph or something pretty on the cover. They wanted all the things that would make the book more salable, but less

Historians and researchers have debunked most myths surrounding Columbus's discovery of America. Apparently, learned men of the fifteenth century already knew the earth was round; maps in existence in 1492 documented the existence of the continent Columbus "discovered." The *Nina*, the *Pinta*, and the *Santa Maria* were only nicknames and not the real names of the ships that made up his expedition, and while Columbus died on the outs with the King and Queen of Spain, he was not in pennlless disgrace.

Charles Downey, "Scholars Run Columbus Myths Aground," *Los Angeles Times* (10/12/87)

Human bodies and minds can be viewed as systems of information, through which matter is continually passing. Within the whole are subsystems that communicate with each other.

Richard Rabkin, "A Tower of Babble: The Sociology of Body and Mind," *Family Process* (3/86)

clear. The book is about its cover, about somebody's words, the difficulty he had with the clarification of ideas, the working over and over of an idea, trying to find his way through the mistakes and the failures to the clarity. The book isn't about Kahn's buildings; it is about his ideas of the man-made world and of learning. How do you express an idea? How do you avoid being seduced and allow that feeling to flow into a finished product that has clarity? How do you make a connection between the idea and the image?

Ideas that aren't attached to images are forgotten. If you are trying to understand the DNA molecule, you could memorize all the formulas or you could read the story of Francis Crick and how he unlocked its secrets. The image of the man and his work would help you remember the formulas.

Learning is like Velcro. An unfiltered fact is not a complete fastener. Only one side of learning is made up of facts; the other consists of stories, i.e. ideas and images.

ED SCHLOSSBERG CONVERSATION

Ed Schlossberg is a maverick exhibition designer who is a master at the art of making connections between images, between the picture of the thing and the thing itself, between art and science. Schlossberg is the author of many books and holds doctorates in science and literature from Columbia University. His Ph.D. dissertation was an imaginary dialogue between Albert Einstein and Samuel Beckett. His radical views have prompted museum and exhibition designs that are sexy and dramatic, and eminently understandable.

ES: My vision of a brave new world is not the opportunity for me to create, but for us to create a maze which becomes the context for us to find our way to each other. The things that interest me most are environments that make me learn about you—the occupants, not the designer.

RSW: This has a parallel in the design of museums today where you are more conscious of the design of the museum building than of what is in it.

ES: I think that the idea of letting these spoiled brats design things which are awards to their own ingenuity is outrageous. The task of a museum is to create an event that doesn't tell you how wonderful the designers are, but instead provides a context where you can feel better about and understand the people around you.

I think the thing that was so wonderful about Shakespeare was that in addition to being a great writer, he knew that his audience was full of drunken kids and very fine ladies and that all of them came from different levels, so he tried to entertain all of them at different times. So many things that we do are really geared to a specific audience—other designers or very wealthy people. The fact is that they are a very exclusive, small segment of things. It shouldn't be a choice between mass or class, and it should be a choice to do something well that has broader appeal.

RSW: Part of this *information anxiety* is about who is anxious. I know damn well you are not anxious about the information. You can blast by this stuff. But some people, when they look at something, are put off because they immediately think the information is not for them; it is not in their language. The idea of anxiety is the idea of immobilized fear. I had a great definition of neurosis the other day. It is what you do to yourself to protect your parents. Being anxious is part of a neurotic pattern. Information anxiety is parents not giving you the word when you understand something.

ES: The dangerous part of doing any kind of exhibit or entertainment is that you finish the circle, make it hermetic, as if the whole story has been told and we don't need you, but if you want to look at it, fine. That is how most exhibitors feel when they walk into a place. What you want to have is an exhibit that says we have been waiting for you to finish this, and if you are not here, it doesn't work.

RSW: There is a misnomer that you can take a book and make it into an exhibit. You can't. There is a belief that you can switch ideas between different media: books into exhibits, plays into movies.

ES: They are different, not only in the sense that it is a different kind of story, but the way that you communicate in a three-dimensional event is very different from the way you communicate in a two-dimensional event. In an exhibit, the drama ought to be happening around me. Most exhibits are designed as books; you see a little thing and you read about it; you see another little thing and read about it. If God had wanted us to read standing up, he'd have given books legs.

In *Macomber Farm*, there was a desire on the part of the ASPCA to talk about cruelty to animals. The way they thought to translate that to the public was to make a display of all the different ways that people were cruel to animals. What was quite obvious to me was that people wouldn't learn; they would just feel sorry for the animals. We wanted to make the experience one where people could understand what it was like to be a particular animal, what it was like to smell like that animal, see like that animal, or walk like that animal. So we invented masks that you put on your face. You could actually see like a horse or a cow, instead of doing a chart or a book or a graphic about it. In front of the masks, we put these signs saying "I am seeing like a horse or a pig" because we thought it might be intimidating to try one. We thought it would be a good contextual experience to have something that was funny so people could take a photograph of other people doing it. I wanted to talk about how the sense of smell in pigs was critical. Their sense of smell relates to a part of their brain. They use their smell amazingly well. The olfactory lobes are quite large in a pig's brain, compared to those of other farm animals. Pigs smell bad to humans, so we invented the scent maze. The only way you could find your way through a series of areas was to sniff your way rather than look your way through it. It's amusing because it is out of the realm of experience for

On being asked what he thought about Western civilization, Mahatma Gandhi responded by saying "I think that it would be a very good idea."

Those who know that they are profound strive for clarity. Those who would like to seem profound to the crowd strive for obscurity.

He is a thinker; that means, he knows how to make things simpler than they are . . .

Friedrich Nietzsche, *The Gay Science*

most people to use their sense of smell as a guide. So what they were doing was putting themselves in the behavioral set of the pig.

WHAT YOU TAKE FOR GRANTED YOU CANNOT IMPROVE

Ed Schlossberg is a master observer. He pulls himself back from any endeavor and looks at it from different vantage points. Thus he enables the viewers to look at the world through different eyes. By refusing to take the way we look at exhibits for granted, his exhibit designs present a fresh way of looking at the world.

What we take for granted we give up the possibility of changing or improving. This applies to monumental issues, like marriages, jobs, law, religious doctrine, and to more pedestrian concerns, such as a recipe or a room color.

People take it for granted that if they go outside when it is raining, they will get wet. But why couldn't cities be built with arcades—like Bologna?

The information traps outlined in this chapter exist because people take them for granted—looking good is being good; if it's accurate, it's information; an expert opinion is an objective opinion. We accept that tax forms should be confusing, legal documents should be written in legalese, and that we should spend hours everyday trying to decipher charts and graphs.

All of these conceptions cloud our understanding of information because we accept them as givens. If we questioned them, we would see them with different eyes. In this way, we wouldn't be such easy victims of them and we might begin to see the new paths around them to understanding.

LEARNING IS REMEMBERING
WHAT YOU ARE INTERESTED IN

Just as eating against one's will is injurious to health, so study without a liking for it spoils the memory, and it retains nothing it takes in.

Leonardo da Vinci

Learning can be seen as the acquisition of information, but before it can take place, there must be interest; interest permeates all endeavors and precedes learning. In order to acquire and remember new knowledge, it must stimulate your curiosity in some way.

Interest defies all rules of memorization. Most researchers agree that people can retain only about seven bits in their short-term memory, such as the digits in a Zip Code or telephone number. Yet most people who saw the movie *Mary Poppins* and liked it could remember the word "supercalifragilisticexpialidocious." Children who couldn't for the life of them remember the capital of Idaho could not only remember, but probably could spell this word.

Learning can be defined as the process of remembering what you are interested in. And both go hand in hand—warm hand in warm hand—with communication. The most effective communicators are those who understand the role interest plays in the successful delivery of messages, whether one is trying to explain astrophysics or help car owners in parking lots.

Multilevel parking garages are generally pretty threatening places. They conjure up frightening images—a favorite site for nefarious activities, clandestine meetings, rapists, and mob hitmen, to say nothing of the fear of remembering on what level you parked your car.

In downtown Chicago, there is a multilevel parking garage that uses the names of countries instead of numbers to denote each level. In the elevator, the buttons are labeled France, Canada, Greece, Turkey, Germany, etc.,

About twenty-five years ago, the psychologist George Miller found that only about seven "chunks" of information—such as the digits in a phone number—can be held easily in a person's short-term memory. This is borne out in current research. We design machines today recognizing that one's short-term attention span is as important as long-term memory in determining how much data can be usefully displayed.

Daniel Goleman, "Ideas & Trends: Learning to Mesh Mind with Machine." *The New York Times* (2/15/87)

each in a different typeface. In the elevator lobby on each floor, the national anthem of the country is broadcast through an intercom. While parking garages don't seem to inspire the imagination of the public, foreign countries do. People don't forget where their cars are parked, and almost everyone is smiling when they leave the garage.

The developer of the parking garage has taken a mundane thing and has not only made it work, but has made it into a cultural learning center as well. This parking garage exemplifies the principle that we learn only if we are interested in the subject.

In his book *Freedom to Learn*, Carl Rogers states that the only learning which significantly influences behavior is "self-discovered, self-appropriated" learning. Only when subject matter is perceived as being relevant to a person's own purposes will a significant amount of learning take place.

When designing a building, an architect considers observers' interest. As Eugene Raskin explains in *Architecturally Speaking*, the sequence of interest points in a structure—what comes first, what comes next, how long it takes a person to experience each hallway, each entrance—determines the extent to which the structure will intrigue the eye. Like interest in learning, interest in a building "flags and needs to be revived and renewed by constantly increasing doses of stimulant. While these doses . . . may be alternated for effect with transitional periods of relative dullness, the overall plan must be one of rising interest," said Raskin, a professor of architecture at Columbia University.

Information anxiety results from constant overstimulation; we are not given the time or opportunity to make transitions from one "room" or idea to the next. No one functions well perpetually gasping for breath. Learning (and interest) require "way-stations" where we can stop and think about an idea before moving on to the next.

SEEK AND YE SHALL REMEMBER

Some research indicates that users of information are more likely to value information which they themselves seek out, as opposed to information which is merely presented to them without solicitation.

Amy S. Knicely, "A Study of the Use of Social Information in Decision Making," *Dissertation Abstracts International.*

Without learning, life is but an image of death.

Cato

Learning without thought is useless; thought without learning is dangerous.

Confucius

Most things are easy to learn, but hard to master.

William Scarborough

YOU CAN'T GET LOST ON THE ROAD TO INTEREST

The importance of piquing and maintaining interest crosses all media or forms of expression. Any written or spoken presentation should be developed to incite interest along the way. The path should be flexible enough to allow the reader or listener to see the connections between the topic at hand and other topics. If you are presenting a proposal to do a marketing study on a new analgesic, you are not bound to discuss only the drug itself. Relate it to other analgesics, the development of painkillers, the history of medicine. Understanding the connections between one interest and another encourages people to chart their own paths.

You can follow any interest on a path through all knowledge. Interest connections form the singular path to learning. It doesn't matter what path you choose or where you begin the journey. A person can be interested in horses, or automobiles, or color, or grass, or the concept of time, and, without forcing the issue whatsoever, can make connections to other bodies of information.

Someone who's interested in cars could move into a fascination with the Porsche and the German language, or the physics of motion, or the growth of cities and the pattern of movement and defense, or the chemistry of fuels. Various cars are made by various countries that have different languages and histories. By studying Italian automotive design, you can gain entry into the study of roads, the Appian Way, the plan of Rome, and the history of transportation itself.

INTEREST CONNECTIONS

The idea that you can expand one interest into a variety of other interests makes your choices less threatening. You can jump into a subject at any level, and not only can you follow the subject to greater levels of complexity, but you can follow it to other subjects.

If a computer company wanted to develop an exhibit that would make computers less intimidating to the public, they could start at a basic level with the idea of opposites, which could move into "on" and "off," then into binary numbers, the workings of a circuit panel, and into computers themselves. Everyone can identify with the idea of opposites. Its simplicity and universal appeal aren't threatened with self-limitations or exclusivity. They form a path to new interests and higher levels of complexity.

Part of the trauma of decision making is the fear that you must eliminate alternatives which you fear may have been more viable than the one you selected. But when you realize that one interest can always be connected to another, you dispel that fear. If you choose to study automobiles, it doesn't mean you can't study history as well.

DISCRIMINATING BETWEEN INTERESTS AND OBLIGATIONS

The problem with interests is less one of making choices than one of distinguishing interests from obligations. Many people can't distinguish their genuine interests from the subjects they think would make them more interesting as individuals—true interest versus guilt or status. The trick is to separate that which you are really interested in from that which you think you should be interested in. The pursuit of the first will provide pleasure; the pursuit of the second will produce anxiety. Are you memorizing football scores so your husband will talk to you or because you have a genuine interest in the sport? Are you living your life with the idea that before you do you are going to have to take a test?

Sometimes it is easy to separate interest motivated by genuine curiosity as opposed to guilt, responsibility, or status seeking. But other times, the distinctions are not so clear. They may become clear in time, or they may require asking yourself some questions:

Play used to be regarded as a harmless release of surplus energy, but it has come to be regarded as useful to the process of learning. Under the guise of play, new forms of behavior can be invented with impunity and thus it becomes an inspiration to innovation. According to Jerome Bruner, the invention of tools came after a long period of pressure-free existence when man didn't have to worry about defending his terrain. Thus, technology can be seen as an extension of play.

Jeremy Campbell, *Grammatical Man: Information, Entropy, Language, and Life*

141

● Do you find yourself compelled to read every line of a book or magazine despite the fact that your mind keeps wandering off to what you are going to wear tomorrow? Chances are you are probably reading only because you think the information gleaned will improve your cocktail-party ratings and not because you really want to know the information.

● Do you change your opinion about movies after having read reviews of them?

● Have you ever asked a teacher, "Will we have to know this for a test?"

● Have you ever asked a teacher, "Are there other books I could read on this subject?"

● When someone mentions a PBS program, do you get a queasy feeling remembering that you were watching "Dallas" at the time?

● Or worse, do you quickly switch the television channel to the PBS station when you hear someone walking toward your room? Do you listen to classical music only when you have company?

● Do you look forward to the destination or the journey of any new endeavor? Do you have a cod-liver oil attitude toward the trip, patting yourself on the head with the promise of how good you will feel when it's over, or do you relish the process with joy?

Once you have determined your interests, you can develop your potential for curiosity by maximizing the connections between your interests. How do you move from your interest in Ming vases to Chinese history and then to your job as a claims adjuster? How does the word **interest** figure into your daily life? What do you pursue in any planned way to increase your involvement in these interests? Your work should be an extended hobby.

I have always been passionate about architecture, and it was as an architect that I started my professional career, but I discovered that just about everything interested me, and I couldn't channel the practice of architecture to recognize my curiosity. I needed quicker gratification; I needed to be able to follow my interests. As an architect, you can't do anything until someone asks you to do it. You can't get up in the morning and say, "I've got this great idea for a factory. I think I'll design one today." You are always dependent on the client.

The most creative project that we can undertake is the design of our lives, so I set to work to redesign mine in such a way that my curiosity could manifest itself in my career. It was sort of an adaptive or re-use project. I followed my path of interests into graphic design and into the architecture of information.

George Simmel, a turn-of-the-century sociologist, was the first to recognize the concept of information overload when he described a phenomenon of urban life where people shield themselves from "indiscriminate suggestibility to protect themselves from an overload of sensations, which results in an incapacity . . . to react to new situations with the appropriate energy."

ACCESS® *GUIDES*

Literate people possess the means to organize their surroundings and establish personal connections with what they see organized before them. Personal relevance depends on organization and perception.

The fact that people learn in different ways and have varied interests was the inspiration behind the guidebooks to cities, sports, medicine, and finances that I have been publishing for eight years. We structure them so they can be read and used selectively and unpredictably. We want readers to feel nothing is being asked of them. We give them permission not to read from beginning to end. They can skim, concentrate on one section, look at the pictures, do whatever seems comfortable. We provide traditional background information that I believe a number of people who use the books never read. But it's there for those who do.

The **ACCESS®** guides to cities were the first I developed and were perhaps the clearest examples of my principles of organization. To describe them in a sentence, one could say I mix up the pieces as they exist in a traditional guidebook and put them next to each other, as they exist in the city.

143

Kenneth A. Kiewra argues
that most teachers do not
understand the nature of
human memory and that
memory-compatible in-
struction can be designed
to facilitate knowledge re-
cording and retrieval.

Kenneth A. Kiewra,
"Memory-Compatible
Instruction,"*Engineering
Education* (2/87)

When you're visiting a city, you either are someplace or you're going someplace. If you are someplace, you want to see what's around you. If you're going someplace, you want to know what you'll pass by.

Our books are about adjacencies that often seem seren-dipitous. I learned from drawing maps that categories of information can be indicated by color, so I transferred that to the city guides.

The format involves the use of color to categorize text: red for restaurants, blue for architecture, black for narra-tive, museums, and shops, green for parks, gardens, and piers. Each city is divided into areas, with brief entries on the topics listed organized according to their location and proximity to each other.

Deciding how to break a city down into manageable pieces is a vital part of our process. The division into areas and their geographical relationships decides how our data will be collected and our maps drawn. This breakdown is based on research—reading, talking to people who live in the city for sensible ideas about shopping, etc., finding areas that are already known as cohesive entities, and reacting to what other books have portrayed. In planning area divisions, we also consider landmarks that will help people orient themselves when switching from one area map to the next.

Individual sites are described or graphically represented not by any set formula, but by whatever means seems ap-propriate. I ask myself, "What is the key to this particu-lar space or place? Is it a section diagram, a floor plan, an elevation drawing, a story, an anecdote?"

One vital link in an interest connection chain is familiar-ity. In our New York guide (and in the Washington, D.C., and Tokyo books) we accomplish this partly via cartoons by well-known local artists, by listings of songs and movies about the locale, by contributions from famous citizens about their city. On the one hand this provides a familiar flavor. On the other it surprises readers in what we hope is a delightful manner. You never know what you are liable to find on any page.

We don't have the inside track on information. But we provide a unique format and a way to gain access to it. In other guides, you seldom get to know the fabric. Fabric is an important part of understanding a city or any subject. How are the parts woven together in a cohesive whole? Fabric involves overlaying layers of use—neighborhoods, sports facilities, or hospitals—the way they are, rather than arbitrarily delineated into sections for the sake of convenience. Cities would be far less interesting, for example, if they were arranged the way most guides are arranged, with all the restaurants in one area and all the hotels in another. More than the space shuttle or any other new technology, the city is man's most complicated invention. It is a mix of a jewelry store next to a restaurant next to a bookstore next to an office building.

Everybody experiences far more than he understands. Yet it is experience, rather than understanding, that influences behavior.

Marshall McLuhan

GETTING PERMISSION TO LEARN

A good facilitator or teacher, says Carl Rogers, tries to "organize and make easily available the widest possible range of resources for learning." One way to learn, Rogers found, is to state your own uncertainties, to try to clarify your puzzlements, and thus get closer to the meaning that your experience actually seems to have. My guidebooks attempt to facilitate learning by allowing free interaction with as close a mirror of a given environment as a reader is likely to get on a printed page.

I believe that people cannot enjoy an overly structured city. City planners who design a walk in the sky, say a linear walk, are not really thinking humanely. People do not walk in straight lines, except when they are running for a train. Our books attempt to offer multiple paths to learning.

Unity of concept is important to any creative endeavor. An architect must form a clear concept of a project in human and social terms before beginning. Then shapes, scale, color, harmony, ornament, rhythm, dominance, subordination, and other devices are used to enhance the basic concept.

LEARNING IS REMEMBERING WHAT YOU LIKE TO EAT

A study at the Veterans Administration Medical Center in Sepulveda, CA, has shown that a gastrointestinal hormone released in mice during feeding can enhance memory by activating fibers in the peripheral nervous system. Hungry mice who were fed immediately after learning a task remembered it much better than the other groups. Findings suggest that after-dinner speeches would be more memorable if delivered before the meal.

Stefi Weisburd, "Eat to Remember," *Science News* **(5/23/87)**

The scale of Paris is small and personal compared with many major cities. It's more walkable than most. This is why I organized **PARIS**ACCESS along seven paths. Each path is mapped in conversational style like the example (right), and each is essentially linear in nature.

Tokyo is larger and in many ways, at least for the Westerner, more complicated. If you think of a line as a two-dimensional representation of a moving point, then imagine what the two-dimensional represen-tation of a moving line would be—an area. This is how **TOKYO** ACCESS is organized.

If you move an area in three dimensions, the result is a volume. In **DC**ACCESS, where an idea of the scale and form of the structures is so important to the understanding of the place, a depiction in three dimensions is helpful.

A point is a one-di-mensional shape.

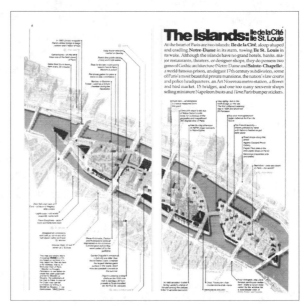

from **PARIS**ACCESS

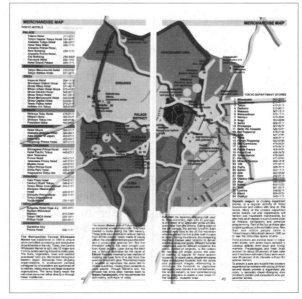

from **TOKYO**ACCESS

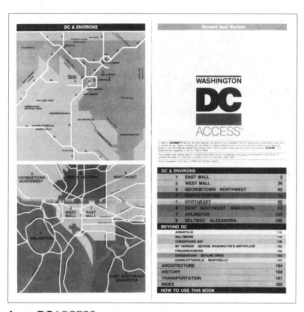

from **DC**ACCESS

from **DC**ACCESS

Moving a point describes a two-dimensional line.

Moving a two-dimensional line describes an area.

And moving an area describes a three dimensional volume.

My work has to do with overcoming the thoughts with which I have discomfort. My own understanding or lack of it is enough. Committee meetings and market research are not part of this process. I don't believe in using such methods to determine what subjects or cities to tackle. Having confidence in your own understanding, acceptance of your ignorance, and determination to pursue your interests are the weapons against anxiety.

THE IMPORTANCE OF BEING INTERESTED

If my premise is correct that you only remember that in which you are interested, then interest becomes a key word in assimilating information and reducing anxiety. Yet interest is cast in at best a supporting role in our lives. It is tinged with the insignificance of a hobby. A category that is disappearing from résumés is "Interests." They have become "Outside Interests." They have almost become something people are not supposed to have—distractions from your ultimate purpose or mission. We should all look closely at what the word "interest" means to us. I think *all* interests should be inside interests. We should figure our interests into our activities every day, into our reading habits, into the news to which we pay attention, into our personal relationships.

The concept of interest may be simple-minded, but I believe that because of this, it should be a word of special delight, because it represents a way to get in touch with clarity.

EDUCATION IS TO LEARNING AS
TOUR GROUPS ARE TO ADVENTURE

**Learning and seeing are
more important than
education.**

Sten Nadolny, *The
Discovery of Slowness*

*C*ontrary to Voltaire's Dr. Pangloss, we are not living in the best of all possible worlds. Not only are we overwhelmed by the sheer amount of information, most of us are also hampered by an education that inadequately trains us to process it.

School is the place where our information habits are formed, yet most of us graduate ill equipped to handle the avalanche of new information that we will have to continuously acquire. We suffer from *information anxiety* primarily because of the way that we were, or were not, taught to learn.

Theoretically, the goal of our educational system is learning, but it is bound by the limitations of any bureaucracy, in that the demands of administering the system often take precedence over the initial purpose of the system. A principal objective of any operational system is to keep operating, to maintain the status quo. But this is often done at the expense of the people who move through the system.

It's a bureaucratic Catch-22, similar to the one that operates in the health-care system. Being awakened at 2 A.M. to have your temperature taken is not conducive to healing, nor is being awakened again at 6 A.M. to have the bed sheets changed, breathing airborne contaminants, or having to make yourself available to well-meaning but sadistic friends and relatives for four hours every day because the hospital has proclaimed this time for visiting hours. This schedule is primarily conducive to hospital administration.

Thus the day-to-day demands of administering the educational system distract from the quality of education and inhibit learning. One has only to look at the way the educational system is covered by the press. The headlines are about teachers' salaries, crime in the schools, reading levels, prayer in the classroom, test scores, and building improvements. The quality of education and joy of learning are in fine print.

According to a report on "60 Minutes" on February 7, 1988, the Japanese company Matsushita uses high school graduates to do statistical quality control for its semiconductor lines in its facility in Japan. In the United States, the company had to hire people with a graduate-school education to do the same job when the company opened a branch in North Carolina because it couldn't find any high school or college graduates who could be taught the technology.

GIN-RUMMY MEMORY

The single most counterproductive element of our educational system is the importance placed on puzzle solving and memorization. The predominant measure of success is the test; thus the mission of schools is to raise students' test scores. Across the country every day, teachers are saying, "He's such a bright boy, but he doesn't test well," and shaking their heads with the tragic somberness you might expect from a doctor telling a patient to get his affairs in order.

This places extraordinary emphasis on short-term memory, at the expense of long-term understanding. How much can you cram before tomorrow's test? This doesn't further your understanding of things, and you will remember what you learn this way about as long as you will a gin-rummy hand. It is garbage in and garbage out. Students are forced to compete against other students rather than against their own aspirations.

While the debate rages on about what makes an intelligent student and educators scramble to compile lists of facts that everyone should know, we lose sight of the fact that the lists are arbitrary and the judges are biased.

SACRED BULL FIGHTING

Our education system is riddled with sacred bulls which we take with us into our lives after school. They affect the way we conduct our lives and perform in our careers, and most of us would increase our productivity if only we weren't afraid to question them. Do these "truths" sound familiar?

● **"If only everybody could read well and get high scores, everything would be fine."** Of late, educational theorists have come to realize there are two kinds of intelligence—one academic and one practical. They have found there is little to indicate that faring well in one will assure the same success in the other. The neat structure of school, with only one right answer to every question, bears little relation to the ambiguity we face outside. More "educated" students won't necessarily produce more "successful" human beings.

● **"The one who always has the right answers wins."** In school, we are measured by our ability to answer questions and, in one form or another, this occupies most of our time. What we need to know is how to ask the questions. Most of us are surrounded by answers and solutions in our lives. Our adeptness at asking questions will determine how we reach the solutions.

● **"Classes should have thirty students and last for one hour."** This precept has given birth to the inflexible rule which is responsible for a good many of the unproductive business meetings taking place around the country every day. People feel cheated unless the meetings last for an hour, yet an hour is a highly arbitrary unit of time. Because this is the way we are taught, we assume that this is the way things should be. Just as there is no such thing as an ideal class size or length there is no such thing as an ideal meeting size or duration. Some subjects could be best addressed by a few people in fifteen minutes, others by five hundred people in an hour. As the size of meetings will change the character, the subject should determine the time and amount of people involved.

● **"Students should be stuffed with facts like sausages."** Facts are meaningful only when they can be attached to ideas. Unless students are taught a system for learning or processing information, facts are of little use to them. Several books have come out in the last two years about what students know, don't know, or should know. Some have even attempted to make lists of what a person needs to know to qualify as a culturally literate human being. In addition to the sheer presumption of making such a list, these books tend to distract readers from the real issues as they try to memorize lists.

● **"Classes should be held during the day and homework done at night."** Just as some people learn faster by reading, by trial-and-error, or by example, people learn more easily at different times of the day. Everyone should pursue their education in the manner that best befits their learning preferences—in their own time. In this way, homework will become "homejoy."

● **"Halls and corridors are nonspaces for lockers."** Circulation space accounts for more than any single other space in schools, yet it is treated as a throwaway. Instead, hallways could be great arcades where people meet, talk, learn, and fall in love.

● **"Senior faculty teach senior classes, junior faculty teach the freshmen."** This is backwards. Freshmen are more impressionable than seniors. Their educational future is more fragile and needs the benefit of the most experienced faculty. By the time students have spent four years in college, they should be more able to direct themselves.

Educational researchers have identified more than twenty components that affect how individuals learn, ranging from room temperature and background noise preferences to memory capacity and analytical ability. This information enables educators to compile individual learning profiles of students.

Lucia Solorzano, "Helping Kids Learn—Their Own Way," *U.S. News & World Report* (8/31/87)

SEEING, HEARING, EXPRESSING

If we are lucky, we learn reading, writing, and arithmetic, but what we need to learn in the information age are seeing, hearing, and expressing. We need to know how to make connections from one interest or subject to the next. In an ideal system, teachers shouldn't be expected to be fact machines, police officers, or psychiatrists. They should be guides down interest paths, with special insights about the path-to-path and interest-to-interest connections.

But it is not the best of all possible worlds, after all. So if we have been hampered by our education, it is incumbent upon us to develop our own models for learning.

FEAR OF LEARNING

Learning involves nurturing an interest. The greatest threats to learning are guilt and anxiety. Guilt and anxiety are parent and child, and they stop interest cold. They stop the movement of information into memory, into utilization, and into communication. They stop you from genuinely commiting to your interest, which is what gives you a sense of ownership of the information and enables you to use and communicate it.

You feel guilty that you haven't kept up your college French course and fear that your verb conjugations may be slipping, so you don't admit to being able to speak the language, and thus you close off a chance to exercise your skills and improve at a subject that once interested you.

A widely held myth, fostered by the regimen of school, is that people should learn continuously. But when do people really learn? We learn at moments rather than continuously, and it's the acceptance of moments of learning that allows you to make full use of them. If you believe you're supposed to learn continuously and you don't continuously learn, then you'll be full of anxiety and guilt. You'll be distracted from learning because you're too busy worrying about *not* learning.

THE ANTIJOY OF LEARNING

. . . In the early stages of acquiring any really new skill, a person must adopt at least a partly antipleasure attitude: "Good, this is a chance to experience awkwardness and to discover new kinds of mistakes!" It is the same for doing mathematics, climbing freezing mountain peaks, or playing pipe organs with one's feet. Some parts of the mind find it horrible, while other parts enjoy forcing those first parts to work for them. We seem to have no names for processes like these, though they must be among our most important ways to grow.

Marvin Minsky, *The Society of Mind*

Difficulties illuminate existence, but they must be fresh and of high quality.

Tom Robbins, *Even Cowgirls Get the Blues*

Our educational system doesn't have exclusive rights on the guilt and anxiety associated with learning. Learning inherently involves some trauma; it requires a certain amount of exertion and implies giving up one way of thinking for another. Added to this is the puritanical attitude that we are put here on this earth to suffer and that suffering is good for us; therefore, learning shouldn't be too pleasant.

Given this, it is inevitable that learning is regarded somewhat like cod-liver oil, as something that might taste pretty bad but may do some good in the long run. Learning is invariably perceived, to varying degrees, as a source of anguish.

Fear of learning is endemic in our culture. Carl Rogers notes that although humans have a natural potential for learning, they approach the process with great ambivalence because "any significant learning involves a certain amount of pain, either pain connected with the learning itself or distress connected with giving up certain previous learnings."

To avoid suffering the "pain of learning," people will go to great lengths to trick themselves with sugar-coated approaches to knowledge in much the same way that those who are fearful of the unknown approach travel: they try to make the trip as easy as possible by having every moment planned in advance, by turning over the arrangements to someone else, by trying to turn travel into a neat package. This deters the traveler from ownership of the experience. And while the tour-group approach to travel can make a trip easier and reduce the anxiety of the unknown, it is not always the best way to explore new territory. It is a defensive response and is done from a position of fearfulness. The same can be applied to learning: trying to turn knowledge into a neat package or, worse, trying to protect yourself from new information won't foster learning; you will succeed only in making yourself more anxious.

A phobia is generally represented as a psychological and emotional state characterized by phobic anxiety, where the anxiety involves dread at having to face an object or to be involved in a situation. The dread, usually seen as irrational by the non-phobic observer, leads to strenuous avoidance efforts.

Geoff Simons, *Silicon Shock: The Menace of the Computer Invasion*

Make your friends your teachers and mingle the pleasures of conversation with the advantages of instruction.

Baltasar Gracian

DEFENSIVE EXPENDITURES

Friedrich Nietzsche, in *Ecce Homo*, discusses how destructive this anxiety can be. "The rationale is that defensive expenditures, be they never so small, become a rule, a habit, lead to an extraordinary and perfectly superfluous impoverishment. Our largest expenditures are our most frequent small ones. Warding off, not letting come close, is an expenditure—one should not deceive oneself over this—a strength squandered on negative objectives. One can merely through the constant need to ward off become too weak any longer to defend oneself."

LEARNING ABOUT LEARNING

Education will also become creative—a game more under the control of the person being educated. In addition to going to school, youngsters will hook up their home computers to the contents of a huge computerized library. This will allow them to explore whatever they want—to work at their own speed, in their own way, on subjects of their own choosing. Everyone will have a chance to discover exactly what he or she enjoys.

Lee Kravitz, "Future-Bound: Glimpses of Life in the 2lst Century (Four Futurists Speculate on the Future)," *Scholastic Update* (12/1/86)

Defensiveness is unavoidable in a test-based system founded on reward and punishment. We spend our years in school trying to zero in on the information that will reward us by raising our grades or test scores and avoiding the "extraneous" that may distract us from our goals, even though it may well be relevant to our own interests.

Corroborated by the findings of such people as Ivan Pavlov and B. F. Skinner, psychologists have long espoused the theory that we learn only by reinforcement or "reward." But this is a limiting, overly rigorous concept, restricting of creativity and of those divine leaps that the human mind is able to make from simple observation to global idea. If we are dependent upon reward, we are also dependent on someone else's vision of success.

In *The Society of Mind*, Marvin Minsky calls for new ways of learning. "The answer must lie in learning better ways to learn. In order to discuss these things, we'll have to start by using many ordinary words like goal, reward, learning, thinking, recognizing, liking, wanting, imagining, and remembering—all based on old and vague ideas. We'll find that most such words must be replaced by new distinctions and ideas."

CONVERSATION WITH ALAN KAY

One person at work on developing new ways of learning is Alan Kay, a fellow at Apple Computer, Inc., and a major folk hero in the computer world. Kay founded and runs the Vivarium, an ambitious, breakthrough program sponsored by Apple Computer to teach children how to think. Kay was a former National Quiz Kid on the radio, a jazz musician, and principal scientist at the Xerox Palo Alto Research Center.

AK: I have always felt that there are these internal impulses that are basically artistic even if you are trying to learn science. Most great scientists are incredibly involved aesthetically with the systems that they are studying. And I don't think a person who goes through school learning physics without finding that it is beautiful or elegant is going to get anywhere. So all of the things I have done with technology first involved wondering what is actually going on in the person and then wondering what the technology could do to amplify it rather than covering it up like a prosthetic.

One of the reasons I have worked with children for the last twenty years is that children are very intelligent beings, but they don't think the same way we do. Just trying to work with them and understand their way of being is a way of getting new ideas. The Vivarium program was founded on the theories of Jerome Bruner, who divided child development into three stages of learning mentalities. The child of four and five thinks kinesthetically by doing—actively. Everything is done by direct actions, very tactile. Children a few years older are dominated by the visual. Their attention moves around the way your eyes move around on a bulletin board. The third stage is symbolic thinking, the practicality of translating their creative ideas into things or symbols. What seems to happen in our society is that adults turn into basically sequential processors and shut down the creative things that children are able to do. The Vivarium program attempts to rotate people's mentalities from the kinesthetic, to the visual, to the symbolic.

Everytime we teach a child something, we keep him from inventing it himself.

Jean Piaget

THINK FIRST, ASK QUESTIONS LATER

A Cambridge University professor, Edward de Bono, a leading advocate of teaching thinking, offers a program of sixty thinking lessons geared to turning students into competent thinkers, a prerequisite to sorting out the abundance of data with which we are all confronted.

Researchers have identified four types of learning styles: activists, who learn best from activities while they are engrossed in them; reflectors, who learn from activities which they have had the chance to review; theorists, who benefit from activities when they are offered as part of a concept or theory; and pragmatists, who learn best when there is a direct link between the subject matter and a real-life problem.

Alan Mumford, "Learning Styles and Learning," *Personnel Review* **(UK 1987)**

It is impossible for a man to learn what he thinks he already knows.

Epictetus

RSW: It is also giving permission.

AK: Right, and they don't even know it. In fact, the mouse is not just for pointing on the screen; it engages your body in the knowledge of things. That is the kind of thing you want to know even if you are blind. Where am I and what is around? It is kinesthetic understanding.

RSW: A lot of people think my books are very visual, the organization of them doesn't stem from the visual, it stems from another kind of organization.

AK: I have pointed that out to people many times and they mistakenly think that the orientation of space is visual which it isn't at all.

RSW: You are the first person I have talked to who understood that. The significance of your work whether you own up to it or not is the idea of menu and window.

AK: I think the idea of a window was around; I invented the idea of the overlapping windows. What I got credit for was recognizing how those ideas could actually fit into a learning context. I was taught to look below the surface messages and ask what the medium is doing to the person.

Fifteen years from now technology will be such that people can make their own artificial intelligences, so we will be able to shape semi-intelligent agents that can essentially be extensions of our own will and our own goal structure. And instead of having to go to a central database and sit there for a couple of hours puzzling through it, a lot of this kind of work will be done by our agents, who will be constantly rummaging for us.

I designed a program called Newspeak at The Media Lab in 1980, as an example of an agent. It stays up all night logging into Nexis (a database) and *The New York Times* and the Associated Press, trying to retrieve personalized news for you. Then, when you come down to breakfast, there is your copy.

RSW: The news of the day customized for you.

AK: Customized for you to the extent that a headline might well say your three o'clock meeting was canceled because that would be the most important news of the day for you. It reads your electronic mail. A side bar might say the children slept well last night. The idea again is a redefinition of what news means just as the telegraph redefined news as being stuff that was very current and from afar.

When we were creating the Vivarium, we wanted to exploit the potential of these networks. Children love animals. What would it be like to have children learn about animal behavior and learn a whole variety of strategies? Instead of just allowing them to make a clay model of the animal and talk about it, we tried to come up with computer tools that would allow them to bring the animal to life, to give not just the form of the animal but to give it a brain.

LEARNING FANTASIES

The Vivarium seeks to create an ideal learning environment that facilitates "moments of learning" by encouraging interaction between students and their subjects. Students are exposed to diverse topics, which increase the likelihood of inspiration and are provided with an ideal framework or system for learning.

An ideal school would be like a smorgasbord where you could take large or small plates and eat fast or slow, where you could construct the meal going forwards or backwards, and you could start again. You would be given permission to have dessert first, and the people who fill up the plates would have conversations with you. You could pick up a plate called fancy cars and have somebody advise you that this salad here, the road system and mode of transportation, go with it.

"In order to tolerate experience, a disciple embraces a master. This sort of reaction is understandable, but it's neither very courageous nor very liberating. The brave and liberating thing to do is to embrace experience and tolerate the master."

Tom Robbins, *Even Cowgirls Get the Blues*

Never believe on faith, see for yourself. What you yourself don't learn, you don't know.

Bertold Brecht

A man has no ears for that to which experience has given him no access.

Friedrich Nietzsche

Who learns by finding out has sevenfold the skill of he who learned by being told.

Arthur Guiterman

IF SHAKESPEARE CAN, SO CAN YOU

But most of us don't have that kind of experience with school. In an attempt to overcome any shortcomings in my education, I try to create learning environments in my life. I have developed a list of imaginary courses that I thought would be good courses and would inspire me. They inspire me to look at the world differently.

● **Learning About Learning.** For me, this should be the only course taught for the first six years in school.

● **The Question and How to Ask It.** Asking questions is the most essential step toward finding answers. Better questions provoke better answers.

● **What Do You Want.** We don't pay enough attention to the old adage: be careful what you wish for because all too often it will be exactly what you get.

● **A Day in the Life.** Studying in intimate detail a day in the life of anything—a truck, a building, a butcher— would not only provide a memorable understanding of what it means to be something else, but would also permit us a better understanding of ourselves in comparison.

● **What Are We to Ants.** This would be an advanced version of *A Day in the Life*. The whole idea of how a thing relates to something else is often left unexamined in school, yet it is the essential doorway to knowledge.

● **Time, Fast and Slow.** If you studied all the things that take place in a minute or a day, or a week, or a year, or a thousand years, you would have a new framework for understanding and for cataloging information.

● **The Five-Minute Circle.** What could you do or see in five minutes from where you are sitting?

● **The Five-Mile Circle.** What could you do, see, and understand about sociology, the fabric of schools, urban life, and systems within five miles of where you are sitting?

● **This Is Your New World.** If you were king of this five-mile world, how would you run it, change it, understand it, communicate with it?

● **A Person Course.** You could have a course on Albert Einstein, Louis Kahn, or Yasir Arafat.

● **Hailing Failing.** More learning is possible by studying the things that don't work than by studying the things that do. Most of the great technological and scientific break-throughs are made by examining the things that fail.

● **Wait-Watching.** We spend a great deal of time wait-ing—in checkout lines, in ticket lines, in doctors' offices. How could we better occupy this time?

● **How to Explain Something So Your Mother Could Understand It.** The recognition of someone else's ability to understand is essential to all communication, yet it is something we rarely think about. We assume that others can understand the same things we can.

● **The Difference Between Facts and the Truth.** Facts are only meaningful when they can be tied to ideas and related to your experience, yet they are offered in place of the truth.

● **The Obvious and How to Hug It.** In our zeal to appear educated, not only do we often forget the obvious, we avoid it. Yet it is in the realm of the obvious that most solutions lie.

COME BACK IN TWO YEARS, I'M ON HOLD

Michael Fortino, a time-management expert, concluded from his firm's studies that the average American will, in a lifetime, spend five years waiting in line, one year searching for belongings at home or office, three years attend-ing meetings, and eight months opening junk mail.

Dan Sperling, "Study: Time's a Wasting," *USA TODAY* (6/24/88)

We have used our wealth, our literacy, our technol-ogy, and our progress to create the thicket of unreality which stands between us and the facts of life . . . experiences of our own contriving begin to hide reality from us, to confuse our sense of reality, taking us headlong from the world of heroes to a world of celebrities, transforming us from travelers into tourists.

Daniel Boorstin, *The Image: A Guide to Pseudo-Events in America*

PARALLEL LEARNING

Everyone should have his or her own imaginary course list, which would function as a way to encourage learning in one's own life. There are always opportunities for education if you keep in mind that your life is the place for learning.

Researchers are beginning to recognize that the kind of intelligence rewarded in school may have little to do with the wits that will determine how well one will fare in life. We've all met people who can't balance their checkbook and think that "the classics" are a series of golf tournaments, but who can turn hot-dog stands into multimillion dollar businesses.

Heretofore, most scales of intelligence were measured by a standard known as IQ, or intelligence quotient. But this only measures certain mental processes that have to do with vocabulary, logic, reasoning, and numeric skills. These tests don't recognize people skills, creativity, or even the practical intelligence that seems to propel some people through life.

Howard Gardner at Harvard describes several different types of intelligence: physical, verbal, spatial, musical, social, and personal. Other researchers, such as Robert J. Sternberg at Yale, divide intelligence into categories such as practical, experiential, and mental.

These theories acknowledge the role of "street smarts" in intelligence for the first time. Dr. Sternberg demonstrates that while standard IQ tests are fairly good for predicting how people will do in school, they have a very low correlation with job performance.

The tests are composed of questions for which there are only right or wrong answers. They measure a person's ability to perform within a limited arena where all problems can be solved with black-or-white solutions. In the workplace, situations are rarely so unequivocal or even so quantifiable. Yet employers often require their staff to take these intelligence tests.

Not only are the tests an inaccurate indicator of career success, they brand a person for life with a number that they must either live up to or live down. This discourages people from acquiring new skills and new learning that might be defined as beyond the accepted reach of their intelligence rating.

Supposedly designed as the test you couldn't study for, the Scholastic Aptitude Test has spawned an industry of preparatory courses from private tutoring, expensive coaching courses, and special extracurricular high school cram sessions. Some students begin preparing for their SATs as early as the eighth grade.

Yet, college admissions officials insist that the test scores are only one element in the selection process and many think that grades and class ranking are a more important indication of how well students will do in college.

Deirdre Carmody, "Cram Courses for S.A.T. Are a Booming Business," *The New York Times* (11/7/87)

Because our educational system is based on cultivating the kind of intelligence that can be measured in IQ tests, the responsibility of cultivating street smarts lies with the individual.

As I was growing up, my parents fostered the concept of parallel or applied learning that happened outside our schooling. We were encouraged to pursue subjects outside of or independent from the classroom. Any reasonable interest that we expressed was indulged by buying us books on the subject, finding special courses for us, and, most important, taking our interests seriously. We were thus able to develop confidence in our own interests.

I became interested in art as a child. From the first grade on, I was always the "best drawer" in the class. Yet despite the fact that art was something of an anathema in our family, my passion was encouraged. When I was in high school, my father got special permission for me to take courses at the Stella Elkins Tyler School of Fine Arts at Temple University, where he knew the dean.

I was also interested in design as a teenager. So when I was about fourteen, my parents gave me the attic as my bedroom. I separated the space into two rooms—one for working, which I painted white, and one for sleeping, painted black. In my work area, I designed sloping bookshelves that weren't parallel to the floor. The lower end of each shelf acted as a bookend, so the books didn't tip over.

Remembering does not happen as a matter of course whenever a person is exposed to information. It does not even happen automatically if the person wants and intends to commit the information to memory. [Psychologist James L.] Jenkins proposed that, if memory is to work well, the rememberer must pick up those aspects of the events or material to be remembered that make possible a well-defined personal experience. For this he needs to be attuned in some way to what is put in front of him . . . It is the quality of the experience that counts . . .

Jeremy Campbell, *Grammatical Man: Information, Entropy, Language, and Life*

I have tried to encourage my own children's interests, even if they departed from my own. My son, Josh, got half of the family freezer for storing his insect collection.

TERROR AND CONFIDENCE

Everyone should develop personal tests for information. Exercise noncomplacency. How can you apply it to your life? The best kind of learning occurs in situations, not in the classroom.

Throughout my whole life, I have created tests that determine how well I have applied information. Up until I was eighteen, I had a comfortable, middle-class upbringing. I decided then that it was important to put myself in jeopardy to understand what kinds of things terrified me. I thought that if I found out what my fears were, I would function more comfortably as an adult. I didn't expect to overcome my terrors, just to know about them and about myself. My first expedition was to go across the country with a friend, a sleeping bag, sixty dollars in my pocket, and a topless, doorless old Army Jeep that had a front seat made out of a plywood board with two cushions on it. We begged our way across the United States and kept to our pact never to sleep under anything.

From this trip, I made the important discovery that not everyone is afraid of the same things. My most terrifying moment came in Chicago. We were filthy; our limited apparel had begun to decay; and we had perfected the look of vagrants. I wanted to see Mies van der Rohe's twin apartment buildings on Lake Shore Drive. The idea of talking my way into those elegant buildings by claiming I was a former tenant terrified me, but I did it. Looking like the wrath of God didn't bother my friend at all.

My next expedition was to spend a few months on an island off the coast of North Carolina with two friends. We slept on the sand and lived off of what we caught. It was a time devoid of decision making because the regimen of survival determined all of our activities. The experience taught me something about mental relaxation, and I probably ate more crabs and clams than most people do in a lifetime. Despite this, I still love them.

After this, in 1958, I ingratiated myself to the director of

MEMORY SOUP WITH NOODLES

If things go well in the kitchens of Thomas J. Lipton, Inc., next year, you'll find a new flavor of soup in your supermarket. You might call it a memory broth, although it may not be advertised as such to avoid regulatory hassles. It's Lipton's basic chicken noodle soup laced with purified lecithin at the request of researchers who have successfully used it to improve the memories of Alzheimer's victims. Apparently it contains a raw material the brain needs to make acetylcholine, a neurotransmitter that is scarce in Alzheimer's patients.

Judith Hooper, "All in the Mind," WholeMind (2/88)

an archaeological museum at the University of Pennsylvania. Claiming that I knew how to survey, I convinced him to send me on a dig in Tikal, Guatemala, the site of the largest and oldest Mayan city. I didn't know the first thing about surveying, but by the time the team discovered this, it was too late to send me back, so I learned—in five days—and spent six months there.

These trips were all tests; I use these trips even today as measuring devices against which I gauge fear and panic. By putting myself in unpredictable situations for which I was ill-equipped, I was forced to discover new ways of accomplishing things. Often I discover that there is a simpler, clearer way which I didn't know before I committed myself to the test.

The fundamental lesson of my travels and travails has been learning that without prior knowledge, without training, you can find your way through information by making it personal, by deciding what you want to gain from it, by getting comfortable with your ignorance.

Learn to listen to your own voice and to balance your confidence and your terror.

These two forces have driven my life. Confidence propels me to try new things and terror keeps me from getting too cocky. The balance of these two—arrogance against assuredness—to conquer the fear of not knowing, of the unknown, of the new. Confidence is the belief that this can be accomplished, giving yourself permission to try.

Applied learning outside the formal structure of the classroom is likely to result in the possession of long-term understanding based on information acquired from interest and not from anxiety. This kind of learning permits an essential sense of ownership.

AHA! RATING

The sudden hunch, the creative leap of the mind that "sees" in a flash how to solve a problem in a simple way, is something quite different from general intelligence. Recent studies show that persons who possess a high aha! ability are all intelligent to a moderate level, but beyond that level there seems to be no correlation between high intelligence and aha! thinking.

Martin Gardner, "Aha! Insight," *Scientific American*

INFORMATION OWNERSHIP

Interaction with information is what enables possession. By putting yourself " in situ," you will create a conversation that will permit learning. You can ask questions, correct mistakes, and adjust to new ideas in an active environment.

This doesn't necessarily mean that you must apprentice yourself to a woodworker if you want to learn about woodworking. It can also mean taking the time to look up a word or term when reading through a text, finding out about the history of wood joints, asking a few questions about new information with which you are confronted, or just repeating something you have heard to someone else.

All of these will allow you to personalize the information in some way that is likely to make it more valuable to you in the future.

YOU ONLY LEARN SOMETHING RELATIVE TO SOMETHING YOU UNDERSTAND

The hypothesis has been proposed that if the mind of Man is exposed to the economy of Nature, as revealed in the workings of living systems, he will become sensitized to recognize the necessity of balancing values. Thus measure is established as the source of wisdom.

Jonas Salk, *The Survival of the Wisest*

*T*he origin of the word "Eureka" is attributed to Archimedes on discovering the principle of specific gravity. As the story goes, he was sitting in the bathtub and, as the water ran over him, the idea came to him, and he shouted, "Eureka, I understand!"

We all live for those moments of clarity, but the amount of information with which we must wrestle is making them fewer and farther between.

In the fourth century B.C., Aristotle observed that a person's memory of a given item of knowledge was facilitated by associating that idea with another, either in contiguity, in sequence, or in contrast.

Comparative learning, making connections between one piece of information and another, is a concept from which I derive my "first law": you only learn something relative to something you understand.

Among learning theorists, this is known as apperception, which was first put forth in the nineteenth century. It is defined as "a process where new ideas associate themselves with old ones that already constitute a mind," in *Learning Theories for Teachers* by Morris Bigge.

Apperception is based on the work of the seventeenth-century English philosopher John Locke, who wrote the ambitious treatise *An Essay Concerning Human Understanding*. Locke believed that through chance, habit, or natural relationship ideas become associated in our minds. These ideas "always keep in company, and the one no sooner at any time comes into the understanding, but its associate appears with it . . . This wrong connexion in our minds of ideas, in themselves loose and independent of one another, has such an influence, and is of so great a force as to set us awry in our actions, as well moral as natural, passions, reasonings, and notions themselves, that perhaps there is not any one thing that deserves more to be looked after."

A mind is constantly forming and changing and the ideas with which we come into contact can redefine our minds.

The theory of apperception differed from the previous view of the mind as an already formed substance that could be nurtured or trained. Apperception implies that the mind is like a framework on which ideas can be hung. Thus teachers function like architects and builders of children's minds rather than as merely trainers of prede-termined mental faculties.

This theory reached full flower with Johann Herbart, who believed that ideas combine and recombine in the mind like chemical elements.

By looking into his own mind, Herbart thought that its "chemistry" could be observed and described. His theory held that all perception involves apperception—new ideas relating themselves to the store of old mental states. Memories in the subconscious theoretically helped one to interpret experiences of the moment. Indeed, Herbart felt that without a background of experience "any new sensa-tion would mean almost nothing at all."

eureka (yŏo-rē´-kə), *interj.* 1. Used to express triumph upon finding or discovering something. *[<Gk heurēka, 1st person sing. perf. indic. act. of heuriskein, to find, discover; attributed to Archimedes on discovering the principle of specific gravity.]*

MOTIVATING MODELS

For teachers, this meant that pupils could not be regarded as "clean slates" and that they must start with experiences their pupils had already had and then enrich and build upon them.

In *Mindstorms*, Seymour Papert talks about how his childhood passion for the workings of gears helped him learn multiplication tables and math equations. "By the time I had made a mental gear model of the relation between x and y . . . the equation had become a comfortable friend." Papert, who developed the computer-programming language Logo for children and adults with limited education, maintains that a fundamental fact about learning is that "anything is easy if you can assimilate it to your collection of models. If you can't, anything can be painfully difficult."

THEME AND VARIATIONS

For this reason, I love collections of things. What is only a fact alone can be information if it is collected with other facts. Knowledge is gained by understanding the theme and variations. If I put a cabbage in front of you, you would think that cabbages are round, green, and leafy. That is a fact. But if I showed you a red cabbage, a green cabbage, and a Chinese cabbage, you would begin to understand the essential characteristics—the smell, texture, and density—that define cabbage. That is information. Together, you can understand much more about each of them, by seeing the relationships between them, the variations on a theme.

The designer Charles Eames used to talk about change ringing, the traditional English art of ringing tower bells where the goal was to explore all possible sequences or changes of tones. The number of possible changes was calculated using the mathematical formula of permutations, by multiplying the number of bells together. With three bells, only six changes, or variations, in the order can be produced ($1 \times 2 \times 3$).

Einmal ist keinmal or *once is nothing* as the Germans say. For an idea or a thing to be meaningful, there must be more than one of it.

I tend to buy things in threes. With only two objects, you can see the differences; with three, you begin to see the patterns.

In Rome there is a room in a church with 10,000 human skulls. One skull is kind of frightening, but 10,000 are spectacular. You begin to see the structure of the human head, how much it can vary and still look like a human form. This is valid with ideas as well. People waste so much energy looking for the best example of their point, when their point might be better made with three mediocre examples.

LEARNING MEANS MAKING CONNECTIONS

I am convinced that the grouping of ideas is vital to communication. One number in an annual report—for example, gross sales—doesn't tell you very much. Even a time line that shows the figures over the course of ten years does not tell you what you want to know. You want to know the profits every year, and how the profits of one company compare to the profits of another in the same industry.

Eugene Raskin notes the impact on architecture of minds "crowded with ideas and associations in a way that may be likened to a random card index file . . . cross-referenced way down into the subconscious." A person viewing a building must find in his mental file a card that says "bank" or "church" or "store." The design should evoke recognition, "otherwise, he will be forced to fumble through his file at random; his chances of achieving any perception of unity will be slim indeed," states Raskin, a professor of architecture at Columbia University.

Scale in architecture has to do with easing perception by establishing the relationship of a building's units (doorways, windows, ceilings, etc.) to man. The simplest means of achieving this is to offer things that are familiar in size. As Raskin says, a person "knows the size of railings intimately, because he has walked beside them innumerable times. He knows just how far he bends his arm to put his hand on them, and just where on his hip he would feel the pressure should he lean on them. He knows

The way we make sense out of raw data is to compare and contrast, to understand differences. Using the analogy of a map, a map isn't the territory, it's the difference—be it in altitude, vegetation, population, terrain.

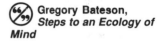 Gregory Bateson, *Steps to an Ecology of Mind*

stairs, too, from his first disastrous encounters with them during infancy. He is familiar with doors and windows . . . with units of construction he had handled, such as brick . . . You must give your observer things that he knows . . ."

Just as all architecture is making connections—the way that two rooms are connected, the way the floor meets the wall, the way a piece of wood meets a piece of metal, the way a building meets the street—so is all learning.

In teaching or communicating anything, we have no choice but to make connections between a new idea and that which is already known. The only alternative is to fool ourselves, which happens all the time. When we gloss over what we don't understand, when we fail to question it, we're lying to ourselves. It is unconscionable, yet pervasive, to read a word, not comprehend it, and continue reading. These become surface words that peel off and disappear from memory. If you don't remember something, it never happened.

We test communication by conveying a message and having the recipient understand it, be interested in it, and remember it. Any other measure is unimportant and invalid.

Failing to make connections between the known and the unknown prevents us from grasping new ideas and new opportunities.

> An organism's ability to perceive information is dependent on the capabilities of its internal systems to process it—the nature of its sense organs and the speed at which impulses are carried through its neural systems. A worm can transmit signals at the rate of 100 cps (characters per second). In humans, the rate is 30,000 cps, but a computer can transmit billions of times faster. Our sensory limitations mean that many events "occur too fast for us to follow, and we are reduced to sampling experiences at best. When the signals reaching us are regular and repetitive, this sampling process can yield a fairly good mental representation of reality. But when it is highly disorganized, when it is novel and unpredictable, the accuracy of our imagery is necessarily reduced. Our image of reality is distorted."
>
> **Alvin Toffler, *Future Shock***

HOW BIG IS AN ACRE?

Facts in themselves don't solve the problem. Facts are only meaningful when they relate to a concept that you can grasp. If I say an acre is 43,560 square feet, that is factual but it doesn't tell you what an acre is. On the other hand, if I tell you that an acre is about the size of an American football field without the end zones, it is not as

> **1 acre = 6,272,640 square inches**

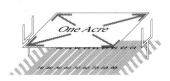

One Acre

accurate, but I have made it understandable. I have made it infinitely more understandable to most Americans because it is as common a plot of ground as we have. We have a sense of that size. And you don't have to play football to know this.

You only understand information relative to what you already understand. You only understand the size of a building if there is a car or a person in front of it. You only understand facts and figures when they can be related to tangible, comprehensible elements.

New information is created by the connections made by the receiver in the radio of the mind.

THE NUMBERS GAME

The importance of setting information into a comprehensible context permeates any endeavor. In the business world, context should be the primary concern of anyone trying to sell a new product or idea. How can a new product or idea be related to something the market already understands?

Numbers, with their absolute value, are the easiest form of information to compare. However, many people suffer from "innumeracy," an inability to comprehend numbers. According to Douglas R. Hofstadter in *Metamagical Themas*, the inability to make sense of numbers is a problem on par with illiteracy in this country. Numbers have the ability to summarize salient aspects of reality, yet the inability to comprehend numbers, large numbers in particular, is widespread. How many people know the difference between a million and a billion? How many people would understand the difference in defense spending in the billions versus the trillions of dollars? Yet these numbers affect all our lives.

For this very reason, we imbue them with an undeserved power. We live our lives by them, regarding them with awe—from scholastic aptitude tests to football scores. Sports fanatics expend energy memorizing the scores of games, yet the only important statistic is who won or lost. Numbers are often not as important as they seem.

Literacy is more than a skill. We know instinctively that to understand what somebody is saying, we must understand more than the surface meanings of words. We have to understand the context as well. To grasp the words on a page, we have to know a lot of information that isn't set down on the page.

E. D. Hirsch, *Cultural Literacy: What Every American Needs to Know*

Time magazine did two pages on the stock market crash in 1929. After Black Monday in October 1987, it came out with a twenty-five-page section.

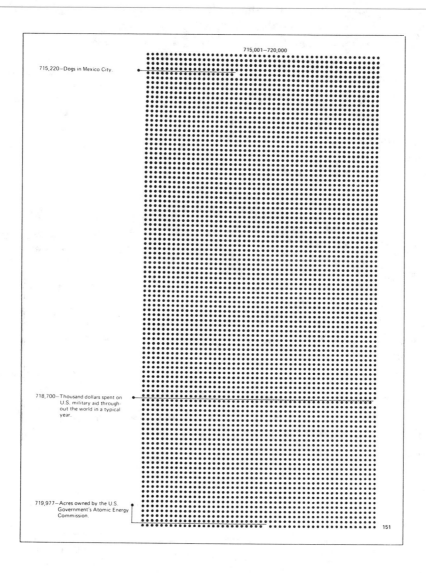

715,001—720,000

715,220—Dogs in Mexico City.

718,700—Thousand dollars spent on U.S. military aid throughout the world in a typical year.

719,977—Acres owned by the U.S. Government's Atomic Energy Commission.

151

It is difficult to understand how big one million is without ever having seen one million things. Hendrik Hertzberg's book *One Million* (published in 1970) makes the number understandable by giving us a visual model—one million dots to look at, to hold in our hands. We see the size of what the figures and statistics we hear about in the news really represent.

SAY I DO OR DIE

A set of numbers, without any reference or verification, can dramatically change our values, behavior, and emotions. We rarely question the figures quoted by the news because we assume them to be correct and valid, or at least important. But many times, these statistics are misinformation, disinformation, or just plain non-information.

Anyone who disputes this probably didn't talk to any single women after the findings of a study regarding the marriageability of women over thirty were published. In its June 2, 1986 issue, *Newsweek* did a cover story based on a so-called Harvard-Yale study on the marriage chances of college-aged women over thirty. Among the incendiary findings was that women over forty-five were more likely to get assassinated by a terrorist than they were to walk down the aisle.

The article wreaked despair in the hearts of thousands of single women, inspired a flurry of media coverage worthy of Pearl Harbor, was the sole topic of conversation in certain circles for weeks afterward, probably increased revenues for dating services, and surprised *schlubs* everywhere when their proposals were accepted.

Few people, at the time, bothered to question the validity or accuracy of the findings because the ensuing turmoil was much more entertaining. Not only did the public not question the report's validity, but the media itself didn't.

Yet after the first volleys, the suspicions of statisticians were aroused and some interesting facts about the findings were uncovered. Number one: the study was not conducted under the official aegis of either Harvard or Yale, but by two professors at the respective universities who were "tinkering" with some figures. Number two: they used a four-year-old census report that surveyed only around 1,500 college-educated women and based their conclusions on this, assuming that there were few subsequent changes in demographics and marriage patterns. Number three: they assumed that women always married men older than themselves.

HOW MUCH IS 42 MILLION GALLONS OF WATER?

It's enough water to:

● **Fill a glass that's 100 feet in diameter and 715 feet high.**

● **Allow each person in Chicago to brush his teeth seven times in one day.**

● **Provide the one-day water needs for all the people in South Dakota.**

● **Fill one 29-gallon fish tank for each person in New Mexico.**

● **Allow every person in Maine to take a bath in a 36-gallon tub.**

● **Flow over Niagara's Horseshoe Falls in 1 minute and 14 seconds.**

USA TODAY (8/10/87)

The counterclaims started to surface. The U.S. Bureau of the Census report, more carefully done, although not infallible, found that thirty-year-old women had a 58 to 66 percent chance of getting married, not a 20 percent chance as reported by the Two Tinkering Professors Study.

What the professors came up with was highly suspect and could be shot full of holes by a high school freshman with a pocket calculator, but the aura of Harvard and Yale imbued these predictions with the patina of the absolute and the important.

The sensationalistic aspects of the story eclipsed all questions of its accuracy. People didn't even ask themselves what it meant if the report was correct or why it mattered. The media went further to assume even more aspects that just weren't true, loaded their articles with personal examples of tales of woe, and in some cases even invented information that was never in the report.

And we didn't question it.

DON'T RAIN ON MY PARADE

Statistics about the distribution of income may not mean much, but imagine if people's height reflected their income. An hour-long parade of 38 million British income-earners would start with several minutes of people with no height at all (people who, although working, are losing money), to more than a half-hour's worth of very short people (mostly women, pensioners, and teenagers). Only after forty minutes would people of average height appear, followed by a few people who would be ridiculously tall, towering 20 miles over the heads of the people who started the parade.

The Economist (12/26/87)

SCREENPLAY RIGHTS ON ANNUAL REPORTS?

Annual reports, which have long been accused of glossing over bad news, are becoming positively panegyric in these days where the profit seems to be disappearing from profit and loss statements.

An article by Lee Berton in *The Wall Street Journal* on September 9, 1987, cited several examples. Bear Stearns & Co. ran a list of "selected" corporate underwritings that didn't include two of its biggest—an $81 million convertible debt issue for the financially troubled Crazy Eddie Inc. and a $75 million bond issue for the scandal-rocked Wedtech Corp.

Owens-Corning Fiberglas Corp. used to run an upfront table of financial highlights showing earnings gains from the previous year. The table was dropped the year profits plunged 88 percent.

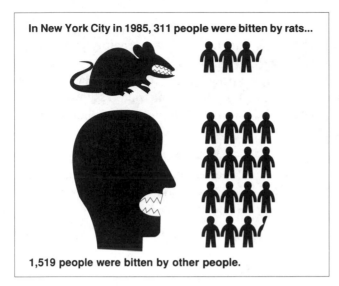

In New York City in 1985, 311 people were bitten by rats...

1,519 people were bitten by other people.

This simple chart is all the more effective because the numbers are expressed in a visceral and visual way. Sara Self, a student of Krzysztof Lenk at the Rhode Island School of Design, created this interpretation of a statistic from *Harper's* magazine

WHAT CAN $3 BILLION BUY?

Penzoil was awarded $3 billion in its suit against Texaco. What could the money buy?

● A "small" Fortune 500 company.

● Every NFL franchise and enough leverage to acquire every professional baseball and hockey team, too.

● Thirty 747 jets.

● Prime Manhattan real estate like the World Trade Center Towers and the RCA Building.

● Enough $100,000 homes to create a suburb.

● The contents of the Guggenheim Museum.

According to William P. Dunk, a New York consultant, annual reports are often more interesting for what they leave out, citing the 1986 reports of the seven Baby Bell companies that glossed over immense service problems with fancy graphics and emphasis on new technologies.

We let information (especially in the form of statistics) push us around and make our decisions for us. If we do not question the facts and figures that come our way, we cannot understand them, and we are more likely to be misled. You are usually much better off ignoring information that you do not understand than trying to act upon it.

Even the most powerful number in business—the Dow-Jones Industrial Index—isn't really in itself all that omnipotent. It is only a modified average of the stock prices of thirty large industrial companies.

Re-examining the role that numbers play in your life can make them less threatening and can help you use them more effectively. Which numbers are of real value to your life and which are psuedo-scientific cant? Has your life ever been affected by the barometric pressure or by the national debt? What does a billion or a trillion mean to you?

Numbers become meaningful when they can be related to concepts that can be viscerally grasped. A billion and a trillion are meaningless without a frame of reference. What can a trillion buy?

Numbers are symbolic of all information in that they are useless unless they can be compared to something you already understand.

The British-born Nigel Holmes, executive art director of Time, Inc. and author of several books on the diagramming of information, suggests that the key to making sense of facts and figures is to "reduce them into bite-size chunks, which the reader can pick and choose."

He developed a delightful example of the problem of translating numbers into comprehensible information— using toothpaste. How much toothpaste is used in the United States every year? How would you go about understanding this? Multiply the population (240 million people), minus 50 million for the toothless or careless, by the average amount used, 1/2 inch per person twice a day. Then multiply by 365 days. You come up with a huge number: 1.1 million miles. This is a hard distance to comprehend. How far is that? Most people have no conception of this. It is over two round-trips to the moon, which is an average of 240,000 miles away. To translate figures they must be relative to what you can comprehend.

So let's look at toothpaste usage in a day. Divide 1.1 million miles by 365, and you come up with about 3,000 miles, which is about the distance from New York to Los Angeles, a distance most people can understand. As Holmes lectures, he actually squeezes out toothpaste on the floor. "The audience can suddenly see all these other

Each night the television newscaster intones the Dow Jones industrial average. Amateurs can then debate whether the "market" will hold there or move up or down, a practice about as relevant as tracking dinosaur migrations by the paw prints in the dried mud . . . The Dow Jones . . . is roughly where it was in 1967. The new companies are unrepresented by the old totem—the average— and are unseen by the news. If you see only the old totem, you can begin to feel rather grim about this country.

Adam Smith, "And Now the Real News," *Esquire* (9/82)

relationships quickly. Not only are they laughing because someone who is supposed to be lecturing is instead squeezing toothpaste on the floor, but they are really seeing the numbers. It's a gimmick but it is another way of making people remember things," said Holmes.

What this implies is that constantly making comparisons and being open to new ways to chart and present information releases meaning.

SLICING THE PIE: THE NATURE OF RECREATION

In 1972 I was asked to develop a handbook on recreation for the National Gallery in Washington, D.C., which was presenting a show on Frederick Law Olmsted, one of the

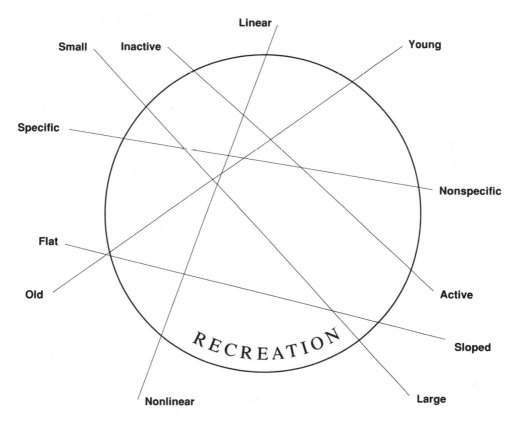

A diagram of the organization of the book, *The Nature of Recreation: A Handbook in Honor of Frederick Law Olmsted Using Examples from His Work.*

Two double-page spreads organized by continuum from *The Nature of Recreation: A Handbook in Honor of Frederick Law Olmsted Using Examples from His Work.*

Slicing the subject in these ways allows for a more meaningful focus on the subject.

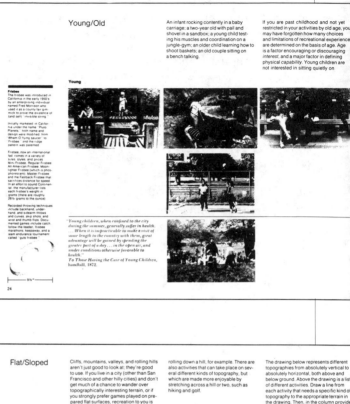

Young/Old

An infant rocking contently in a baby carriage; a two-year old with pail and shovel in a sandbox; a young child testing his muscles and coordination on a jungle-gym; an older child learning how to shoot baskets; an old couple sitting on a bench talking.

If you are past childhood and not yet restricted in your activities by old age, you may have forgotten how many choices and limitations of recreational experience are determined on the basis of age. Age is a factor encouraging or discouraging *interest*, and a major factor in defining *physical capability*. Young children are not interested in sitting quietly on

Young

Frisbee
The frisbee was introduced in California in the early 1950's by an enterprising individual named Fred Morrison who used it as a county fair gimmick to prove the existence of (and sell) "invisible string."

Initially marketed in California under the name "Pluto Planets," both name and design were modified from Wham-O flying saucer' to 'Frisbee,' and the ridge pattern was patented.

Frisbee, now an international fad, comes in a variety of sizes, styles, and prices. Mini-Frisbee, Regular Frisbee, All-American Frisbee, Moonlighter Frisbee (which is phosphorescent), Master Frisbee and the Fastback Frisbee that sacrifices distance for speed. In an effort to sound Continental, the manufacturer lists each frisbee's weight in grams (there are roughly 28½ grams to the ounce).

Recorded throwing techniques include backhand, underhand, and sidearm throws and curves, skip shots, and wrist and thumb flips. Documented games include catch, follow-the-leader, frisbee marathons, keepaway, and a team endurance tournament called "guts frisbee."

"Young children, when confined to the city during the summer, generally suffer in health. . . . When it is impracticable to make a visit of some length to the country with them, great advantage will be gained by spending the greater part of a day . . . in the open air, and under conditions otherwise favorable to health."
To Those Having the Care of Young Children, hamhull, 1972.

|— 9½" —|
24

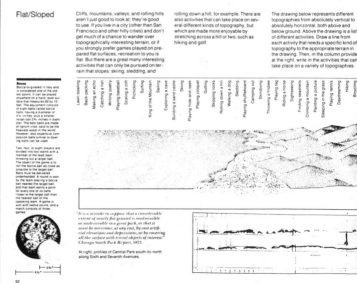

Flat/Sloped

Cliffs, mountains, valleys, and rolling hills aren't just good to look at; they're good to use. If you live in a city (other than San Francisco and other hilly cities) and don't get much of a chance to wander over topographically interesting terrain, or if you strongly prefer games played on prepared flat surfaces, recreation to you is flat. But there are a great many interesting activities that can only be pursued on terrain that slopes: skiing, sledding, and

rolling down a hill, for example. There are also activities that can take place on several different kinds of topography, but which are made more enjoyable by stretching across a hill or two, such as hiking and golf.

The drawing below represents different topographies from absolutely vertical to absolutely horizontal, both above and below ground. Above the drawing is a list of different activities. Draw a line from each activity that needs a specific kind of topography to the appropriate terrain in the drawing. Then, in the column provided at the right, write in the activities that can take place on a variety of topographies.

Bocce
Bocce originated in Italy and is considered one of the oldest sports. It can be played anywhere on a hard, level surface that measures 60 by 10 feet. The equipment consists of eight balls called bocce balls, having a diameter of 4½ inches, plus a smaller target ball 2¾ inches in diameter. The best balls are made of lignum vitae, said to be the heaviest wood in the world. However, less expensive composition balls similar to bowling balls can be used.

Two, four, or eight players are divided into two teams with a member of the lead team throwing out a target ball. The object of the game is to roll the bocce ball as close as possible to the target ball. Balls must be delivered underhanded. A round is won by the team placing a bocce ball nearest the target ball, and that team earns a point for every one of its balls closer to the target ball than the nearest ball of the opposing team. A game is won with twelve points, and a match consists of three games.

Lawn bowling
Back-packing
Making an echo
Catching a fish
Writing poetry
Playing baseball
Picnicking
Scaling a cliff
Surfing
Sailing
King of the Mountain
Exploring a cave
Building a sand castle
Skiing
Playing hide-and-seek
Playing croquet
Golfing
Skipping rocks
Rolling down a hill
Walking a dog
Sledding
Playing shuffleboard
Camping out
Skindiving
Throwing a frisbee
Playing tag
Riding a horse
Sightseeing
Finding seashells
Climbing a mountain
Painting a picture
Sleeping in the grass
Playing tennis
Daydreaming
Hiking
Bicycling

"It is a mistake to suppose that a considerable extent of nearly flat ground is inadmissible or undesirable in a great park, or that it must be overcome, at any cost, by vast artificial elevations and depressions, or by covering all the surface with trivial objects of interest."
Chicago South Park Report, 1871.

At right, profiles of Central Park south-to-north along Sixth and Seventh Avenues.

|— 2¾" —|
|— 4½" —|
32

These pages focus on how people of different ages relate differently to recreational spaces, from the young on the left to the old on the right.

benches; infants cannot climb jungle-gyms; older children don't like to play in sandboxes; and older men and women don't have the stamina for basketball. It is easy to forget, in thinking about the recreational profile of a neighborhood, how much people's age influences their need for particular recreational opportunities.

There are, however, many activities that are appropriate to several different age groups. Camping, for example, can be enjoyed by a two-year-old or a seventy-year-old and by almost anyone in between. A hike or bicycle ride appeals equally to the young person and the middle-aged.

Finally there are activities that can be enjoyed equally by all groups and in which they can participate together. Sun-bathing, people-watching, picnics, sports events, outdoor plays and concerts, and outings are activities which can bring all the generations together.

Mixed age groups

Old

"Cultivate the habit of thoughtful attention to the feebler sort of folk—of asking, for instance, can this or that be made easier and more grateful to an old woman or a sick child, without, on the whole, additional expense, except in thoughtfulness? If so, ten to one, the little improvement will simply be that refinement of judgment which is the larger part of the difference between good and poor art, and the enjoyment of every man will be increased by it, though he may not know just how."
Mount Royal.

Shuffleboard
Shuffleboard, a derivative of lawn bowling, began in England around the thirteenth century. The earliest record of the game in New England was its denunciation as a gambler's sport, and it was outlawed in certain areas in 1845. The game appears to have picked up again in the 1870's when it became a chief feature of entertainment for passengers on the ocean liner voyage between England and Australia.

It was re-introduced in Florida after World War II and by 1951 it was estimated that there were about 5000 public courts in 455 cities. It is played by all ages, although it is especially popular among older people.

The court is 52 by 6 feet with a concrete or terrazzo surface. The composition disks are one inch thick, six inches in diameter, and weigh between 11½ and 15 ounces. The strategy of the game is to knock a rival's disk out of position in a scoring box replacing it with your own. Each player or team shoots eight disks each round.

25

The nature of the terrain clearly bears on the types of recreational possibilities inherent at a given recreational site. Topography and its relation to recreation is presented here as a continuum from flat to rugged.

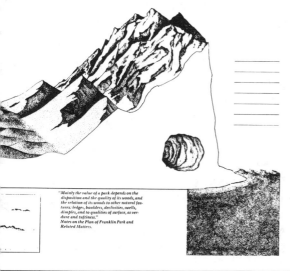

"Mainly the value of a park depends on the disposition and the quality of its woods, and the relation of its woods to other natural features; ledges, boulders, declivities, swells, dimples, and to qualities of surface, as verdure and tuftiness."
Notes on the Plan of Franklin Park and Related Matters.

Skiing
The earliest ski edges were bones from large animals strapped to the skis with leather thongs. The oldest pair of skis (purportedly 5000 years old) was found in Sweden.

Skis were first used in warfare in the Battle of Oslo in 1200 A.D. and proved so effective they became standard army equipment by the 1500's.

The bone ski had no standard size and was not turned up at the ends. Centuries later, when wood was substituted, the standard size became 7'8" long, about 2" thick, and 5" wide with about one foot of the front end of the ski turned up.

Skiing was introduced into Central Europe via Austria in 1590. It is not known how skis originated in North America, whether they were fashioned by native Indians or evolved out of the Canadian snowshoes. However, during the rush to the Pacific coast for gold in the 1850's, skis were in evidence in the Sierra Nevadas and in 1840 it was stated that "wooden blades for use on ice and snow" were brought from Norway and were used by the immigrants along the north Atlantic coast.

33

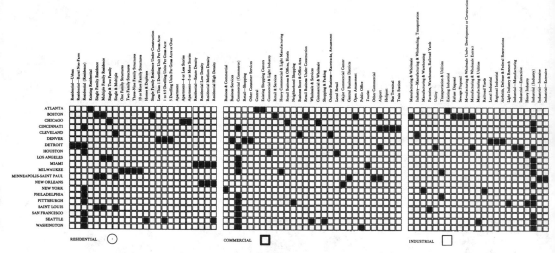

The matrix above, from *Urban Atlas: 20 American Cities,* summarizes the state of affairs in the mapping of major cities of the United States.

A black box indicates that maps *are* available from the city named on the topic in question.

The overall preponderance of empty boxes is not surprising in our times of urban frugality—cities can't afford to map everything.

What is surprising is the almost random "shotgun" pattern made by the black boxes, showing clearly the lack of correspondence in map subject matter from city to city.

Such a situation causes confusion and an inability to meaningfully compare mapped urban demographic information.

creators of Central Park in New York. The problem was how to break down the vast, complex, and ambiguous concept of recreation, which means something different to everyone.

You can't sum up the opportunities, problems, possibilities, physical and personal characteristics, age groups, desires, needs, and locations of recreation in a simple paragraph.

So I treated the subject as if it were a circle. Then I drew lines through the circle, the ends of which represented extremes on a continuum of the components of recreation—public and private, summer and winter activities, needs of the elderly and the very young. One line represented people. At one end of the line was a single person; at the other end of the line was a huge group of people.

Another line represented the contour of the land. One end of the line was flat; at the other end was a sheer cliff.

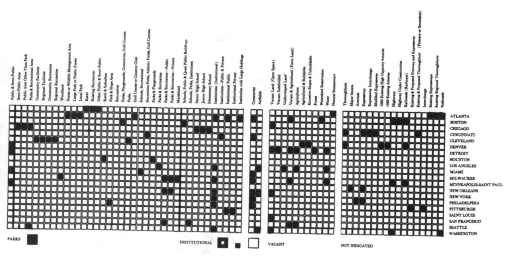

PARKS ■   INSTITUTIONAL ■ ▪ □ VACANT   NOT INDICATED

I drew another line and looked at the things people do and the equipment they use to do it. Some were very specific, i.e. a jungle gym. The line moved on to places that were less and less specific, until you had an open field on which you could do many things: picnic, run, play baseball or football, walk, or ride a bicycle.

The subject was divided into slices so I could deal with how landscape architecture performs to meet the varying needs that humans have for recreation—how physical places interact with personal desire.

Any larger subject can be broken down into slices. Each slice helps you understand what you cannot grasp as a whole. By breaking up a subject, you are less likely to be overwhelmed by it.

This can be applied to creating reports or to reading the reports of others. If the author hasn't broken a subject down, perhaps you could divide it in your own mind. By dividing a subject into manageable components, by experimenting with different ways of breaking it down, then comparing the components, you can really see the information.

Man has been called the symbol-making animal, and his talent for naming things frequently outstrips his capacity to understand them. Everyone knows the name of infinity, eternity; few people, if any, know what they are . . . Knowing the name—spoken or written—of a number is a prerequisite to using that number as well as understanding it. Among certain primitive peoples, there are only four number-names: one, two, three, and many.

Hendrik Hertzberg, *One Million*

COMPARING COMPONENTS

This is especially apparent when working with statistics. I was doing research for an urban atlas that I was developing and I discovered that most of the available information on income distribution consisted of dividing the total income by the number of residents. But this doesn't tell very much about disposable income. One person living on ten acres who earned $1 million would have a higher average income than 10,000 people living on ten acres sharing $1 million. But if you were thinking of establishing a business, such as a shoe repair or grocery store, you would want to locate in an area of higher density. A very wealthy area with low density has much less disposable income than an area that has low income and very high density. One person can buy only so many groceries. To get this information, I multiplied the average income by the total number of people per block. I found out that the map of total income was quite different from the map of average income.

Comparing data can answer the question "where is the money?", not how much disposable income there is or where the rich people are. Those are different questions.

That is part of that information process; you have to build off things you understand. Comparisons enable recognition. We recognize night by its difference from day. We recognize all things by their relationship to other things, by the context in which they exist.

HOMES BY THE POUND

Despite the high cost of housing in the Bay Area, homes still are cheaper per pound than hamburger. According to one estimate, an average 2,000-square-foot house weighs about 339,000 pounds and sells for $98,000 in the West, (1986 figure) so the house would run 29 cents a pound—considerably less than ground chuck.

"Homes by the Pound," *The San Francisco Chronicle* **(12/15/86)**

CONVERSATION WITH JOHN SCULLEY

As chairman of Apple Computer, Inc., John Sculley has been a seminal force in the world of computers. The company has set a standard of usability for the entire industry, and, in part, the success of the company is due to its response to the problem of context. A new technology was introduced that people could use with the skills they already had.

JS: I think we have a data overload and yet we have very few people who are actually able to use information successfully. When we say information, it somehow suggests that it informs you and "informs" means you are understanding and learning something and that possibly you are interested in it. I think "data" is a better word than "information," because it is more of a machine nomenclature and [what we're discussing] is just something that is extremely unfriendly. The two extremes are data at one end and knowledge at the other.

Knowledge should be interesting, understandable, and relevant to your interests. Data, on the other hand, is without context. How do we take this data without context and give it context? Most data doesn't meet that test.

I think the hardest job is getting information into a recognizable form so that people find it important enough in their lives to be willing to change their behavior.

Today all we have done is to take the way that machines create data and scale it up; we are finding that it is machine scaleable, not human scaleable. It is just not very useful to have these massive amounts of data.

RSW: If it is such a major issue, how come nobody is really in that business?

JS: Most intelligent people appreciate that information is a much bigger part of our lives. The problem is that we are still overlaying more and more information on top of the old ways of processing it; there is no conceptual link between the ability to create information and the technology that could really create information. This link isn't going to be measured in pounds of paper or even in the megabytes of information, but in the usefulness of it to people.

We measure productivity by the quantity of things that are given out. Everything was reduced to a process that

The breakdown of human performance under heavy information loads may be related to psychopathology in ways we have not yet begun to explore. Yet, even without understanding its potential impact, we are accelerating the generalized rate of change in society. We are forcing people to adapt to a new life pace, to confront novel situations and master them in ever shorter intervals.

Alvin Toffler, *Future Shock*

creates more. So now we have a process that created more and it really has nothing to do with productivity at all. It is really the process that created less. Everything we have learned in the industrial age has tended to create more and more complication. I think that more and more people are learning that you have to simplify, not complicate. That is a very Asian idea—that simplicity is the ultimate sophistication.

RSW: And that is a value in itself.

JS: Within the context of the Industrial Revolution, complexity had some value. In the context of the electronic age, it has no value at all.

RSW: The frightening thing for me is that as we sit here, complexity and not simplicity is the value for all the school systems. Everybody who graduates from high school comes out with twelve years of this kind of indoctrination.

JS: Even at our best schools we are preparing young people for a world they won't live in.

RSW: Why aren't there more people who break out of that circle?

JS: I believe that when we put the idea of simplicity in front of people that understand, they recognize it right away. There are intelligent people in the world who recognize it. It has to do with a point of view. Years from now, we will come up with a totally different view of this. The facts won't have changed; it is just that our point of view will have shifted.

The development of the Macintosh™ illustrates this idea. No amount of research would have created the demand for the Macintosh™, but once we created it and put it in front of people, everybody recognized it as something that they wanted.

We don't need to invent anything. Things are already there; they are just waiting to be discovered. What we have to do is go out and harvest the things that are already there.

If my theory of relativity is proven successful, Germany will claim me as a German and France will declare that I am a citizen of the world. Should my theory prove untrue, France will say that I am a German and Germany will declare that I am a Jew.

Albert Einstein

Human history is replete with evidence that devolutionary processes also operate, with deterioration of the human condition, unless foresight, imagination, ingenuity, determination, and wisdom are brought to bear, to increase self-awareness and self-discipline in the choice of ends as well as means.

Jonas Salk, *The Survival of the Wisest*

RSW: That is what I say about information. All I do is allow it to reveal itself. It is there; I am just helping it to reveal itself.

JS: Like sculpture by Michelangelo.

RSW: Right. Moses was inside the stone.

JS: That says something interesting about intelligence because things that seem so obvious to us today were brilliant insights at some point in time. Yet they don't seem so brilliant from our vantage point.

RSW: It is the "of course" factor. How do we develop ourselves to see the things we have seen, but have never really seen?

JS: That is what recognition really is; it is not inventing things.

THE JOY OF DISCOVERY

Recognition is finding things. I always delight when I suggest an idea to someone and they say, "That is obvious. I could have thought of that." That means that they have seen how one idea is connected to another.

> **We know a thing when we understand it.**
>
> **George Berkeley**

New ideas are not so much discovered as uncovered by moving from what you already understand into the realm of what you would like to understand. Sometimes simply by reorganizing the information you possess, by using and comparing what you already know, you can uncover other information. You also probably have some sense of how big a football field is. When you hear that a football field is about 43,560 square feet, you now can understand what an acre is—in a way that most likely you will remember.

These connections differentiate raw data from meaningful information.

I find this reassuring. I don't worry so much about discovering new information, but in connecting existing information in new ways. I think that all things are connected and that once you realize that, you will feel immediately justified to start your search at any place.

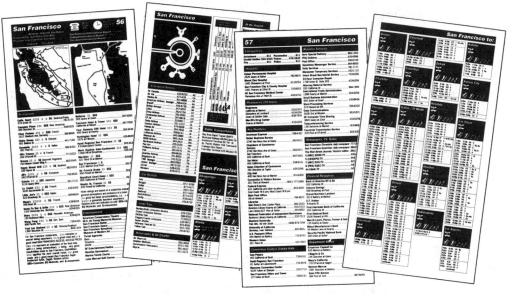

These designs for a new kind of airline travel guide include arrival and departure time schedules such as might be found in the *Official Airlines Guide*®. In addition, information about transportation between the airport and the city, information about hotels, restaurants, and business services, and information about other travel-related services is included.

Guides such as this, which take a broad view of an experience, allow the reader to more easily connect those bits of information relevant to his or her needs and to ignore the rest.

HAILING FAILING AND STILL SAILING

Nowadays most people die of a sort of creeping common sense, and discover when it is too late that the only things one never regrets are one's mistakes.

Oscar Wilde

*T*he winds of Puget Sound twisted, contorted, and destroyed the Tacoma Narrows Bridge—but also prompted urgent and exacting aerodynamic research that ultimately benefited all forms of steel construction.

● Beauvais Cathedral was built to the limit of the technology in its day, and it collapsed—but succeeding cathedrals made use of its failure. Who's to know where any technology ends if its limits are not stretched?

● The machines of the world's greatest inventor, Leonardo da Vinci, were never built, and many wouldn't have worked anyway—but he was trying solutions where no man knew there were even problems.

● Clarence Darrow became a legend in the courtroom as he lost case after case—but he forced re-evaluations of contemporary views of religion, labor relations, and social dilemmas.

● Edwin Land's attempts at instant movies (Polarvision) absolutely failed. He described his attempts as trying to use an impossible chemistry and a nonexistent technology to make an unmanufacturable product for which there was no discernible demand. This created the optimum working condition, he felt.

Doubts that cloud the faith of an era will excite its geniuses.

Frederic Morton,
Nervous Splendour

190

AN ODE TO ERROR

These people understood, tolerated, and even courted failure. They were alternately exhilarated, confident, and scared to death, but they didn't perceive failure as a stigma. They were able to say, "Sure, that didn't work, but watch *this*."

They saw failure not as a sign of defeat, but as a prelude to success, a stage or step to be understood and then used to best advantage—a *delayed* success. They embraced failure and manipulated it as a creative agent to drive their work. Their lives were failure-success cycles. Their submarines sank, their rockets exploded, their domes collapsed, their serums didn't work. But they documented their mistakes, they tried something else, then something else, then something else.

From the artist's studio to the scientist's laboratory, for the satisfaction of a problem solved or a fortune gained, those who seek to live their dreams, and to conquer the new or simply to challenge the status quo, all risk failure.

R. Buckminster Fuller built his geodesic domes by starting with a deliberately failed dome and making it "a little stronger and a little stronger . . . a little piece of wood here and a little piece of wood there, and suddenly it stood up." He edged from failure to success.

A television program on "The Mystery of the Master Builders," part of the "Nova" series, made reference to how architects learned from mistakes to create some of the world's most beautiful Gothic cathedrals.

Builders of Notre Dame in Paris discovered that wind velocity increases with elevation, causing greater stress to taller buildings. "Pressures at the top of Notre Dame were much greater than anyone had foreseen," said the show's narrator. "The builders here had pushed into unknown territory. They faced new challenges, made

After the success of *South Pacific*, Oscar Hammerstein put an ad in *Variety* that listed a dozen or so of his failures, in case anyone had forgotten them. At the bottom of the ad, he repeated the credo of show business, "I did it before, and I can do it again."

DARE TO BE STUPID

Yoshimichi Yamashiti, head of Japanese operations for Arthur D. Little, has a theory about the executive's role in creative processes that yield great ideas. "The manager must learn to be stupid." Personal authority must be set aside, and homage paid to the ideas of workers, whose working knowledge and insight can lead to breakthrough products and processes.

P. R. Nayak and J. M. Kettringham, "The Fine Art of Managing Creativity," *The New York Times* (11/2/86)

mistakes, and devised new solutions. Notre Dame established the fashion for flying buttresses, but it was a fashion forged by necessity." And by trial and error.

These discoveries led to the addition of flying buttresses to the cathedral at Bourges, France, which was not originally designed to have them.

But most of us equate failure with inadequacy or rejection. Failure suggests a shame to be borne in secret. Mistakes in school, on the job, or in social milieus are the switches with which we beat ourselves.

A major form of *information anxiety* exists because of the fear of failing to understand, or of admitting a lack of understanding. Assimilating information means venturing into the realm of the new and unknown in order to come to understand them.

And with any new undertaking, the risk of failure increases. Some people shun new information and new technology to avoid the risk. Others persist despite their fears, but the burden of their fear of failure will make the acquisition of new information that much more difficult.

Perhaps if we kept in mind that many extraordinary people *expect* failure, we wouldn't fear it so much and could begin to learn how to use it.

THE PROPER MANAGEMENT OF FAILURE BREEDS SUCCESS

Success exploits the seeds that failure plants. Failure contains tremendous growth energy.

Human efforts which fail dramatize the nobility of inspired, persistent human endeavor. Great achievements have been built on foundations of inadequacy and error. The discovery of America was made when Christopher Columbus took a wrong turn en route (he thought) to the East Indies. Charles Goodyear bungled an experiment and discovered vulcanized rubber. Sir Isaac Newton failed geometry and Albert Einstein lacked an aptitude for math. Paul Gauguin was a failed stockbroker, and Alfred Butts invented the game of SCRABBLE® after he lost his job as an architect during the Depression.

You learn balance by losing it.

If failing can be seen as a necessary prelude to impressive achievement, then the process of succeeding itself can be better understood.

The aspiration and determination of an athlete to succeed when his body is ruined, of an engineer to build again when his bridge falls down, of a nation to prosper after its economy has crashed, or of a scientist to conduct years of unsuccessful experiments help us understand the origins of success. Their failures, sometimes quiet and interminable, sometimes quick and spectacular, define the foundations of success and the spirit it needs.

While thinking about how I was taught values, I realized I was taught to value the effort and the exploring that come before success. I have found that failure and the analysis of failure have always been more interesting to me and I learn something from them. I don't learn anything by basking in success. When I can honestly say " I don't know," I begin to know. "I think of information as the oil in a piece of machinery," said Nathan Felde, a communication specialist in charge of the NYNEX Media Lab. The information permits operation. There are a lot of systems now that are being designed by people who fail to notice that the exhaust pipe runs back into the passenger compartment. They are running along at quite a clip pouring exhaust into the cockpit or the passenger compartment—people have gotten used to it; they have adjusted to a very high level of exhaust.

"So you think that you're a failure do you? Well, you probably are. What's wrong with that? In the first place, if you've any sense at all you must have learned by now that we pay just as dearly for our triumphs as we do for our defeats. Go ahead and fail. But fail with wit, fail with grace, fail with style. A mediocre failure is as insufferable as a mediocre success. Embrace failure. Seek it out. Learn to love it. That may be the only way any of us will ever be free."

Tom Robbins, *Even Cowgirls Get the Blues*

Jonas Salk spent 98 percent of his time documenting the things that didn't work until he found the thing that did.

Every exit is an entry somewhere else.

Tom Stoppard

WHAT YOU DON'T KNOW IS AS IMPORTANT AS WHAT YOU DO

As the former president of the New York Public Library, Vartan Gregorian was at the helm of one of the world's most significant collections of information. And as a former professor who has a Ph.D. in history and humanities from Stanford University, he is well aware of the problems in assimilating it. Gregorian, now president of Brown University, has been awarded twenty-two honorary degrees, and was provost at the University of Pennsylvania before being named to his library post, blames the educational system for fostering *information anxiety* by not teaching students to cope with adversity and failure. He describes the problems as follows:

> In 1983, when I was in Mexico City attending an International Publishers Association meeting, I was shocked to hear Akio Morita, chairman of Sony, saying that "Every year we're able to use less and less information because while there is an explosion of information, at the same time our capacity to retrieve it is declining." We're able to retrieve, according to his investigations in Japan, only five percent of the available supply of information.
>
> I've been thinking since then of the implications. Is the information explosion equivalent to a knowledge explosion? The answer is no! I've talked with my friend Carlos Fuentes, who said, "The greatest crisis facing modern civilization is going to be how to transform information into structured knowledge." In order to do that, people must learn to overcome their lack of dimension and discover how to make better information connections.

People often peddle non-information as information, or obsolete information as true information or nonobsolete information as obsolete. If Orwell were writing

1984 now, he would not say," Destroy the information." He would say, "Inundate people with information, they'll think they're free. Don't deny them. Give them more." Undigested information is no information at all, but it creates the fiction that you have accessed it, even though you didn't benefit from it.

The sole task of an educational system should be to give you the tools and provide you with a critical mind, so that you can ask the right questions, make the right connections.

The educational system currently confuses means and ends. The means are the tools. The ends are the meaning. I remind people in educational institutions when they talk about how well organized they are by citing St. Augustine's *City of God*, in which he said, "Rome was a well-run city, but where was it going?"

There is a doubling every five years of the information supply. But you do not know if what you've got is distilled or undigested information. On top of it you have the fragmentation of knowledge. There is not only an explosion, but a fragmentation of knowledge owing to specialization, overspecialization, subspecialization.

Specialization in colleges and universities is bringing about this phenomenon, which is making the problem far more acute. People are not trained to recognize sources. They think that if it's not in the computer data bank, it doesn't exist. They don't know that you can have archival sources. You can have many things which are not on-line.

Their notion of what composes or constitutes the totality is defective. Our educational system has to bring integration of knowledge between disciplines. I've proposed that we should have courses taught by five professors around one topic. For example, five professors teaching together, not lecturing at each others' class. A course on the cosmos to be taught by a physicist, a biologist, a geologist, a philosopher, a mathematician.

He who lies on the ground cannot fall.
Yiddish Proverb

How often I saw where I should be going by setting out for somewhere else.
R. Buckminster Fuller

The classical notion of knowledge has two parts. One half is to know what you know. To know what you don't know is the other half. To know what you know and to know what you don't know is total knowledge. In our schools and in our fast-moving society, we teach people to know what they know at least. But we don't teach students to know the limitations of their knowledge. As a result, we kill the act of curiosity, to discover more.

Part of the problem now is we don't teach people how to cope with adversity and failure. We think people ought to know how to learn only from success. And that's part of the instant gratification, instant knowledge they demand. "Just give me the pill; spare me the agony of learning"—that's what they are saying. One of my favorite quotes has always been from Richard Sheridan's *The Critic of 1799*, where one of the characters says, "The number of those who undergo the fatigue of judging for themselves is precious few."

The task of education, I always tell my students, ought to be to increase the number of those who undergo the fatigue of judging for themselves.

We make strenuous efforts for our body, but not the same strenuous efforts for our mind.

CONVERSATION WITH PAUL KAUFMAN

While Vartan Gregorian laments the overemphasis on success placed on the individual, Paul Kaufman (cited in Chapter One) has a special interest in how this affects the corporate environment and how large corporations acknowledge the idea of failure.

RSW: I use a memory of my youth as a paradigm for hailing failing. I saw a man in a wheelchair. My mother said he had been ill and bedridden for a long time and they had to teach him how to walk again. He hadn't walked in a long time and he had forgotten how. That was a revelation to me. I never knew you had to be *taught* how to walk because I couldn't remember learning to walk and assumed I always knew how. As I thought about it, I realized that relearning to walk must be a process of continually putting yourself in jeopardy. You put a leg out, deliberately lose your equilibrium and begin to fall. Walking is a succession of falls.

You learn from the thing that doesn't work because it speaks to you; it blueprints the next step. Yet we are not allowed to talk about failure.

PK: I work with large corporations. The prospect of failing or—to use your metaphor—falling is understandably threatening to managers. Falling means losing control, and many managers believe that control is the essence of what they do.

Unfortunately, their efforts to stay in control interfere with their productive use of information. Consequently, they don't see things as they really are. True breakthroughs in understanding—the kind of perceptions that can revitalize a business—often come only after a fall of sorts.

In this fall, the manager, as it were, hits bottom. In hitting bottom, the manager has the traumatic experience of discovering that he or she has actually had a hand in creating the mess, the system that just hasn't worked. That particular realization is an important first step toward seeing things in a new way.

Henry Thoreau tells a story about a traveler on horseback who comes to the edge of a bog. He asks a local youth if it has a hard bottom. The boy assures the traveler that indeed it does, but as the traveler proceeds across the bog, he starts to sink. "I thought you said that this bog had a hard bottom," says the traveler to the boy.

SOMETIMES WRONG WAY IS RIGHT WAY

When Douglas Corrigan was denied permission to fly his ramshackle airplane across the Atlantic during the 1930s, he requested permission to fly from New York to California instead. The U.S. Bureau of Air Commerce granted it. Corrigan took off from Brooklyn's Floyd Bennett Field and landed 28 hours and 13 minutes later—in Dublin, Ireland. When airport officials informed him where he was, he replied, "I must have flown the wrong way," earning him the nickname Wrong Way Corrigan.

> I have learned throughout my life as a composer chiefly through my mistakes and pursuits of false assumptions, not by my exposure to founts of wisdom and knowledge.
>
> Igor Stravinsky

> There is much to be said for failure. It is more interesting than success.
>
> Max Beerbohm

"So it has," replies the youth, "but you've not got halfway to it yet."

Thoreau is saying there is a solid bottom everywhere. Corporations are no exception, but it takes a courageous executive to get to the bottom of things.

YOU WON'T BELIEVE WHAT WENT WRONG

In order to get to the bottom, in order to find what is there, you really do have to fail. We have a culture that sustains only the manifestation of success.

While many people probably aren't consciously aware of it, we all possess the capacity for endowing failure with more nobility—or at least with more humor and affection. When we look back on our lives, sometimes the things that we remember most fondly are the times when everything went wrong. I know a woman who could write a book about the terrible things that have happened to her on first days—the first day of school, the first day of a new job. Once she wore two different kinds of shoes and didn't discover it until the day was over. Another time she was beset by a case of static cling. After performing in what she thought was an exemplary manner during her first four hours at a new job, a coworker informed her that she had a pair of rainbow-colored panties clinging to the back of her white blouse.

When people talk about their vacations, invariably what they recount with the most delight are the misadventures. Long after they have forgotten the names of the cathedrals and museums, they will remember the time they went to California and their luggage went to Caracas, when the Hilton Hotel in Hong Kong lost their reservations and they spent the night in the hotel sauna, when they rushed to the JFK Airport in New York to catch a plane that left from La Guardia.

In all my travels, one of my fondest memories was getting stuck on a hot runway in Jodhpur, India. I was en route to Jaipur and the plane had mechanical difficulties. Airport personnel told us that we would be there for seven hours and would have to wait on the plane. I was the only foreigner on the plane. After an hour, I started berating the airline personnel. I insisted that they find a bus and take us into town so at least we could see the place and have lunch. They did. After letting everyone else off the bus at a restaurant, the driver turned to me and said, "You stay on the bus. You're going to get a tour of Jodhpur." We returned to the restaurant to find everyone else still waiting for lunch. Someone from the airlines came and, glaring directly at me, made an announcement, "The plane is ready now, but you are going to eat first."

We all happily recount our misadventures when it comes to travel. We should be able to do more of this in our professional lives. When John Naisbitt was questioned for acting as a business consultant after his own company almost went bankrupt, he asserted that for this very reason, he was a better consultant. He understood from experience what could go wrong in a company.

In my company, I respect the person who can come to me and say, "I'm sorry. I tried something and it didn't work." I know that the person has learned something.

THE BREAKING POINT

I am interested in failure because that is the moment of learning—the moment of jeopardy that is both interesting and enlightening. The fundamental means of teaching a course in structural engineering is to show the moment when a piece of wood breaks, when a piece of steel bends,

MINI-MUSEUM OF FAILURE

Device for shaping the upper lip.

Eye protector for chickens.

Massage apparatus.

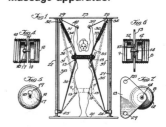

Adapted from *Absolutely Mad Inventions* by A. E. Brown and H. A. Jeffcott, Jr., drawings from the U.S. Patent Office

when a piece of stone or concrete collapses. You learn by watching something fail to work. William Lear, who invented the jet that bears his name, invented a steam car and all sorts of other things that he was certain would fail. He felt that there was a cyclical relationship between failure and success, and that failure was the necessary first part of the cycle.

I often think one's life is molded more by inability than ability. When I visited the aerospace museum in Washington, D.C., as marvelous as it is, I missed the epiphany of things that failed. A few years ago, to celebrate the anniversary of the Wright airplane, there was an article in *Scientific American* about the Wright brothers and their inventions. It made me think about the beginning of that wonderful film, *Those Magnificent Men in Their Flying Machines*, in which you see a litany of failed aircraft. You laugh, but you also see how seriously involved everybody was in trying to fly. All the failures, all the things that didn't work, make you realize that the Wright brothers were really something. All the paths taken, all the good intentions, the logistics, the absurdities, all the hopes of people trying to fly testifying to the power we have when we refuse to quit.

Half the failures in life arise from pulling in one's horse as he is leaping.

A. W. Hare

He who never fails will never grow rich.

C. H. Spurgeon

MUSEUM OF FAILURE
IS OVERNIGHT SUCCESS

There should be a museum dedicated to human inventive failure. The only problem it would face would be its overnight success. In almost any scientific field, it would add enormously to the understanding of what does work by showing what doesn't work. In developing the polio vaccine, Jonas Salk spent 98 percent of his time documenting the things that didn't work until he found the thing that did.

A scientist's notebook is basically a journal of negative results. Scientists try to disprove their ideas; that is the work they do. "Images become useful to scientists to the extent that they contain information that contradicts conventional wisdom, forming the basis of a polemical understanding of nature," according to Chandra Mukerji in a paper, "Imaginary Dialogues: The Practice of Picture-Making in Scientific Research," delivered at the International Sociological Association and published in 1986.

As economist Kenneth Boulding said, "The moral of evolution is that nothing fails like success because successful adaptation leads to the loss of adaptability . . . This is why a purely technical education can be disastrous. It trains people only in thinking of things that have been thought of and this will eventually lead to disaster."

If you put a camera on the Golden Gate Bridge and photographed it for twenty years, you wouldn't learn very much because the bridge succeeded. You learn much more from the documentation of failure. So failure can be defined as delayed success.

The anxiety associated with failure inhibits us from exploiting our creativity, from taking the risks that might lead us into new territory, and from learning and thus assimilating new information. An acceptance of failure as a necessary prelude to success is imperative to reducing anxiety.

> A failure is a man who has blundered, but is not able to cash in the experience.
> **Elbert Hubbard**

> Nearly all my successes are founded on previous failures.
> **Louis Parker**

> My definition of failure is delayed success.

INFORMATION BULIMIA: A READING DISORDER

One failure we are destined to experience in an information age is a failure to be as informed as we could be.

The fear of failing to be one of the "informed" in an information age has created a condition similar to the eating disorder known as bulimia, characterized by binge eating followed by purges.

Your feelings of not keeping up with your field or with events in the world send you into a stage of manic subscribing. You decide that your stable subscriptions to

Time, The New York Times, The Wall Street Journal, and *Esquire* are inadequate. You actually find yourself picking up those pesky subscription cards that fall out of your old familiar magazines; next you start sending them to the publishers. In six to eight weeks, a procession of new magazines starts filing into your home or office—*The New Republic, Harper's, Foreign Affairs, The Atlantic, The Nation.* You greet each one as if it will be the instrument of your salvation, your membership in the elite Informed Persons Club.

Then you realize that by virtue of their presence in your home or office, they are all silently demanding to be read. No Jewish mother could make you feel as guilty as an unread magazine. Suddenly your salvation becomes a burden, a constant reminder of how far you really are from that blissful state of being informed.

Some of us can let this go on for months, others for years. But inevitably at some point, you decide that if you got rid of the guilt-inducers, you would find peace. You fire off cancellation notices to the magazine circulation departments and you blithely ignore the ominous notices composed by melodramatic subscription departments about what will happen to you if, God forbid, "you let your subscription expire."

In six to eight weeks, if you are lucky (magazine subscription departments being more stubborn than stockbrokers), the flood of periodicals across your desk will begin to dwindle to a trickle. You will feel like Prometheus unbound, or at least unsubscribed.

Then a friend will casually mention, "Did you see the article in *The Hydraulic Bench Press Digest* on catalytic converters?" And you had just canceled your subscriptions. The cycle starts again.

This binge-purge syndrome is not a healthy response to the problem.

There is no failure except in no longer trying.

Elbert Hubbard

Flops are a part of life's menu and I've never been a girl to miss out on any of the courses.

Rosalind Russell

In one year, the average American will read or complete 3,000 notices and forms, read 100 newspapers and 36 magazines, watch 2,463 hours of television, listen to 730 hours of radio, buy 20 records, talk on the telephone almost 61 hours, read 3 books, and spend countless hours exchanging information in conversations.

Thus we spend most of our waking hours with information.

Linda Costigan Lederman, from "Communication in the Workplace: The Impact of the Information Age and High Technology on Interpersonal Communication in Organizations," *Interpersonal Communication in a Media World*

W

e are what we read. In both our professional and personal life, we are judged by the information we peruse. The information we ingest shapes our personalities, contributes to the ideas we formulate, and colors our view of the world.

Americans' appetite for information is increasing, but their attention span is decreasing. According to publishing executives, instant books that elaborate on people and events of the moment are disappearing, owing to public preference for the immediacy and brevity of the electronic media.

Michael Freitag, from "On the Endangered List: The 'Instant Book,' " *The New York Times*

What we choose to read and what we choose to ignore are, therefore, some of the most critical decisions that we make, yet they are invariably made with little thought, almost unconsciously.

The information we take in becomes a part of us. As we get older, we grow more diverse and individualistic because our viewpoints and outlooks are shaped by our own peculiar collection of information experiences.

Even planning one's reading diet carefully doesn't solve the problems. Those who do are often overwhelmed by the enormity of the selection. Case histories of information junkies abound.

The mass media instantly and persuasively disseminate new images, and ordinary individuals, seeking help in coping with an ever more complex social environment, attempt to keep up. At the same time, events—as distinct from research as such—also batter our old image structures. Racing swiftly past our attention screen, they wash out old images and generate new ones.

Alvin Toffler, *Future Shock*

CONFESSIONS OF AN INFORMATION JUNKIE

Wilbur Schramm, who, with William Porter, co-authored *Men, Women, Messages, and Media: Understanding Human Communications,* claimed, "At the moment, I feel it necessary to be familiar with the contents of about fifty scholarly journals. Those are the ones I know I should be familiar with: how many of the hundred thousand I do not know, but should be familiar with, I am not prepared to say. To keep up professionally, I should read several hundred new books each year, and a very large number of duplicated drafts or preprints that circulate among scholars. I should also keep in touch with fifty or more scholars who are working on problems that interest me, and answer the letters of another fifty to one hundred who ask information from me. In addition to these things, I must work on my own articles and books. What I have listed is already an impossible task, even if I had no other work to do, had no need of sleep or relaxation, and could read and write twenty-four hours a day. But it illustrates what the information explosion means to a communication scholar."

ABSOLUTELY ESSENTIAL VS. GUILT

In *Thoughts from a Victim of Info-Overload Anxiety,* Warren Bennis, a writer, educator, and co-author of *Leaders*, said that the stacks of journals, letters, books, documents, periodicals, memoranda, and newspapers in his office look like "mobiles of Dutch colonial homes gently swaying."

He divides the stacks into the "Absolutely Essential," which go onto the "Guilt Shelf"—they topple onto the not–Absolutely Essential piles. "I spend a lot of time feeling guilty about the amount of time I spend feeling guilty about reading less than one percent of what I receive.

"I cannot distance myself from this chronic anxiety. Who among us can argue with Daniel Bell, John Kenneth Galbraith, Bertrand de Jouvenel, and others who have defined our 'post-technological' period as one in which only those who have the right information, the strategic knowledge, and the handy facts can 'make it' in the last quarter of this century?"

Bennis's reading diet reflects his determination to "make it." He admits to subscribing to about 225 magazines and periodicals, but his secretary claims that number is "definitely conservative." In addition to

It is estimated that the world's great libraries are doubling in size every 14 years, a rate of 14,000 percent each century. In the early 1300s, the Sorbonne Library in Paris contained only 1,338 books and yet was thought to be the largest library in Europe. Today, there are several libraries in the world with an inventory of well over 8 million books each.

Wilbur Shramm and William Porter, *Men, Women, Messages, and Media: Understanding Human Communication*

Selective reading habits are taking hold as Americans read more magazines and newspapers to gain information of significance or personal value to them. "New generation" consumer magazines, books, and newspapers cater to specialized interests, from home repair, to gardening, to computer programming, to you-name-it. Readers are reading books that fit their "lifestyle" and not necessarily for the pleasure, if they even see it as such, of reading.

Lena Williams, "Studies Find More Reading for Information and Less for Fun," *The New York Times* (5/2/88)

skimming two local daily papers and *The New York Times*, he tries to read thoroughly *The Wall Street Journal*, along with a daily digest of general news, *Sports Illustrated*, and selected articles from *The Atlantic, Commentary, The Public Interest*, and *Fortune*.

"The best metaphor I can think of to describe the process by which I make choices of what to read and in what order is 'The Ambush.' A colleague tells me about an important article he has recently read in the last issue of *The Wilson Quarterly*. It's on 'Changing Patterns of American Families,' a topic which happens to interest me. It turns out that very day I receive an interesting ad from *The Wilson Quarterly* which features that particular issue. The following day another colleague sends me a reprint of that article, and the week after, the article is loaded into tissue paper for briefcase #2. In my mail, two weeks later, I receive an invitation from the president of Bankers Trust asking me to address their annual executive committee meeting (for a lovely honorarium) on—you guessed it—'Changing Patterns of American Families.' *The Wilson Quarterly* reprint moves up to briefcase #1.

"A long time ago I read a story which was all about the proliferation of words. The country's dictionaries grew from 40,000 words to 4 million and were in danger of doubling every ten years . . . By the year 2000, as I recall the story, the common dictionary was expected to weigh more than the earth. Then one day a massive explosion, some kind of verbal accident, occurred, and the world was reduced to one word, IRTNOG, or something like that—a nonsense syllable.

"I suppose that story comes to mind because the verbal pollution which fouls up our lives makes us anxious about all we do not, cannot, maybe should not, read or know. I do not want our precious English language heritage to metastasize beyond comprehension; at the same time, could we live with only IRTNOG?

"My own solution is possibly too simple. It consists of two parts. First, we need theories to live by. A theory is an intellectual armature which allows only certain facts in; other inconsequential facts can be screened out, untouched, not to be worried about. We will all die of word pollution if we allow our minds to become empirical dustbowls where every fact is as salient as any other. Secondly, in an information-rich age, it really is impossible to know everything. Even if I were to read every single journal, book, periodical, abstract in my teetertottering library . . . even then, I wouldn't even be close to what Palestrina, Erasmus, Galileo, or Aristotle knew about their worlds.

"So what I must learn to do is to ask the right questions. And that, it seems to me, must come from having some working theories about what's important."

TO READ IS WONDERFUL, BUT TO FORGET IS DIVINE
Forgetting meanings is not a matter for excuses, an unfortunate defect in performance; it is an affirmative value, a way of asserting the irresponsibility of the text, the pluralism of systems . . . it is precisely because I forget that I read.

Roland Barthes, *S/Z*

One of the most anxiety-inducing side effects of the information era is the feeling that you have to know it all. Realizing your own limitations becomes essential to surviving an information avalanche; you cannot or should not absorb or even pay attention to everything.

Many people recognize the problem, but don't know how to say. no to something without feeling the weight of remorse. Business people used to have "In" and "Out" baskets; many of the people with whom I consult now have "Guilt" baskets as well.

Steve Smith, executive editor at *Newsweek*, admits: "I never feel relaxed unless I am out of range of *The New York Times*. It is my first source of information and it is the first thing in my guilt pile. When I get beyond *The Times*, when I am in Europe or something, there is a great load off me. I love being in London and buying a great load of British papers and dabbling in them. With *The New York Times*, I have this sense of duty to plow through story by story and to master the thing."

The key to reducing the oppressiveness of this duty is learning to decipher what is germane to your life and to your interests. Many time-pressed executives use vicarious readers who sort through material and weed out the impertinent.

**SCIENTISTS TOO BUSY
READING TO EXPERIMENT**

The number of scientific
articles and journals being
published around the world
has grown so large that it
is starting to confuse researchers, overwhelm the
quality-control systems of
science, encourage fraud,
and distort the dissemination of important findings.

Desktop printing, electronic
transmittal of material, and
the proliferation of vanity
presses have increased
the number of scientific
journals to such an ex-
tent that the majority of
scientific articles go virtually unread, according to
some surveys. One side
effect is overtaxed editors
and referee panels that are
supposed to scrutinize
journal submissions,
evidenced by several cases
of fraud in which gross
errors of fact and logic
have slipped through the
safety nets.

William J. Broad, "Science
Can't Keep Up with Flood of
New Journals," *The New
York Times* (2/16/88)

If you lack the resources or staff to sort for you, establish your own criteria. If you are a sociologist, examine the journals that cover your field. In your own and valid opinion, determine the two or three best ones. Explore the journals that cover your specific area of interest within the field of sociology. If you study health-care organizations, for example, select a few journals that cover hospital administration. Refuse to read those which don't convey useful information to you.

I follow the shard approach to reading. Every day, I get about a dozen periodicals. I let them pile up on the floor of my office. When the stack starts to get desk-high, I flip through them and tear out only the articles that interest me or that I have some reason to read. The rest get thrown out. The pile immediately becomes less threatening. I can now attack it with optimism. It now contains only the shards that will be meaningful to my life, the material or information that I might be able to use.

I am a consultant to *Road & Track* magazine. Every month, the magazine provides an extensive analysis based on a road test of a particular car. One day, I asked the magazine's art director and the man who tested the cars why some of the items were on the list. Neither had any idea why some of the items were on the list. Certainly, they were of little concern to someone contemplating the purchase of a car. Consequently, the list was shortened.

The same lessons can be applied to your life. Time spent collecting information that doesn't pertain to your life is not only wasted, but the information you have acquired is probably wasting valuable memory space.

PAPER WEIGHT-WATCHERS

According to Lance Shaw, in an article in *Technology Review* (July-August 1979), there is a disorder brought about by our "poly-saturated, paper-polluted," information-mad society characterized by an "obsessive-compulsive tendency to read everything about everything. When the amount of reading matter ingested exceeds the amount of energy available for digestion, the surplus accumulates and is converted by stress and over-stimulation into the unhealthy state known as IOA (Information Overload Anxiety)."

And the cure pushers are as prolific as the information pushers. Nobel laureate Herbert Simon claims that reading daily newspapers is the "least cost-efficient thing you can do" and suggests reading *The World Almanac* once a year. Some tout speed-reading courses; others make millionaires out of abstract and digest publishers with subscription fees; and others hire fleets of assistants and do their reading vicariously.

Shaw, a "reformed IOA patient," suggests that these approaches are unnecessary and recommends instead the Fat-Free Daily Reading Diet (FFDRD), which is an individually tailored program of reading material composed of publications selected from four basic reading groups for their practicality, consistency, and absence of bulk. The FFDRD diet is as follows:

Group I. **Newspapers.** One daily. But proceed slowly and check first with your physician. Choose from the following: *The Wall Street Journal, The New York Times, The Washington Post,* or *The Los Angeles Times.* Absence of bulk clearly makes *The Wall Street Journal* the preferred choice, and only *The New York Times* is delivered outside its region on the date of publication. The *WSJ* does not suffer any regional virus, such as the *Post*'s "Potomac virus," leading to feverish stories about the identity of presidential tennis partners or *The New York Times*'s "Big Apple syndrome," leading to information about where one can

PERIODICAL PROLIFERATION SHOCK SYNDROME

"Do you have *Women?*" Marilyn Imhoff asked the newsstand clerk. "No," replied the clerk, who said he had lots of *Womans*, but no *Women*. "I have *Woman, New Woman, Complete Woman, Working Woman, New York Woman*—all those *Womans*."

"I guess I don't know what I want," said Ms. Imhoff, who seemed suddenly dazed and confused, and turned on her heel and left—another victim of Periodical Proliferation Shock Syndrome.

The Magazine Publishers Association said that 265 more magazines are being published this year than last year, which works out to about one a day if magazine creators take weekends off.

The newsstand on the concourse level of the Pan Am building offers about 2,500 different magazines.

William B. Geist, "Magazine Chaos: From Hot Tubs to Talking Birds," *The New York Times* (5/20/87)

buy Albanian sausage on Second Avenue or on which Thursday you can dance the *hora* on Prince Street with your children.

Group II. **Newsmagazines.** One to be selected from the following: *Newsweek, Time, U.S. News & World Report.* Diet must be limited to one. Ingesting two reveals serious addiction. Since the basic contents of *Newsweek* and *Time* do not vary significantly, reading both will throw your metabolism out of kilter.

Group III. **General Culture and Ideas.** Few temptations here. Needed is one unsweetened, streamlined packet with reviews of books, movies, dance, theater, music, TV, the plastic and performing arts, architecture, urban aesthetics, graphic design, and the commercial arts. No such item exists in the U.S. In waiting rooms, try *Vogue;* in England, sample *The Listener;* on Sunday, read *The New York Times.* A warning about the Sunday *Times*: it has unquestionably brought more patients to terminal IOA than any other single diet component. It must be read only under doctor's supervision, and you must first remove bulk—all lingerie ads, travel pages, reports of recent polo deaths in Zimbabwe. Leave in essential ingredients: discussions of architecture, drama reviews, essays on arts and culture.

Group IV. **Reference Books.** Do not be hooked by book clubs or by friends' seductive shelves of Encyclopaedia Britannica. This diet includes only one reference book—a dictionary with intellectual heft and clarity; an untrendy dictionary, but one that doesn't shy away from "DNA" or "glitch," a dictionary with helpful pictures, but no drawings of nailheads or cows; one with first-rate etymologies and with type that can be read without an accompanying magnifying glass. The dictionary that comes closest to meeting our minimum daily requirement is the Random House Dictionary of the English Language—unabridged.

Reference Supplements. To help you adjust without regressing to book clubs, libraries, and binges resulting in a three-year subscription to *Mother Jones* or to *Popular Mechanics*, I refer you to the following extras containing no fat. They may be read only by those who have their appetites under control.

The National Directory of Addresses and Telephone Numbers, a paperback, includes addresses and phone numbers of all U.S. companies with annual sales of $10 million and more, and governmental agencies, foundations, educational institutions, museums, ballparks, symphony orchestras, public libraries, hotels, airlines, hospitals, and all those organizations you've been wanting to write hate letters to all these years.

Free Items. Morgan Guaranty Trust in New York offers a monthly report on the U.S. economy, and Metropolitan Life publishes a monthly *Statistical Bulletin* tracing important demographic trends and their consequences.

Lance Shaw suggests that "for the lucky few who do not require a strict regimen," publications devoted to business and science may be added as a supplement to the basic maintenance program.

RÉSUMÉ VÉRITÉ

Before you can curb your information intake, though, you have to come to an understanding of who you are. What kind of information is essential to your life, to your work? What information answers directly to your need to know? And what are you amassing only for the sake of some ideal image you have of what an "informed person" should be? The pursuit of the former will provide satisfaction; the pursuit of the latter will produce anxiety. Information that is essential to you will help define who you are and what you do. Information that is extraneous to your life will further reinforce the unsettling distance between who you are and who you think you should be.

I have a writer friend who is periodically struck with a fear that she doesn't get enough done in a day. Ordinarily, she is an extraordinarily relaxed person who is perfectly happy to watch rocks grow, but every once in a while she wishes she were more informed, more well read, more politically astute. During one of these phases, she read that while Henry Kissinger was Secretary of State, he would sleep for 1.5 hours three times during a 24-hour day, and that as the most salubrious sleep occurs during the early stages, he was able to get the maximum benefit of sleep in a minimum of time. So she decided to adopt this schedule, hoping that she could get more accomplished if she slept for only 4.5 hours a day. She immediately discovered that 1.5-hour periods were too short. So she increased them to 2 hours, then 3, then 4. After two weeks, she was up to sleeping for three periods of 6 hours each when she decided that maybe it wasn't her nature to be so well informed.

One exercise to determine your own information needs is to write what I call a résumé vérité. See how you would describe yourself verbally to somebody in five hundred words or in five minutes, whichever occurs first. The difference between this and a conventional résumé is that this one really answers the questions of who you are and what you do while the formal résumé that gets sent to potential employers is often so laden with self-aggrandizement that it is more a picture of who you wish you were.

"What do you do?" is probably one of the questions most frequently asked when two people first meet. The answer is also one of the most critical pieces of information that we give away about ourselves and is a microcosm of the problems of information dissemination. Trying to make ourselves and our work understandable to someone else—given that each bit of information we convey will be construed differently through the experiences of the other person—is an endeavor laden with the potential for

---

Thus as radio, television, newspapers, magazines and novels sweep through society, as the proportion of engineered messages received by the individual rises . . . , we witness a profound change: a steady speed—up in the average pace at which image-producing messages are presented to the individual. The sea of coded information that surrounds him begins to beat at his senses with new urgency.

Alvin Toffler, *Future Shock*

perpetrating misconceptions and misunderstandings that can result in someone being judged erroneously.

If you are asked what you do and you say you work at Channel 13 (in New York, Channel 13 is the public television station) people normally say, approvingly, "Oh really?" You could be working at Channel 13 sweeping floors or you could be the president, and people still say, "Oh really?" There is a respect you get for working anywhere near certain jobs, and there are other jobs that could be extremely creative at a very high and powerful position and yet your association with them wouldn't get an "Oh really?" If you say you work at General Motors, many people will be unimpressed, possibly imagining you on an assembly line, although you could be chairman.

Describing yourself in understandable terms—your life-work, your image of yourself, your priorities, what you would like people to think you do, what you do, and what you would like to do next—is a telling slice of reality and aspiration. Yet the question is asked and answered with little thought. It is one of the pieces of life that we do inordinately poorly.

We should all have a personal curriculum vitae or résumé that attempts to describe who we really are and not who we are trying to pretend to be (the motivation behind most conventional résumés). The following are two examples of possible approaches. They are amusing, intriguing, humane. One is by Loring Leifer, a writer and editor who lives in New York. The other is by Sally O'Malley, president of O'Malley and Company, Ltd., a marketing and public relations firm in Chicago.

Although I wouldn't recommend using this kind of résumé to get a job interview with any traditional company, I think you would be curious to meet the people who composed them. They tell you not only about the tasks people perform, but of their attitudes toward life and work. They tell you about humor and intelligence and provide models that could be used to describe yourself, if not to a prospective employer, at least to the person next to you at a cocktail party.

RÉSUMÉ OF LORING LEIFER

(The company names have been obscured to protect the identity of her employers, who admirably chose to hire Loring despite her penchant for the absurd and for whom she still feels a great deal of affection.)

WORK HISTORY
DESIGN EDITOR ■■■■■■■ *MAGAZINE*

Duties: I was in charge of cranking out filler to keep the pictures from bumping into each other for a glitzy, monthly magazine devoted to interior design. I served the same function that Styrofoam pellets do in packing crates, and my prose was accorded about the same attention. This actually made my job quite entertaining. I could intersperse my copy with recipes for Waldorf salad, anecdotes from my childhood, and long passages from page-turners like *Utility Rates in Ottawa*, and no one noticed. Among my other responsibilities were trying to outdrink publicity people on press junkets (something at which I failed miserably on numerous occasions) and to appear sincerely interested in anything for which someone else was picking up the tab. My most important task was to locate designers on tropical islands to justify tax-deductible trips to exotic locales, and wherever possible, to convince the designers to pay for the trips by promising cover stories on their work. (In one year alone, we promised 437 covers.)

COMMUNITY RELATIONS DIRECTOR/
THE ■■■■■■■ *HEALTH AGENCY*

Duties: After three years of highly praised work for the Health Agency, I still had no idea just what this federally funded agency was supposed to do. I think it had something to do with telling doctors and hospital administrators how they could spend their money, so you can imagine what our relations with the community were like. We were about as welcome as Hitler was in Poland. Given this, my main responsibilities were to cheer up the staff and to write upbeat speeches to be delivered by our volunteer board of directors at monthly performances aptly named "Board Meetings." (These made the movie *Death in Venice* seem action-packed.) I also acted as the resident authority on where to have lunch, when to use hyphens, and concocted explanations as to the whereabouts of the executive director after the local newspapers got word that we were being investigated for the misuse of government funds.

STAFF WRITER & POTENTIAL WIFE/ THE ███████████ JEWISH NEWSPAPER

Duties: This was a very delicate position—providing equal attention to ten women on the staff of a weekly newspaper who all thought they were my grandmothers. I also had to spend numerous Saturday nights with their real-life grandsons who would have made Alexander Portnoy seem well adjusted. Every time I sneezed at the office, four of my coworkers got wedged in my doorway with jars of chicken soup and physicians' samples of cold remedies. When I left for the day, the entire staff waved their sweaters at me, simultaneously shouting a chorus: "You'll catch pneumonia, take mine, it's all right, so I'll freeze, you've got your whole life ahead of you."

DAUGHTER OF THE PRESIDENT/ THE ███████████ FABRIC COMPANY

Duties: Believe it or not, I actually did a lot of work. I answered phones, unloaded trucks, typed threatening collection letters, counted hog rings into envelopes, and did numerous other menial tasks that the other employees realized they could pawn off on me to assuage my guilt at having a father who owned the company. Strangely, my sister transcended this guilt. She was the only employee my father ever fired in the history of the business. He overheard her telling the other employees that if she had to work here for the rest of her life, she would kill herself. He decided it would be better for company morale if he paid her not to come to work.

MEMBERSHIPS

First I was a Brownie; next I was a Girl Scout; then my troop leader had a nervous breakdown. I never joined anything after that.

EDUCATION

Although I was a model student during my two years at Arizona State University and then at the University of Wisconsin, where I was graduated with honors with an English degree, I have always suspected that somehow the educational institutions just missed with me. I managed to go through college during the Vietnam War era without turning on, tuning in, dropping out, marching on, or spitting at. Maybe I saw too soon that we would all eventually compromise our principles and join the establishment and decided to send in my membership early. What else would you expect from a fatalist who lamented to her mother at the age of four when she was struck down with the flu: "It's not right that someone so young should suffer so much."

Loring Leifer ©

RÉSUMÉ OF SALLY O'MALLEY

Excerpts from Sally O'Malley's story about herself:

"An attempt to explain who I am since I have none of the background normally associated with a person in my profession."

BORN: Inspiration, Arizona

EDUCATION:
Anaconda Mining Camp Schools, Cananea, Sonora, Mexico (ages 6-10) and at home, where my father read Plato for his private pleasure and Gertrude Stein aloud, laughing his delight, and played complex games based on pure mathematics. My mother expostulated: "Chagall? No, no. Can't you see, it's Miró!"

My father died when I was 10.

All Saints School, Sioux Falls, South Dakota (ages 11-18), where I learned to conjugate 101 irregular French verbs; where I confided in my mathematics teacher that all numbers were colors and she in turn made calculus simplicity itself; where my mother was discussing architecture, art, poetry, literature, and world affairs, expecting her two children to make intelligent contributions to the conversation. My sister suggested I needed "a line" to start a conversation at the once-a-year school dances. I carefully honed: "What do you think of the current international situation?"

Augustana College, Sioux Falls, South Dakota (for one and a half years until rebellious boredom), where my principal interest was to marry a farmer and raise five children. Interest displayed by farmers: zero. Said my mother musingly, "You just don't look the part. Perhaps, a *Vogue* modeling job would be fun?"

BUSINESS EXPERIENCE:

Chicago: 10 jobs in 12 weeks

Knoll Associates (6 years). Where in the early years I typed, walked the sheepdog, waited on customers, watched Hans present one incredible planning unit project after another, called on architectural firms in five states, cut thousands of perfect rectangles out of fabrics and pasted them on plans, flew to Manila to find out why Knoll furniture was arriving in Japan with spool legs, designed spaces, found showroom sites in San Francisco, kept a sharp eye out for imaginative furniture/textile designers, decorated the Christmas tree with cookies flown in from Germany, and cried when Hans was displeased.

DISTINGUISH YOURSELF

The person on your résumé vérité is the one you should nourish, the one around whom your information habits should be structured. The Latin words *curriculum vitae* literally mean "the course or running of your life." Few people probably regard their own *curriculum vitae* in that light and consequently don't take advantage of its potential as such.

The conventional job résumé is regarded more as a possible entry into a higher income bracket; an advertisement of the person you would like to be or think you should be. A résumé vérité should be a narrative of who you are. It should chronicle your interests and your attitudes toward work.

In my professional résumé, my accomplishments were listed under various categories—education, jobs, teaching positions, publications, professional honors. As I have worked in many areas—architecture, graphic design, information consulting—the résumé was quite lengthy. I applied the idea of a private profile to my professional résumé and reworked it in narrative form, using paragraphs to tell the story of my different pursuits. When I showed it to some of the same people who had the older version, they said, "Richard, I had no idea you had done all these things." The narrative version had only half of the information contained in the first résumé of lists, but was more in my personal style and thus more meaningful to others.

A well-crafted personal résumé can be the starting point for planning your information diet. Coming to a better understanding of who you are will enable you to determine the kind of information that will feed your interests and endeavors. You will become more assured about isolating the information that is appropriate to your life and less guilty about ignoring that which is not.

Everything that you hear, read, and see can potentially influence your outlook and personality. The choices, wherever they are yours to make, shouldn't be made lightly, but with a constant sense of who you are.

The promiscuous intake of information, acquired to feed some imprecise or ill-defined desire for improvement or advancement, will likely defeat you by the enormity of the task and by the quantity of information available. Whereas sorting through the information around you with a keen understanding of your own personality and needs will enable you to make more use of less information.

NEWS INFORMATION: VIOLENT WALLPAPER

News is the same thing
happening everyday to
different people.

Anonymous

*W*hen people were dependent on the town crier for their news of the world, the amount of disturbing and anxiety-producing information they came across was rather limited; there was only one channel, so to speak, and people didn't have to spend much time comparing sources. The boundaries of their world were narrow and manageable.

EDITORIAL WHIM

A former editor of the *St. Louis Post-Dispatch*, Jim Fow, was quoted as saying: "On any given day of publication, there are only about six stories that have to be printed. The rest are chosen by editorial whim. Life could go on if most stories were not printed . . ."

66/99 Werner Severin and James Tankard, Jr., *Communication Theories: Origins, Methods, Uses*

Today news comes to us twenty-four hours a day, from all points in the world, over a variety of media. Yet we often absorb it in the same way we listened to the town crier without paying much attention to the form it takes. Few are aware of how a radio account of a fire might differ from a television report on the same fire.

The form in which information is presented will dramatically alter the perception of that information. It will also change the very nature of the information itself. This is often ignored, so that the shortcomings of a particular medium are unfairly blamed for deliberately prejudicing or slanting information when it is only being delivered within the parameters of the particular medium. This would be like blaming AT&T when someone calls up to yell at you. Understanding the nature and limitations of a particular medium will reduce inherent frustrations.

Architects who attempt to visually represent the design of a building have several choices of materials. They can work in either two or three dimensions, with various materials that permit various capabilities. With white plasticine, the nonhardening kindergarten clay of our youth, they can effortlessly change and manipulate such forms in a way that cannot even remotely be paralleled by the use of a straight edge and inking pen. They can use charcoal, where the shadow of past designs can be left with the smudge of a thumb. They can show a slice of the building in elevation or the footprint of a building in a plan. They can create a perspective or axonometric drawing.

The form that they choose will influence the design of the building, in much the same way that a particular news story will be influenced by the medium in which it is reported.

The complexities and nature of the media give us the opportunity to be involved in a perceptive critique of everything we see. We can receive information in a positive state, or we can marshal our inquisitive powers to make information a utility. Within the freedom we have to interpret information lie the means to possess and use it, to make it part of ourselves and our knowledge of the world.

Av Westin, former head of ABC Television News, has pointed out that the first thing people want to learn from news broadcasts is that they and their families are at least safe for one more night. Then they want to learn if anyone else may have been devoured by external evil or internal rot. Then they may be interested in any signs of future danger. Long-term trends (as news, or as knowledge for self-defense) put them to sleep.

John Phelan, *Mediaworld: Programming the Public*

RISK PERCEPTION

Although the events covered by the media may not affect us directly, they help to shape our outlook on the world. The way these events are treated by the media influences our sense of well-being and security. More specifically, the media play a major role in how we assess our risk of falling victim to disease, accidents, or catastrophe.

Our ability to assess the significance of risks depends on our ability to meaningfully assess events and to make comparisons between the relative threat or danger of each of them.

Most Americans worry about their risk of contracting cancer. This understandable concern is fed constantly by the media's attention to the subject. One can scarcely

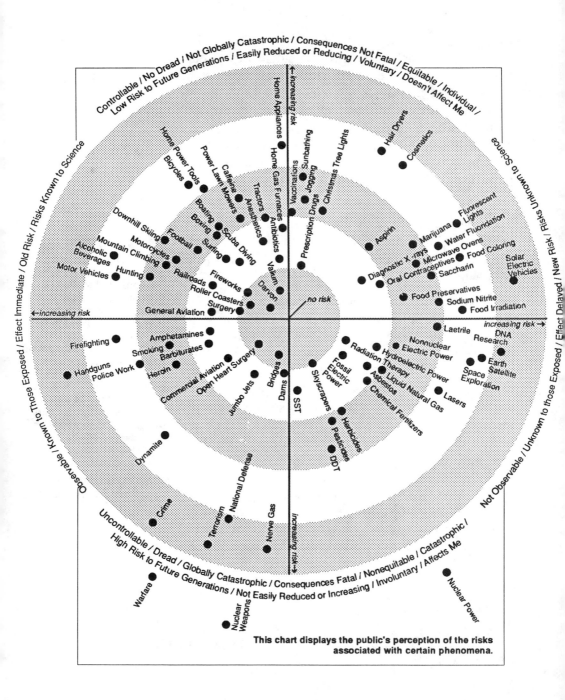

This chart displays the public's perception of the risks associated with certain phenomena.

turn on the television, listen to the radio, or pick up a newspaper or magazine without encountering the results of yet another study regarding some form of cancer. We are told that a certain number of people in the United States will die from cancer in the coming year, that yet another substance has been shown to be carcinogenic, that a particular activity significantly increases the risk of cancer. What such data tend to promote is fear rather than understanding. This is because the data is presented in an information vacuum. What is the risk of contracting breast cancer versus lung cancer, heart disease, or dying in a car accident? Without similar or related data for purposes of comparison, informed judgments regarding risks are very difficult, if not impossible.

When the four-reactor nuclear power complex at Chernobyl exploded in April 1987, there was widespread concern about how the resulting radiation would affect world health. Most notably, there was concern about potential long-term increases in the incidence of certain kinds of cancer. Complex and often conflicting data were bandied about by scientists, politicians, and the press for months after the incident, contributing little or nothing in the end to the comprehension of lay persons, but leaving a distinct residue of fear.

In an attempt to put the incident into perspective, physicist Richard Wilson compared the cancer risk created by the Chernobyl incident to the number of people killed in Russia as a result of their involvement with the coal-burning industry—from its mining to its disposal. He estimated that deaths caused each year from some aspect of the coal industry were between 5,000 and 50,000, while, according to estimates of the U.S. Department of Energy, the total number of cancer cases that may ultimately be caused by the Chernobyl explosion is 20,000.

He concluded that as nuclear reactor accidents happen less than once a year in Russia, the risk is greater for those who work at coal-fired power plants of similar size.

"While the long-term risk created by the Chernobyl incident is not insignificant, it must be viewed in perspective." said Wilson.

The media also play a significant role in our fear of natural disasters, especially weather-related ones. The spectacular coverage of such occurrences as hurricanes, blizzards, floods, and tornadoes has painted a picture of them as extraordinary and devastating disasters. They are perceived as aberrant behavior rather than as normal fluctuations. A rise in the average temperature of five degrees in one area could be potentially much more catastrophic, yet would hardly be perceived as such.

The subtle, less dramatic factors can have a more profound impact on life.

A number of major cities—Boston, New York, Philadelphia, even Washington—are not very far above sea level at all. In New Orleans or Miami, a meter change in the sea level would erode all the beaches away because beaches are about a meter above sea level, and every storm that would happen would be a meter higher. It would be devastating. A number of the cities would have to build dikes around them.

According to meteorologist Josh Wurman, "I think people tend to do that with any event, not just weather. Whatever is kind of peaceful, they think of as normal, and any short periods of deviation are considered abnormal."

The short periods of deviation, however, make the better news stories.

Most Americans feel more at risk in an airplane than in a car, based on the extensive and often gruesome coverage of plane crashes. Yet the number of passenger deaths per mile traveled is much greater in an automobile—about 2,154 deaths per billion miles compared to only 214 in an airplane. But to make these figures useful in judging your own risks, you must compare them to the amount of miles and trips you make in a car versus a plane.

The amount of time Americans voluntarily spend mentally wired to the media is a major percentage of each day, as it is for every modernized and modernizing people. During that time, individuals become members of the mass, drawing their sense of themselves and of the world from the atomistic and sanitized packets of media messages.

... News addicts, hungry for continuous news bulletins, deaden their sensitivity not only to the world, but to their own experience. Whatever the class or age or level of education, one becomes a member of the mass whenever one seeks a mindless connection to concocted propaganda for the head or contrived pornography for the heart. Addiction is the essence of the mass culture experience.

John Phelan, *Mediaworld: Programming the Public*

To get value for your media time, you must apply the information gleaned to your own situation, instead of reacting viscerally to accounts of accidents.

YOUR PERSONAL MEDIA-MEASURING STICK

Too much mass media tends to have a narcotizing effect on society, which is lulled into complacency by thinking that being "informed" is an end in itself and forgets that being informed has no relationship to taking action. According to Reed Blake and Edwin Haroldsen in *A Taxonomy of Concepts in Communication,* large segments of the population of this country could be labeled as "informed but inert," having been bombarded into a stupor by the continuous media stream from radio, television, newspapers, books, and films.

What you perceive, you should filter, so you can focus on those things which are useful and applicable to your own dictionary of the world.

Or, as Philippe Auguste Villiers put it more succinctly, "I have thought too much to stoop to action."

When I watch the news, I try to experience visually everything that is going on. I observe the scenes and try to figure out why they were chosen to illustrate the story. I ask how they relate to other events. Asking the questions makes the news more meaningful to me.

When you watch the news, you should maintain a conversation with it by asking questions:

● Why did the newscaster choose the particular details of the story?

● What do the numbers mean?

● To what other events does this incident relate?

● What is it the announcer isn't telling me?

● Why is this story more important than another?

● And, the most crucial question, how does this story apply to my life?

Sometimes dispelling anxiety can be as simple as giving yourself the right to question. By not accepting information at face value, you can go beyond the surface to understand the vocabulary of information and how particular events are relevant to our life.

Only from your questions and your comparisons can you begin to form a model or measuring stick to decide what kind of information is important to your life. This process catapults you as a receiver into an active state. Weighing events against your own interests and needs is a recognition that your questions and your judgments are valid and worthwhile. You can answer the most essential question of what to peruse and what to ignore.

By the conscientious questioning of what you see, hear, and read, you can make material release information it might ordinarily conceal. Through this questioning, you can begin to see events in context, which is the only way they can be of value.

EVERYTHING TAKES PLACE SOMEPLACE

Everything takes place someplace—hardly a profound observation. Yet when we watch, read, or listen to the news, we often lack a sense of place, not only of the name of the location where it occurred, but the size of the place, the population, the part of the world, the terrain, etc. A sense of place can make a story come alive. Location is the common denominator in all events.

For instance, in reporting the Union Carbide disaster in Bhopal, India, few newscasters mentioned the size of the city. Most people, however, had never heard of the city and probably presumed that it was a village. If the newscasters had said the city is in central India and is the size of San Francisco or Boston, the public perception of the story would have been different.

The media may exacerbate geographic ignorance by failing to make the location of an event a central part of any story, but they don't cause it. Americans are notorious for their poor showings on geography tests. Based on a nine-country Gallup survey conducted for the National Geographic Society in 1988, American adults ranked

---

News does not provide contact with the world so much as small change in the currency of mental money exchanged at meetings and parties.

John Phelan, *Mediaworld: Programming the Public*

MORE PICTURES, LESS COPY

More graphs and charts to explain complex ideas (like the U.S. deficit) and shorter copy are the newspaper predictions of Alvah N. Chapman, chairman of the Knight-Ridder newspaper chain. "We are not in the business of manufacturing paragraphs. We are in the business of moving ideas into the minds of people."

Michael Harris, "The Man Behind Knight-Ridder's Success," *The San Francisco Chronicle* (4/22/86)

Cities, ports, and regions in the Middle East are mentioned in this news article without solid reference as to where they are located in the region or where they are situated in relation to each other. We are told that the Iranians were ". . . in a position to destroy Basra without ever setting foot in the place," but not how, or about what significance this would have. Why use the past tense and not the present tense to report on the apparent siege? Is the Shatt al Arab a river, bay, or lake? What bearing do sales of F-16 fighters and armed personnel carriers have on the Basra situation? It must be easy for foreign correspondents in the field to assume we know more of these basic facts than is common—after all, they're there. Yet facts and figures just aren't understandable without the background and remain truly violent wallpaper.

IRNA—SYGMA

Another bloody stalemate: *Iranian troops run for cover on Bovarian Island in the Shatt al Arab*

Iran Tightens the Noose

Khomeini's victories frighten the Arab states

Where is it?

Basra was on its way to becoming a ghost town. Hundreds of thousands of inhabitants had fled from Iraq's second largest city as Iranian troops closed in on what had been the home of 1.5 million people. With Iran's forward units only six miles away, artillery fire harassed the half-deserted port. There seemed to be no immediate danger that Basra would actually fall to the invaders. The Iranians still had to cross the broad Shatt al Arab waterway and hack their way through elaborate Iraqi defenses manned by as many as 200,000 troops. But the Iranians were in a position to destroy Basra without ever setting foot in the place. Unless the Iraqis could lift the siege with a counterattack, Basra could cease to function as a city.

Have they left because of the siege?

River Bay?

What is the advantage?

Even a partial Iranian victory around Basra could be a disaster for the regime of Iraqi President Saddam Hussein. Despite an overwhelming advantage in warplanes and tanks, the Iraqis have fought timidly. Reports from Baghdad said the armed forces chief of staff, Gen. Abdul Jawad Zannoun, may have been fired because of Iran's gains around Basra. Ultimately, if the Iranians are not dislodged from the area, Hussein himself could be in danger. And if Hussein falls, Iran's fundamentalist fervor could flare across the Middle East, threatening Western interests there. Already Iran's mood is so upbeat that last week the regime of Ayatollah Ruhollah Khomeini allowed more than 100 foreign journalists into the country. "Victory is near with the guidance of Allah," said one of the signs that greeted them in Teheran.

Does he live in Basra?

The Iranians haven't won yet, but they have made enough headway to cause fresh anxiety in the Arab states of the Persian Gulf. Last week President Reagan condemned Iran for seizing Iraqi territory and urged Teheran to negotiate for peace. "We share the concern of our friends in the gulf region that the war could spill over and threaten their security," Reagan warned. "We would regard any such expansion of the war as a major threat to our interests." The statement was intended to reassure Washington's friends, who had been shaken by Reagan's secret arms sales to Iran. The administration also hoped to buttress the Arabs by selling 12 F-16 fighters to Bahrain and 200 Bradley armed personnel carriers to Saudi Arabia.

Attacking in waves: By the end of last week the war on the southern front seemed to be settling into another bloody stalemate. Iranian troops crossed the Jasim River and took the town of Duayji and attempted to advance around man-made Fish Lake. U.S. intelligence sources said the Iranians attacked in waves, with volunteers called the Basidj—some of them only 14 or 15 years old—leading the way, followed by Khomeini's fanatical Revolutionary Guards. As many as 25,000 Iranians have died in the campaign, while Iraqi losses were estimated at fewer than 10,000 dead—and perhaps fewer than 5,000. An analysis by Israeli experts predicted that the campaign would end indecisively, with the defenders hanging on to Basra but with the Iranians controlling a large piece of Iraqi territory.

On the central front, another Iranian Army had executed what appeared to be a feint toward Baghdad, pinning down Iraqi troops that otherwise might have been used in the south. Farther north, Iranian-backed Kurdish rebels stepped up their guerrilla activities against the Iraqi government. Iraq and Iran also fired missiles at each other's cities, and Iraqi warplanes bombed many Iranian towns and cities.

Out on the Persian Gulf, Kuwait, a staunch supporter of Iraq, was harried by the Iranians. Since last fall Iranian patrol boats have fired on 12 ships bound to or from Kuwait. Last week a missile reportedly hit a Kuwaiti island, and three suspicious fires flared up at Kuwaiti oil facilities. Iran apparently was trying to disrupt an Islamic conference scheduled for this week in Kuwait. The Islamic summit is expected to produce a call for an end to the war, but Iran, which plans to boycott the meeting, has said it will not be bound by any such resolution.

Iran's advances on the battlefield were bad news for Arab nations such as Kuwait and Jordan, which have given Iraq their undivided support. Many of the gulf states, including Saudi Arabia, have hedged their bets, clinging to the possibility of reconciliation with Teheran. But now that Iran is making some headway near Basra, gulf Arabs are anxiously looking to Egypt, with its large Army, to offset the Iranians. Egyptian President Hosni Mubarak plans to attend the Islamic conference, and not since Camp David have the Egyptians seemed so welcome in Arab councils.

What does this mean? Who would this help?

Mubarak's pro-American government is one of those that might be threatened by fundamentalist subversion if Iran scores even a limited victory. Some analysts, including Israelis, believe that if Iran gets the upper hand the United States might be forced to intervene militarily to help protect the relatively moderate gulf states. An Iranian victory also would be a blow to Moscow, which is Iraq's principal patron and is fighting against Islamic fundamentalism in Afghanistan. With so much at stake, a negotiated settlement to the war would be welcomed by Iraq and just about everyone else—except for Iran, which continues to demand Hussein's surrender.

Henry Kissinger once remarked that to serve "the ultimate American interest, both sides should lose." Or at least neither of them should win. "The optimum outcome of the war would be a cease-fire in place, with neither side vanquished and with both [armies] tied down by facing each other," says Amatzia Baram, a specialist in Iraqi history at Haifa University. So far, however, more than six years of slaughter has not persuaded the Ayatollah Khomeini to accept a cease-fire. Nothing that has happened recently on the southern front is likely to change his mind.

RUSSELL WATSON *with* THEODORE STANGER *in Teheran,* CHRISTOPHER DICKEY *in Kuwait,* MILAN J. KUBIC *in Jerusalem and* JANE WHITMORE *in Washington*

Where are these places?

36 NEWSWEEK : FEBRUARY 2, 1987

sixth in geographic literacy. In the eighteen- to twenty-four-year-old category, Americans ranked last. When asked to identify sixteen spots on an unmarked map (United States, Soviet Union, Japan, Canada, France, Mexico, Italy, Sweden, United Kingdom, South Africa, West Germany, Egypt, Vietnam, Central America, the Persian Gulf, and the Pacific Ocean), they averaged fewer than seven.

Many educators lament that geography has, in recent years, played second fiddle to courses such as social studies and current events. They have formed a national network to improve the way geography is taught in elementary and secondary schools. In a world that through communication technology and high-speed transportation has become, as Marshall McLuhan predicted, a "global village," a knowledge of geography is essential to understanding world events and relationships between countries.

The mass media select and process information to make it available as fast as possible. The act of selection makes them the chief gatekeepers of the flow of information through society. Gates operate at all levels, from the reporter who selects what facts to write down, to the editor, who decides what to delete, to the cameraman who chooses where to point the camera, to the film editor, who leaves part of it on the cutting room floor.

Everyone is a gatekeeper in their own lives making decisions about what to tell our bosses, coworkers, friends, and relatives.

Nowhere is this selection process more dramatic than in the news business. A paper that receives Associated Press wire service reports may have almost 1 million words from which to choose from one source alone.

Wilbur Schramm and William Porter, *Men, Women, Messages and Media: Understanding Human Communication*

CONVERSATION WITH TOM BROKAW

Lee Iacocca said in *USA Today* (5/25/88) that if he were elected president, he would create a Secretary of Communications post and give Tom Brokaw the job. "In this electronic age you need a concise, no-bullshit reporter to help you communicate clearly with the American people," he said. The position would assuredly be well executed, for Brokaw has set the standard for his field as an anchorman at NBC. In the following conversation, Brokaw discusses how the concepts of geography and orientation are addressed in news stories:

TB: There are lots of dimensions to being informed in television news, as you know, and how we convey that. To a great degree the news is controlled by people who are word-oriented; they are not visual people except in a conventional format like videotape. They are worried about the content of the story rather than the aid that can help you tell the story better.

RSW: Well, that is, in a sense, the myth that accuracy is an end in itself.

Understanding is not the goal. Accuracy is more of a goal than understanding, because I think they find ultimate comfort in accuracy; understanding is nothing anybody was taught.

TB: I think it is something to do with that. We are about to change our life in terms of the look of our graphics at NBC. We have got somebody who at the moment in a preliminary way is deciding about typeface and colors and that kind of conventional, basic thing.

RSW: The whole graphic design world tries to make things look good and many do, but they don't necessarily perform well.

TB: I was watching last night a CBS program on Las Vegas. There was a showgirl who was talking about what she was going to do when her body finally goes. It has held up very well; she is thirty-seven and she works very hard at it. She knows she can't sustain that. She said, "I want to do something with computers." She hasn't the foggiest notion what they are or what she could do with them or whatever. I thought about that; all she knows is that there are computers out there somewhere and that they do something that she probably ought to know about—what she may be able to do with them, what they do, what the range of activities are, and how hard or how easy it is to learn something about them. I think that is a classic demonstration of what happens to a lot of things.

RSW: As far as the news goes, what I constantly see is that much of the news is a listing of pop macabre events and that bad news will always bump off good news. There is a belief that people are interested in bad news more than good news and yet most of those events have little relationship to anything in one's life. Many people have no idea where events take place or what the numbers actually mean.

TB: That concerns me more than the "angels on the head of a pin" argument about what is good news and what is bad news and what is important news. A very good demonstration of the things you are talking about is what is going on right now in Israel. Because of its size, population, relationship, short and long history, the news is making the Israelis out to be an evil force in the world.

We did a report in which we said this is Israel before the 1967 war: 110 miles long, only 6 miles across right here. So when they took the West Bank, they added this area and increased their territory by a third.

RSW: It's basically Long Island.

TB: And there are 3 million Israelis, and there are about to be 3 million Arabs in the Gaza Strip. That is what we did because we thought we had to lay it out there.

RSW: How is the judgment made of what is understandable to your audience and what isn't understandable?

TB: It is on an episodic basis. Take the 1987 stock market crash, for example. Unless there is something dramatic, the stock market is not of much interest for a general news program. There are lots of other sources of information for the public to turn to and that is where they should get it. As we become an increasingly fragmented society, this is what will happen. People have specific needs and they will go to specific sources of information. Therefore, television news programs, especially, but even general circulation newspapers, don't have a need to pay that much attention to that sort of stuff. You cannot ignore something like October 19 obviously. It is a dramatic historic event and it does affect a lot of people. Whenever we do make a decision about doing something in economics—because most people in the news are economically illiterate—it has to be reduced to the common denominator. So we do generally break it down into the simplest terms. We deal with it in broad-stroke ways.

A better example, I suppose, would be how do you make a decision on foreign coverage, for instance? Obviously you cover those countries in which the United States seems to have an active vested interest . . . at a couple of different levels, politically, humanistically. We have a big economic investment now in the Middle East, not just with Israel, but because of the Arabs and their investment in energy. The great failure of television news in the last couple of years and one that we are trying to correct at NBC is Asia. We stayed too long at the dance in Western Europe. Western Europe in terms of our eyes is pretty dormant at the moment. You can make a case about its military significance in terms of the Soviet Union, and it is important culturally, but the action in the world at the moment is in the Far East and that is something that we need desperately to improve.

RSW: Yes, it is quite amazing and nobody has a sense of that. We don't have any of that at our fingertips.

TB: We tend, especially as American journalists, to kind of lump things together. People are Oriental in our mind. What does that mean? There is the Yellow Peril where there is Chinese and Japanese whatever. Such distinct cultures and they are often in conflict with each other over a variety of things—ancient rivalries, economic competition, cultural differences. I don't think we have done a very good job covering news over there and that is something I am trying to correct. We are beefing up our presentation.

NBC did a week in China in the fall of 1987, and I really felt good about that. What we did was look at China not through the rose-colored filter. We explained the enormous diversity of the place, the primitive quality of most of it, the hardship under which most people live. We looked at the difference with which we treat the Chinese and the Russians. Their human rights are no better than the Russians, and yet we are so beguiled by the Chinese, so charmed by them.

I have been there a lot and I am beguiled by it as well. The whole place is extraordinary in a lot of ways. But

News is anything you didn't know yesterday.

Turner Catledge of *The New York Times*

233

I do think we have an obligation to teach geography because it has no meaning unless people know how it fits in the world somehow. I don't think we do a very good job. What happens is there is a certain amount of revisionism that creeps in two or three days later and people lose sight of what the important issue is.

When I get criticized by columnists, my first reaction is to be defensive and combat it, fight back. In a couple of cases, what I have done is waited a few days, read it again, and then wrote them a note that said something like, "You may be right. Brokaw."

RSW: Blows them away, doesn't it?

TB: Makes me feel better; it knocks them off guard.

RSW: That is part of our *information anxiety*; we don't feel we can challenge or say that we don't understand. What I am talking about is the most simple stuff in the world and everything I am saying is so simple-minded that everyone will think it is unscholarly. There is a myth that something must be good if it is hard to understand, when just the opposite should be the case. That is the way television news should be. It should be understandable, and not try to snow anybody with erudite illusions.

TB: I have a good example. The night of the attack on Libya was chaotic, as you might expect. We had some forewarning based on our own reporting that this thing was coming. We were having to be so cautious and so careful, and we couldn't prepare a lot. We may be skipping something if it does happen. We continued with the news beyond the allotted time; we went to the Pentagon after a briefing from Defense Secretary Weinberger to get a quick read-out on that. Our Pentagon correspondent is standing in a place where we often stand, in front of a vast flat world map, and he is saying to me, Tom, the planes took off from England and they had to fly around France because they didn't get permission to go through French air space. I said, Fred, just a minute, stop right there, and the control room was

---

News isn't the event; it's the report of an event. A murder isn't news until it has been discovered and reported.

The newsworthiness of an event is affected by:
(a) where it happened in relation to the audience;
(b) the extent to which it personally affects the audience;
(c) the prominence of those involved in the event; and
(d) competition from other events at the same time.

News, as new information, is perishable. Once it has been reported and understood, it becomes history.

Reed Blake and Edwin Haroldsen, *A Taxonomy of Concepts in Communications*

saying what are you doing? He turned around and walked to the map and showed me. The control room people came down here and people were screaming and yelling, that is brilliant. I said it's not brilliant. It is what every fourth-grade geography teacher does.

ORIENTATION TO EVENTS

The marvels of computer graphics can obscure the basic purpose of the news to inform. The abilities of a technology demand to be explored, but they should not be done so at the expense of clarity or meaning. Sophistication is not synonymous with understanding. I am not saying high-tech computer graphics aren't necessary; sometimes they are. But they are being overused. Sometimes they stand in the way of conceptually informing viewers.

Designers get seduced by a technology that makes graphics that look informative, but may not be, or, if they are informative, may not be necessary. Sometimes, instead of displaying a $100,000 computer graphic, a newscaster could almost say, "I have a grapefruit here. Let's say it's Libya. This lemon is Texas. Libya is about 2 1/2 times as big as Texas." That is all. That is as understandable as anything else. And you become oriented to the information.

Orientation begins with relativity, relating two places, two numbers, two ideas together. Orientation begins the understanding process, as much with geographic location as with numbers. When you hear a place or a number, to what does it relate? How big is Libya? Where does a trillion exist? What is comparable to four square miles? You can begin to turn statistics into meaningful numbers, data into information, and facts into stories with value.

THE GLORY OF STORIES

Storytelling is another way of putting information in context and giving you the golden glow of memory.

Stories are a vehicle for making facts and numbers come alive.

Stories permit information to be imprinted into memory. They encourage the application of information and that is what gives it meaning.

Lessons of wisdom have never such a power over us, as when they are wrought into the heart, through the ground-work of a story which engages the passions: . . . we are like iron, and must first be heated before we can be wrought upon.

Laurence Sterne, *The Life and Opinions of Tristram Shandy, Gentleman*

For the hundreds of thousands of years that preceded the last eight thousand years of recorded history, the only vehicle for transmitting information was speech. Our whole history, which is the history of the world, was communicated by stories told by one person to another. So everything from generation to generation was passed on by storytelling. Primitive tribes do this still. Whenever there is no written language, there is verbal transmission—information about hunting and motherhood and fatherhood and gods. Storytelling is probably in our DNA profile. Memory and learning were locked in the embrace of stories, which can often be much more evocative and even more accurate than facts.

If the Bible was only a list of rules and regulations like "thou shalt not kill" or "thou shalt not be greedy," it would have gone out of print long ago. I imagine two guys sitting around a stone table six thousand years ago inventing the new religion. One says, "Hey, I've got this great idea for a book that would be like a white paper for this religion. We'll collect all these stories we've heard about walls and music and whales and floods and use them as examples of how to be a better person." Then the other guy says, "I've got a much better idea. It's more efficient, wouldn't take so much stone carving or kill so many sheep. Let's just say, 'Don't mess around and do be nice.' That's only seven words." The first guy then responds, "I don't think it will sell."

In fact, it might never have become a religion. The richness of the allusions in the Bible are the stories and the characters. The stories make the religion, not the "thou shalt nots." You hear the story of Joseph and his brothers, and you remember greed in an extraordinary way.

Storytelling is another way of putting information in context and giving you memory. Memorizing all the words to "The Charge of the Light Brigade" is a waste of time; understanding the story and the lessons it holds for your own life is not.

In the Yiddish tradition, if someone in the community had a problem he couldn't solve, he'd go to the rebbe or teacher and ask him for advice. And the advice was almost always given in the form of a story. This way people were forced to interpret the story for their own situation, and through the interpretation they were able to possess the knowledge or message contained in the story.

Even today the medium of the story is used in countless, often unconscious ways. In the world of business, the measure of a successful analyst is his ability to create a story from financial statements, to see in the numbers plot twists and developments. Since most stockbrokers are plugged into the same equipment and have access to the same information, they distinguish themselves by turning profit-and-loss statements into parables about people and business philosophy.

Charles Kuralt has a superb means of giving an enormous amount of information by telling a thorough story in a very brief time, but he is a dying breed. In trying to convey more information in less time, the news media often delete the story that is the event.

There is a misconception rampant among newscasters that there is too much news and no time for stories, especially in television news. With only twenty or thirty seconds per event, reporters favor a collection of hard-hitting numbers. The quantity of stories becomes more important than understanding any one story. Newscasters make a fundamental mistake by talking about an auto crash, a bus crash, a trial, a rape, a murder, and a criminal—all in their twelve minutes. Instead, they should give you a more developed story of only two events. Highlights of the news and a list of the inexorable deaths, accidents, and catastrophes—the violent wallpaper of our lives—could be scrolled on some cable channel.

I don't like music at the beginning, at the end, and in the midst of network evening news broadcasts. It's a matter of principle: the music is a fiction, a part of entertainment and not of journalism. No symphonic fanfare greets me when my morning newspaper arrives. Surrounded as broadcast news is by fiction and entertainment, it is imperative that news be scrupulously careful to draw a sharp line between journalism and the entertainment of fiction.

Richard S. Salant, former president of CBS News and vice chairman of NBC, "Network News: Its Future, If Any," the 1988 William Benton National Lecture

This wallpaper doesn't advance your knowledge of the world or your day. It doesn't inform; it is not memorable. Yet we are weighed down by this litany of violence. I'm always amazed when I hear people who have just returned from Europe say how wonderful it was to walk the streets and feel perfectly safe. Their chances of being victimized are probably just as great; they are only escaping from having to hear about the crimes that are so dutifully chronicled in this country.

Crime and violence are no more representative of news than wars are representative of history. Both make up only an infinitesimal percentage of what is happening or has happened. Yet because bad news has an urgency about it that endows it with the shine of timeliness, it preempts other events, the stories with heart and value that could advance your understanding of the world, make you a more valuable citizen, inform you so you could participate in real issues. Another crash on the highway or another mugging is not news that has to be delivered. There is not an appreciable difference between one car accident and another, between one fire and the next. Most of it isn't even valuable as a curiosity. Networks actually use stock footage now for some events such as floods. Why send cameramen to film yet another flood?

News programs without the violent wallpaper could be forums for stories of events, people, positions, and ideas. That is why "60 Minutes" is so popular. The show tells stories in a memorable way. You have to find the appropriate form for information, and the appropriate form for listing the murders, fires, and accidents is just that, a list. There could be a program called "Murders of the Day." You could have programs of traffic accidents of the day, rapes, muggings taken to an absurd level, which is what it approaches some nights; you would see the meaninglessness of it.

Most news could be divided into three categories: Hope, Absurdity, and Catastrophe. Newspapers could have three columns by those names on the front page. The first category would encompass news stories about progress in the realm of science or culture—stories that show hope for our society, such as medical breakthroughs in the fight against cancer, the signing of a peace treaty, the success of a philanthropic program. The second category would be insignificant events that are transformed by the media into world news—like petty political machinations, William Proxmire Awards, and the farmer who grows fifty-five pound watermelons. The last category would be for anything that promulgates discomforts—crimes, acts of nature, large-scale breakdowns of the system. The contrasts of our lives are the stories of hope, absurdity, and catastrophe.

Categories of News
Hope
Absurdity
Catastrophe

RADIUS OF INTEREST

The interest of most people is piqued by events that are either very close to their experience or very foreign to it—whether geographic or philosophic. Proximity expands the realm of interest. Almost anything that happens on your street is of interest. An event that would be unimportant to you in another state—like a purse snatching or a new zoning ordinance—becomes more important the closer it occurs to your home. Conversely, events that occur in exotic locales or seem extraordinary to our experience attract us. The story about a man who strangles his wife on their honeymoon attracts us for no other reason than the unlikelihood of its occurrence.

While our detailed interest in our immediate environment is natural and harmless, a fascination with the extraordinary is not. An event that we can tie to our lives in some way becomes useful information. An event that only titillates our sense of the macabre creates anxiety.

One of the top ten national news stories of 1987—in the amount of air time or print space devoted to it—was about an infant in Oklahoma who fell down a well. An entire nation was made apprehensive by whether or not she would survive the ordeal. To the family and friends of the little girl, the event was of epic importance, but to make this one of the largest national news stories of the year was patently absurd.

Basing your view of the world on these isolated events is like basing your knowledge of music on what you hear on the elevator. Cluttering your thoughts with events like these inhibits your ability to discern the news that might somehow concern us.

This is not to say that accidents and acts of violence should be ignored—only that they should be filtered through a sieve of meaning and applicability to our lives. Accounts of child abuse awaken the public to a pandemic problem; perhaps, they might enable someone to recognize possible child abuse and avert more violence. But the obsession with random acts is counterproductive and superfluous.

I'd much rather read an article in the papers about a breakthrough in the way things are done rather than another recital of the status quo. If it could be proven to me that accounts of traffic accidents increase road safety or that stories on rape reduce the number of rape or murders, I'd rethink my position. But quite the opposite is true: they only beget additional stories.

Crime stories and sensationalism are not necessarily what people find interesting in the news, yet this is what comprises news programs. They become simply violent wallpaper.

STREAM OF CONSEQUENCE

The effect of reference information in our lives is tangible and immediate. We have some control over this kind of information in that, for the most part, we must seek it. We look up a phone number and we make a call. We read a recipe and then add the ingredients. The impact of this kind of information is readily apparent.

We have little control over the news that we watch, other than to ignore it. We are only coming to understand how we are affected by the news media. While the extent remains elusive and hotly contested, few would argue that our news habits influence our perspective on the world and that we bear a psychic weight from viewing the continuous stream of pain and suffering that parades before us as news.

All the more reason to make conscious and careful choices of what to watch, as well as to take an active role in questioning what we see and hear as news.

CULTURAL INFORMATION: PERSONAL VISION

Some things have to be seen to be believed.

S. Harward

Some things have to be believed to be seen.

Ralf Hodgson

1988 Calendar, Bob Gill, designer. © Strathmore Paper Company

*E*very day we see thou-
sands of "events" that
take place around us. Inasmuch as an event is "anything
that happens or is regarded as
happening," everything we see or
hear can be regarded as an event,
albeit of varying consequence.

How many times in the course of my life had I been disappointed by reality because, at the time I was observing it, my imagination, the only organ with which I could enjoy beauty, was not able to function, by virtue of the inexorable law which decrees that only that which is absent can be imagined.

Marcel Proust

From the simple to the sublime, events become pictures in our minds. We perceive them directly—the scene that greets us as we walk into an office, an argument between two people on the street, a business lunch. We also perceive them indirectly via the news media and the people with whom we come into contact.

These events are the raw data that we compare against our attitudes, our beliefs, our personal vision of the world.

To me, the magic of perception is how we take the raw data of our senses—the sights, sounds, and smells around us—and concoct a mélange of mental images and ideas that become the body of information that comprises our vision of the world. When John Osgood signs off the news with "See you on the radio," I think about how we blend, sort, and redefine our perceptions, mixing mental images, time, and media in the radio of our minds.

We each have our own interpretation of what we see. In much the same way as an artist paints a picture that interprets his or her vision, we use our own perceptions to make a picture of the world. Some people see New York as dismal, cold, and hostile. Others see the city as the vibrant, inviting center of the world. Edward Hopper didn't see the same city that Richard Estes did, even though they may have seen the same scenes. The pictures we see depend on our own perception of events, which is influenced by our own attitudes and environment—by our own cultural framework or perspective.

Cultural information operates at the individual level in determining our own personal visions. Collectively it defines the nature of our society. Although cultural information is the most ephemeral, the hardest to understand and assess, it is one of the most structured forms of information.

News comes to us every day in an endless stream, without categorization, and unrelated to other events. Cultural information is by nature categorized. The minute we have formed an opinion of something, we have categorized it in some way, we have made a judgment as to its value or merit. News happens out of context. By definition, cultural information is always within a context or history. It is a chronicle of our existence.

Our cultural framework is an information pool against which we as individuals compare random events to make sense of them and against which our society compares itself to a cultural ideology or history. Once we have compared these events to our existing ideas, we can transmute them into the categories within our information pool or we can discard or erase them by forgetting at an individual or collective level.

The marvels of transportation, the increased pace of our lives, the larger and more densely populated areas we inhabit have increased the number of events that we must process, constantly assessing and reassessing our beliefs and opinions. The stress produced by this assault of images demanding to be processed escalates with the amount of images. We are more likely to witness events that contradict each other and our own previously held opinions, causing us to question our own ability to observe.

Because the anxiety produced by cultural information isn't experienced at the urgent, immediate, or even tangible level, it is harder to transcend, let alone to under-

Some people, who suffer from a disease known as synesthesia, can actually see sounds or feel taste. The condition, which appears when part of the brain shuts down, allows people to feel an aroma or hear music when they see colors. Richard Cytowic, a Washington neurologist, explained the phenomenon as " a remnant of the way early man viewed the world before his cortex opened, grew more complex and began separating his senses."

"Science/Medicine: Some People Really Do See What You're Saying," *The Los Angeles Times* (6/8/86)

stand. Whereas we can easily understand how we might be shortchanged by or penalized for not knowing how to operate a computer, we can only suspect how we are being assessed, judged, or classified by our perceptions.

Learning to operate a computer is manageable; trying to make sense of all the myriad of events or information we perceive is not.

THE INEQUITY OF PERCEPTION

In part, our anxieties arise because we are reluctant to accept that perception is not just a physiological act that works the same way for everyone. We refuse to accept that human perception isn't an absolute. Yet we stubbornly try to operate as if this is the case. When we try to explain something to someone else, we either automatically assume they can see or understand as we do or we spend inordinate amounts of time trying to force them to do so.

We are destined for disappointment, because even if we all perceived the same event in the same way, we are cursed with the physiological limitation of not being able to process an infinite amount of stimuli. Our perceptions are, therefore, selective.

". . . Each act of perception is unique to the person and to the moment. Seeing is not like holding a camera up to the world, merely registering an image, but a restless searching and scanning . . . Memory is not a tape recorder, storing information at the flick of a switch. It, too, is selective. In part, memory is a way of reorganizing information so as to make it special to the individual who remembers; this process is so variable and idiosyncratic as to confound the formal models psychologists are forever trying to build," writes Jeremy Campbell in *Grammatical Man.*

Werner Severin and James Tankard, Jr., in *Communication Theories: Origins, Methods, Uses* divide the selective processes into four rings of defenses. Selective

---

Because everyone reacts differently to messages, communicators shouldn't assume that their messages will have a universal meaning. For example, a presidential candidate spoke to a group of veterans. One viewer's reaction was to commend the candidate for caring about vets; another's was to criticize the candidate for using the vets to get sympathy.

Werner Severin, and James Tankard, Jr., *Communication Theories: Origins, Methods, Uses*

exposure is the outermost ring, followed by selective attention, then selective perception, and finally selective retention. People can head off undesirable information by not exposing themselves to it, not paying attention to it, or finally by not retaining it.

Selective exposure, perception, and retention are barriers to communication. We tend to perceive the things that relate to our pre-existing interests and attitudes—either to support or refute them. People have a tendency to shun information that contradicts these, whether consciously or not. They will also misperceive and misinterpret communications according to their own predispositions, so that every listener tends to hear his own message. And they will tend to remember messages that are sympathetic with their preheld beliefs and forget those that are not.

Our perceptions are invariably biased by our own point of view. Because of these limitations, our perceptions are idiosyncratic; no one else sees the same way.

SELECTIVE PERCEPTION = EXAGGERATION

All selective perceptions are exaggeration. Since humans are incapable of universal perception, what we perceive is inherently selective. And the minute we select or choose, the mere act of choosing implies exaggeration. What we see of any scene becomes the scene itself for us, even though it is based on our less than complete perceptions. When we get to know another person, we can know only certain aspects of that person; yet in our minds, we define that person by only those qualities that we know. John sees that Mary is charming, articulate, and witty, and that is how he describes her. He doesn't know that she beats her cat. His perception of her is exaggerated because he sees her desirable qualities as comprising her entire person, when they are only a partial list.

In the workplace, any project that you choose to give attention means that its importance is exaggerated.

Albert Einstein once said that his most original ideas came to him in mental pictures, not in words or numbers. But only recently have significant discoveries been made in the understanding of mental images.

A recent Harvard study where people kept a diary of such images found that 80 percent of them were in color; 40 percent moved; and in about 10 percent of the cases faded in and out, shrank and expanded, or acted in other ways impossible in real life. Some reported that images involved more than just the visual sense. About one third of the images were used for decision making or problem solving, and one quarter were used to understand a verbal description. Images were also used to change feelings or motivate the subject.

Daniel Goleman, "Mental Images: New Research Helps Clarify Their Role," *The New York Times* (8/12/86)

All things are exaggerated, including what I've just said. When you use a camera, you focus on something in the foreground or the background. That's an exaggeration because you're focusing on one thing rather than another. Art is exaggeration. Dress is exaggeration. So is style.

Point of View

Exaggeration is a natural way of looking at things. It's the slice of the whole. Because our perceptions are exaggerated, they are also biased by our own selective perceptions. We perceive through our own point of view or bias.

Point of view becomes the basis for categorizing information; we can reduce the world to manageable proportions by assigning value to our perceptions. We accord status to our perceptions based on our point of view.

This encompasses how we regard other people. Based on how they measure up to our particular vision of the world, we decide whom to court or to ignore. Just as we cannot process all the perceptions with which we are bombarded, we cannot pay attention to all the people around us.

According status isn't in itself anxiety-inducing when we apply our own point of view to the process. We are made uncomfortable when we try to apply an external system, i.e. using what we assume to be the values of someone else or even society-at-large.

When I go to a restaurant with my father, he usually asks for "crescent rolls" and I cringe. In my peer group, they were gentrified to "croissants" at least ten years ago. My reaction to hearing them referred to as "crescent rolls" is absurd. I have no particular aversion to calling them crescent rolls. Everyone knows what he is talking about. I am allowing someone else's ideas about status to color my reaction.

Dueling Information

In our interaction with other people, we make thousands of assessments and judgments every day without questioning the source of our opinions. These judgments weigh on our faculties, sometimes threatening our own sense of self-worth, when we overinflate our perceptions of others around us and suspect that we are outclassed, underinformed, or ill-equipped.

In reaction to this, many people become belligerent, trying to mask their own inadequacies with bluster and braggadocio. Although it may not be readily apparent, this is really a response to the anxiety produced by our expectations of what we should know—social insecurity. Information anxiety exists not only because of our relationship to information, but because of our relationship to other people and by what information we assume they expect us to possess.

Nowhere are our insecurities more apparent than at parties, where we are confined in close quarters with our theoretical peers—the people up against whom we are measured. Here we must face the people whom we compete against for jobs, affections, and public stature.

Steve Smith, the executive editor of *Newsweek*, calls cocktail parties "Dueling Information" and admits that when he has been invited to a party he will "rush home and read things that people have written because they will be there and I will want to know what their work is like."

We compete or assume we must compete against others armed with our command of cultural information, an ephemeral weaponry that defies objective classification or even interpretation. Because of its nebulous nature, we are not always aware of the role cultural information plays in causing anxiety. In fact, it causes anxiety because we do not acknowledge how subjective it is.

Everything we see or read is tinged with the subjectivity of point of view—both by our own biases and by the biases of the source.

The author isn't altogether certain that there is any such thing as exaggeration. Our brains permit us to utilize such a wee fraction of their resources that, in a sense, everything we experience is a reduction.

Tom Robbins, *Even Cowgirls Get the Blues*

Even seemingly objective reference guides are colored by the perspective of the creators. The proliferation of data banks has prompted many people to falsely assume that they are or can be connected with all information. But data banks are bound by the biases, by the selective perceptions of the people who compile them. So are dictionaries, encyclopedias, and atlases.

Looking for the point of view, the exaggeration in news, in reference materials, in cocktail party conversation, will ensure that you perceive things with a more critical eye. You can understand by exaggeration. At one scale the earth would look smooth like a bowling ball, and yet, globes are done with enormous exaggeration of vertical components so that we can understand the terrain of the earth.

AS THE WORLD TURNS

The following was excerpted from an article, "Toward a New Global View," by Robert Howe, a retired mechanical engineer who lives in Oregon, that appeared in *The San Francisco Chronicle* (1/11/87).

A while back I got to thinking that it would be nice to be able to visualize the solar system. We know how big the sun and planets are and how far they are from one another, but we can't see them. Thinking like a boy with a science fair project, my mind conjured up a beach ball, a basketball, a tennis ball, and a marble.

The sun would be a $4\frac{1}{2}$-foot beach ball. The Earth, then, would be a half-inch marble and would float 480 feet from the beach ball.

I treated all the other planets in the same way, stringing them out all the way to Neptune, which would be a large marble $1\frac{3}{4}$ inches in diameter and $2\frac{3}{4}$ miles away.

All this was very nice, but I felt something was missing. What I wanted was to reduce the Earth in size to the point at which I could still see some recognizable features and some of mankind's larger works. I wanted to see the Earth as a large ball on which I could see bridges, trains, ships, stadiums, and buildings.

The globes we used in geography class that are still to be seen in public libraries are obviously too small for the purpose. Large cities are just dots; rivers are just lines. How large must a globe be so we can see a ship?

It turns out that if we make the *Queen Elizabeth II* a tiny ship three sixteenths of an inch long, we have stumbled onto a pretty good scale . The *QE II* is roughly one fifth of a mile long. So our convenient scale is one inch to the mile.

If the *QE II* is three sixteenths of an inch long, how large would our scale-model Earth be? Well, the Earth is about 8,000 miles in diameter, and we are talking about a scale of one inch to a mile. So 8,000 miles would be 666 feet in diameter, or just 111 feet greater than the height of the Washington Monument.

We begin now to appreciate the comparative sizes of the Earth and an ocean liner.

EMBELLISH WITH FLOURISH

Through exaggeration, you can perceive the world more accurately. If you accept that you can understand by exaggeration, you must learn to use it without dishonesty, so it clarifies the point you're making.

In order to make a point, to clarify or highlight something, you exaggerate it. After tasting the first morsel of steak at dinner, you exclaim, "This is the best steak I've ever eaten!" In reality, it's probably just a good steak. How many steaks have you eaten? Is it one of the ten best, one of the five best? What were the others? In what context were you eating them? Were you hungry? Were you paying for them? Is this one better because of how it was cooked? Was it grilled or broiled?

"Always exaggerate. It makes life seem more interesting."

Drawing by Weber; © 1987, The New Yorker Magazine, Inc.

We speak in terms of being "the most," "the best." This is the best movie. The most beautiful woman. The worst traffic. It's acceptable. It has its own realm of exactitude.

Yet we are unnecessarily intolerant of the idea of exaggerations. Most parents' favorite admonition is "Don't exaggerate." We waste time and energy hunting for evidence of exaggeration, then do not recognize that it is an element of everything we perceive. Our exaggerations become part of our own distinctive vision. If we each recognize our own exaggerations, we can begin to see how they influence the perceptions of others. By accepting that the act of selection involves some degree of overstatement, we can begin to understand basic problems in communications. If we are alert to the existence of exaggerations, we can begin to examine the possible meanings or purpose for it. We can redirect our focus toward thinking about what is a meaningful description, instead of stalking hyperboles with erasers.

The more we can perceive, the less our perceptions will be colored by the exaggeration of selectivity. The more we are aware of the role of exaggerations in perception, the more meaningful our perceptions will become.

When we look at a painting, for example, if we know nothing of the painter or the circumstances under which it was painted, our perception of the work is likely to be exaggerated. We might assume that Picasso painted only in the style of Cubism.

Many psychologists believe that people are able to make sense of visual perceptions because the brain unconsciously selects reliable elements from the bombardment of impressions. Thus John Ruskin's suggestion that painters develop "an innocent eye" to see the world in a pure and straightforward manner is not only ill-advised but impossible.

Daniel Goleman, "Mental Images: New Research Helps Clarify Their Role," *The New York Times* (8/12/86)

PETER BRADFORD ON PAINTING

In my opinion, Peter Bradford is probably the least-known great graphic designer in the country. He is annoyingly thoughtful and acidly brilliant. Instead of seeking fame, he seeks fundamental definitions of words and ideas and thus comes to a higher understanding of the nature of perception.

ART CAN BE HAZARDOUS TO YOUR HEALTH

An acute mental imbalance apparently brought on by viewing art has been documented at the Santa Maria Nuova hospital in Florence, Italy. Dubbed the "Stendhal Syndrome" after the French writer who suffered a similar experience on his first visit to the city, the condition strikes at least one seemingly healthy tourist a month.

A study determined that Italians and Japanese are immune. Perhaps they are more inured to grandeur.

"Florence's Art Treasures Cause Mental Imbalance for Some Tourists," *The Atlanta Constitution* **(5/15 87)**

I tried to reintroduce myself to painting. It was the methods of painting which interested me, not any particular historical figure. After so much exposure to learned people telling me what the art of painting was all about, how come I knew so little about the science? I thought back and I could remember no single instance when I was told how the sequence of paint was applied. I never felt I understood how painters think, and I certainly never found out the simple things like the different ways painters applied paint. I assumed they all more or less did it the same way and that different methods of painting had little to do with the way painters saw and the way they felt.

Why hadn't my art education dwelt on method as well as result? And how *does* the method shape the result?

In the midst of all this, two fortunate things happened. I saw an article on Caravaggio in an issue of *FMR Magazine*, and I happened to tag along on a visit to the John Singer Sargent portraits in the Fogg Museum in Cambridge.

The two combined to give me a terrific jolt. They showed me what I needed to know just then, and they taught me some of the things I should have been taught long ago.

Painters don't paint at all alike. Obviously they don't think alike, but not so obviously they don't see alike. At the very least, they set about achieving what they see in totally different ways. Caravaggio—whose figures appear as illuminated as Rubens but with richer, warmer textures—paints his shadowy tones on top of his light tones. He "shapes" his figures with dark colors on top of brighter colors. He paints as most art students learn to draw: first lines to suggest general shape, then gradually added darknesses to define bulk and depression. Essentially, most students learn to draw with shadows.

But Sargent goes the other way. His highlights are applied on top of his dark tones. The lights in his paintings are quick flicks on top of shadows. Sargent literally builds up to light.

Sargent's light is high, Caravaggio's light is low. So what? Does the difference help the understanding of them?

I suddenly remembered a book I had designed just a year ago on Franz Kline. I went back to it and, for the first time, read it. Kline—that iconographer of black and white, the producer of those indelible black-on-white calligraphic swashes—painted the white *last*. What's more, he painted the white on top of all sorts of colors. Like Sargent.

But Kline adds a complexity to the issue. His whites were often added to cover colors he didn't like. He struggled to introduce color to his work, painted dense greens, blues, and rusts before his large black marks, rejected them, and hid them with dense white. You can still see hints of color peeking out here and there.

Franz Kline's work dramatically changed, caterpillar to butterfly, when he discovered an opticon projector in Willem de Kooning's studio. His paintings had been representational, then gradually, almost grudgingly, abstract; then they flew into huge, utterly dynamic, unique, and very personal marks. Because he had slipped a small brief sketch into an unfamiliar machine and multiplied the drawing's scale against a far wall.

I don't think you have to like Kline to feel closer to his work because you know that. Do you? I hated not knowing that. I always loved Kline and now I think I feel closer to his mind—what a thrill that evening must have been for him.

Now what does all that mean? I am certainly going to go look at his paintings again and look at them a different way from knowing that. I think I will probably enjoy them more because I know that. I am much more intrigued with them than I ever was before. That kind of information alters your perception.

PERCEPTIVE PERCEPTIONS

Information enriches perception. Information distinguishes the physiological process of seeing in the manner of a camera from perceiving in the manner of the mind. Spending four hours traipsing around the Louvre without any sense of art history is a futile expedition. Reading a few paragraphs on the life of one artist and spending thirty minutes looking at his or her paintings would be a much more meaningful experience and would take one fourth of the time. The former involves only seeing; the latter involves perception.

Seeing is mechanical. Perception implies perceptivity, insight, and intuition—the ability to make meaningful observations about events and ideas, to relate one set of images to another. Perceiving involves our mental faculties, our creativity, our personal vision.

Anxiety arises when we confuse seeing with perception, when we assume that because we have visited the Louvre, we have necessarily enriched our perceptions. The society in which we live awards perceptivity in all endeavors, in art, in business, science, academia. Therefore, in order to rise in stature in our own field of endeavor, we strive to be perceptive.

THE MAP AS COMMUNICATIONS CURRENCY

First, to be perceptive, we must learn to recognize the role personal bias plays in everything we do. Point of view pervades information. Once we acknowledge that our perceptions are selective, we can allow the point of view to enrich our experience with information. When we know that Monet's eyesight was very poor and approached near-blindness as he got older, we can begin to understand his water lily paintings. When we accept that all data bases are limited by the viewpoint of the compilers, we won't be so frustrated when we don't find the information we need.

Perhaps we will also be more understanding of the problems of having to communicate with a common language despite the fact that words may mean something different to each individual. To operate in this world, we must rely on standard forms of communication that bridge individual biases and perspectives. They allow us to trade our ideas, however unique they may be to our own experiences.

The standard forms of communications we use can be seen as maps. They enable us to get beyond our own ideas to those of others. They enable us to find new information. We trade our perceptions and ideas through the currency of maps.

Theoretically, a map can be a language, a symbol, a stick, or a drawing in the sand. A map is anything that shows you the way from one point to another, from one level of understanding to another. A map depicts the route through information, be it a geographic locale or a philosophic treatise.

REFERENCE INFORMATION:
THE *MAP* OR MANKIND'S ABILITY TO PERCEIVE

*Y*ou cannot perceive anything without a map. A map provides people with the means to share in the perceptions of others. It is a pattern made understandable; it is a rigorous, accountable form that follows implicit principles, rules, and measures.

Maps provide the comfort of knowing in that they orient us to the reality of place. They enable us to make comparisons between places and tell us where we are in the grand scheme. Walking through the confusing jumble of streets and alleyways that make up the souk (marketplace) in Fez, Morocco, I felt the necessity to know where I was in relation to the market as a whole, to make a mental map. If I had been following a guide, I would never have felt a sense of the place. When you are always a passenger in a car, you are less likely to learn your way around. To comprehend something yourself, you have to have the impetus to make it understandable.

Cosmological maps, fanciful interpretations of the universe, were popular in Europe during medieval times and were accorded the same importance as geographical maps.

J. B. Harley and David Woodward, *The History of Cartography*

THE POWER OF MAPS

Throughout history, maps have always been equated with power, whether they depicted hunting grounds, trade routes, military sites, or buried treasure.

The South Sea Islanders made maps of shells and twigs. The twigs represented ocean currents and the shells noted islands. The maps gave them mobility.

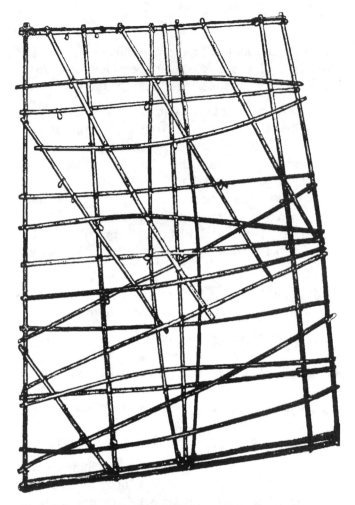

The stick charts of the Marshall Islanders, used for navigation, combined primitive and sophisticated abstract qualities. The mapping technique was fully developed before the Islanders had any written language. A grid of palm sticks, tied together with coconut fiber, indicated open sea over a territory of several hundred miles, while curved sticks showed prevailing wave fronts. Shells indicated the relative location of islands and threads showed where islands come into view. The charts were used on canoes during open-sea journeys. Use of the stick charts ended in the nineteenth century with the introduction of conventional maps by Europeans.

Were all the maps in this world destroyed and vanished under the direction of some malevolent hand, each man would be blind again, each landmark become a meaningless signpost to nothing.

Beryl Markham, *West with the Night*

Maps have been associated with the unknown and mysterious. They beckon the spirit of adventure in all of us. They distill the environment, giving us just what we need to know to explore new territory.

NATURAL MEASUREMENT

The following are examples by Paul Klee of attempts to visually depict fundamental ideas.

Increase and decrease between them, culmination

Increase or decrease

Simultaneous increase and decrease

Crescendo and diminuendo

Drawings by Paul Klee

A map aficionado, Jeff Greenwald explains how he came under the spell of maps in an article, "On Maps," in the *San Francisco Examiner* on March 15, 1987:

"Growing up on Long Island, I had map fever. It was more than a compulsion to cover my walls: it was a need to possess the places those maps represented, to accumulate destinations. Above my desk hung a map of the United States, stuck full of pins, heavy with the destination voodoo of the post-Kerouac generation. *On the Road* was practically mythology to me; I charted Sal Paradise's route through bop America as a scholar of ancient Greece might try to trace Odysseus' travels.

"In 1974 . . . I set off for the West Coast at last, attempting to duplicate Kerouac's journey.

"Needless to say, my path across the country took its own shape. It included some of the cities Sal Paradise visited, like Chicago and Denver, but for the most part I wound my way through territories unknown, an eager disciple of the fates that steer young travelers into the unexpected—but always strangely appropriate—encounters and experiences.

"Maps, I discovered, always seem immutable at first; it's only later, in the heat of an intimate relationship with them, that one realizes they can be redrawn to suit new priorities."

MAPS AS METAPHORS

Most people have a fairly limited concept of a map as a depiction of a particular geographic location. To find our way through information, we also rely on maps that will tell us where we are in relation to the information, give us a sense of perspective, and enable us to make comparisons between information.

Maps can take a myriad of forms. A CAT scan is a map of the human body. A grocery list is a map of a trip to the grocery store. A chart of a company's production over a year maps its output. A loan application is a map showing the route from your actual to your desired financial status. You can map ideas and concepts as well as physical places.

Maps enable us to exchange information, whether about Benares or building codes. Maps are virtually synonymous with reference information in that we use them to direct or influence the course we follow in life. The principles of photosynthesis are reference information or maps to a botanist but not to someone who doesn't own a plant. A TV program guide is reference information only to someone who watches television.

Maps are the metaphoric means by which we can understand and act upon information from outside sources. A map by definition must perform, whether it is a multimillion dollar, four-color production of the National Weather Service or two cans of beer on a counter showing the relationship of a friend's new house to his old one.

You could go right back to Plato for the charting of things. Diagramming goes much further back to the Egyptians. The first person to actually make a visual representation of abstract statistics was a Scottish mathematician, William Playfair. It's claimed that he invented the bar chart. Playfair's brother ran a little business, put the money that they got from the business, the coins, into a little pile. Monday's pile was next to Tuesday's pile and so forth. He published illustrations in a book called *Political Atlas*.

UNIVERSAL MAPS

However, maps are like words; if they don't have a fairly universal meaning, they lose the power to communicate. Although the following lesson was learned from geographic maps, the importance of universal meaning is applicable to nongeographic maps as well.

I realized many years ago that there appeared to be a lack of rigor among varying maps. In the United States, no two cities produced their maps to the same scale or with the same legend. There was no body of work that showed the plans of the cities of the world to the same scale. If maps of different places aren't done to the same scale with the same legends, you can't understand the relationship between places.

Asking "why not do maps to the same scale?" brought me interesting results and a certain exposure. In 1962 I

The simplest map locates a point by referencing it to two known paths. You could describe the location of Mexico City, for instance, by saying "Go straight south of Laredo, Texas, and straight east of Hawaii."

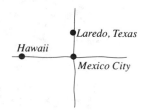

Models, at the same scale, made from Plasticine™ and photographed from above.
Illustrations from *Cities: Comparisons of Form and Scale* by Richard Saul Wurman.

Versailles

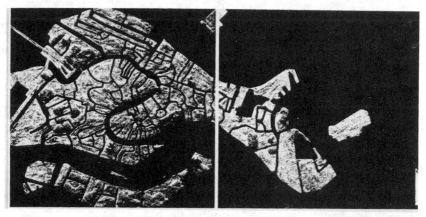

Venice

Downtown Philadelphia

developed a project as a teacher at North Carolina State University in Raleigh.

The class made topographic model maps of fifty cities— all to the same scale. We discovered that Paris is much bigger than Rome, that Versailles is as big as Venice, that Venice is as big as downtown Philadelphia. Once these relationships became clear, a greater understanding of these places was made possible.

The book didn't analyze data or come up with any socio-logical conclusions; it just showed the size of a place relative to other places. Size is something on which you can hang future visual images of a place. By looking at the simple environment of a map, you can understand larger, more complex environments like cities.

Like any number, idea, or concept, maps are understood when we see them in comparison with something else.

MAPMAKERS

Mapmaking demands an understanding of the place or the information and a sense of what can be omitted without diminishing the sense of place or the idea being mapped. A mapmaker is both an artist and a surgeon. In his book *Maps*, Gershon Weltman claims that maps "are not the environments themselves but are, instead, displays de-signed to present an environment in its absence; displays designed to 're-present' in such a way as to allow the map reader systematically to derive attributes of the mapped environment." And despite a proliferation of mediocre or misleading maps, there is an active community of exem-plary designers who have mastered the techniques of mapping.

Joel Katz, a partner in the Katz Wheeler graphic design firm in Philadelphia, is a charter member in the unofficial Understanding Club and well versed in the artistry of maps. For five years he worked for me and with me—the line between the two blurred—and we traded discoveries

WHAT MAKES A GOOD GRAPHIC?

You should apply a stan-dard to the graphics that you peruse. Unless they meet certain criteria, they are likely to waste your time. A worthwhile graphic should reveal data by:

● inducing you to think about the substance rather than the form

● encouraging the eye to compare different pieces of data

● revealing the data at several levels of detail

● avoiding distortion

Edward Tufte,
The Visual Display of Quantitative Information

on numerous projects. His talents span photography and writing, as well as graphic design; he is a mapmaker in the most expansive sense of the word. In the following paragraphs, he outlines the considerations of conscientious mapmakers.

"In the area of maps, particularly, there is no developed aesthetic by the public. People have no concept of what makes a good map, because the concept of a map that they're raised on is so banal. It's the atlas the teacher pulls down in third grade. When people come to us for maps, it's because we make maps that work.

"Anyone who's taken a tenth-grade biology course knows the words to describe certain processes. But the difference between being able to describe it in its jargon and understanding it is being able to image it.

"What are the simplest questions you would ask yourself if you were doing a map? How would you start? There's one question: what's the purpose of the map? Some maps are to get people from here to there, and other maps have nothing to do with that whatsoever. The purpose of a map or the vocabulary of the map relates to the experience that's appropriate for the person using it to have. There are even cases for nongeographic, straight-line maps that depart from reality.

"The clearest, most logical example for the justification of a straight-line, totally nongeographic map is the airplane experience. You have absolutely no control whatsoever. You gain control as you move through the succeeding modes of transportation from trains, subways, buses, and cars to the pedestrian experience, which is at the other end. The kind of map you need is one that relates to what you can see, what you can feel, and the extent to which you can act on information.

"The airplane experience is like a digital experience and the pedestrian experience is like an analog experience. You can cross the street, you can move to the left, you can move to the right. When you're thirty-five thousand feet up, it doesn't matter what you see.

"However, I believe that the fact that there is space between stops is important because what you are doing is imaging the geographical entity with which people have a certain kind of familiarity. A and B, the most important thing in mapping—in nongeographic, diagrammatic mapping, modified-view graph mapping—is consistency. What you have to do is tie the nongeographic diagram with a picture of the nonspecific geography of both. All those things have to connect."

In airline schedules, it doesn't matter what the plane does once it gets up in the air; you want to know where it takes off and where it lands. Headwinds are beyond your control. You can choose a flight that arrives at a particular time, but you can't determine the particular route or the altitude of the plane. Those matters are beyond your repertoire of choice.

But there are aspects that you might want to know about that are hard to find in most airline schedules, such as where does the plane stop? Where are the two stops on my flight to India? What will the plane fly over?

Many flight maps have straight lines between places, many have curved lines because that's supposed to resemble the way an airplane flies. We go up and we come down. But all these lines are of no use. The visual messages don't inform. It would be better to look at a map and understand that there is a plane change, a time change, and a stopover in Mozambique.

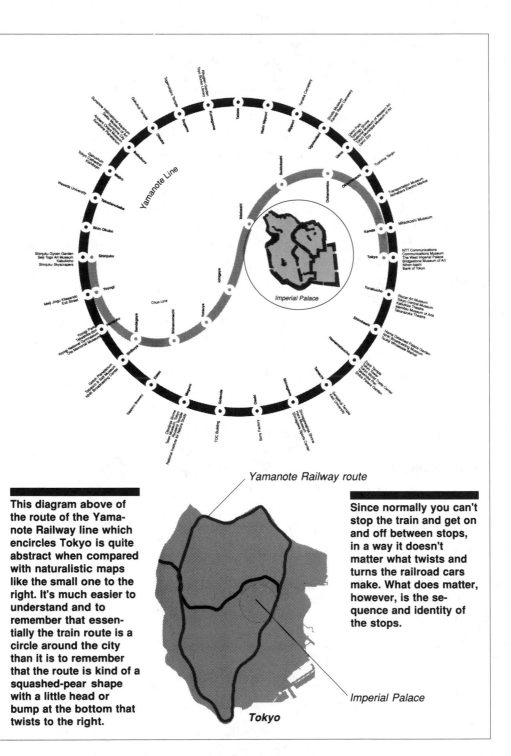

Yamanote Railway route

Imperial Palace

Tokyo

This diagram above of the route of the Yamanote Railway line which encircles Tokyo is quite abstract when compared with naturalistic maps like the small one to the right. It's much easier to understand and to remember that essentially the train route is a circle around the city than it is to remember that the route is kind of a squashed-pear shape with a little head or bump at the bottom that twists to the right.

Since normally you can't stop the train and get on and off between stops, in a way it doesn't matter what twists and turns the railroad cars make. What does matter, however, is the sequence and identity of the stops.

The diagram for the subway system in Mexico City is so abstract it even leaves out lines connecting the picto- grams of the stops to one another. Yet the sequence of stops and the transfer points remains quite under- standable.

OBSERVATORIO   TACUBAYA   JUANACATLAN   CHAPULTEPEC   SEVILLA   INSURGENTES   CUAUHTEMOC   BALDERAS

Detail of the Mexico City subway system diagram designed by Lance Wyman.

MAPS OF NUMBERS AND IDEAS

Albeit not as exotic as geographic maps of faraway lands, charts, diagrams, illustrations, and even forms are also maps—of the written word, of numbers, of concepts. They allow us to "image" information. They can make sense of chaos, define the abstract with the concrete, and generally act as weapons by which we can subdue complex ideas and unruly numbers. Well-crafted maps can reduce anxiety; so can being able to recognize where maps go awry.

"Statistical graphics are the only place where art and science come together in a meaningful way," said Edward Tufte, a professor of political science and statistics at Yale University who wrote the book *The Visual Display of Quantitative Information*. "Clarity, clarity, clarity. You can't draw well unless you respect the reader . . . good visual communications work is like good writing. Clarity in design and complexity in information are what count— just the opposite of the modern world," said Tufte, whose new book *Envisioning Information* is due out this year.

Illustrators have long been concerned with the mapping of ideas. A wonderful example is the book *Maps of the Mind* by Charles Hampton-Turner, which turns the ideas of people like Albert Einstein, Sigmund Freud, or Jacques Derrida into diagrams. Individuals often make at least informal mental maps of their own ideas.

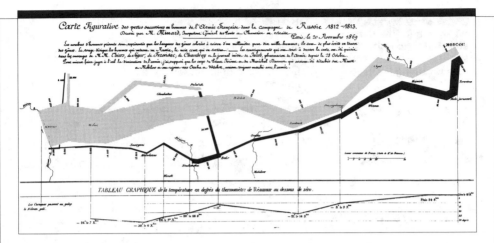

An amazing example of a combined historical and geographic diagram appears above. It charts Napoleon's trek with his army to Moscow and their return to France. The gray section is the route to Moscow, the black is the return trip. The thickness of the line represents the number of men in the army at each point in the journey. It paints a clear picture of attrition. Along the bottom is a temperature scale that shows how cold the winter weather actually was on the grim march home.

Using time as the vertical scale, the last half of a football game is diagrammed play by play on the right. The symbols tell you exactly what happened—where and when. This type of report is more informative than the typical final score in the newspaper and can rival a live newscast for detail. Both diagrams were taken from *The Visual Display of Quantitative Information* by Edward R. Tufte, (Cheshire, CT: Graphics Press, 1983).

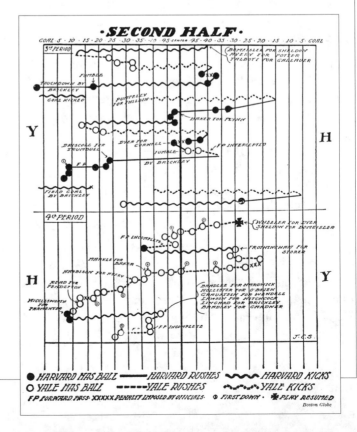

Maps of numbers and ideas can be passive in that they come to us complete, as in the case of charts and diagrams, or they can be active, as in the case of forms and applications that require our participation.

DIAGRAMS AND CHARTS

For many people the first word that comes to mind when they think about statistical charts is "lie." No doubt some graphics do distort the underlying data, making it hard for the viewer to learn the truth. But data graphics are no different from words in this regard, for any means of communication can be used to deceive. Graphics aren't especially vulnerable; in fact, most of us have pretty good graphical lie detectors that help us see right through frauds, claims Edward Tufte in *The Visual Display of Quantitative Information*.

He blames the origins of the preoccupation with deceptive graphics on the early assumption that data graphics were mainly devices for showing the obvious to the ignorant. It wasn't until the late 1960s that the world-class data analyst John Tukey made statistical graphics that were instruments for reasoning with quantitative information.

Elevating the stature of statistical graphics has created two camps, and the mere mention of the words "diagram" or "chart" will likely produce strong reactions. They will set the statistically inclined all aquiver, but will evoke fear and loathing among the poor, angst-ridden verbal types who insist they can't understand numbers. Both reactions are based on a failure to understand or regard charts and diagrams as maps in that they are all patterns made understandable.

A diagram or chart is a map in that its implicit purpose is to help readers through information. Charts and diagrams enable us to make sense of statistics so that we don't lose our way amidst a morass of unconnected numbers. A simple chart is no more than a set of statistics made visible. It shows what has happened in the past and what might happen in the future.

Yet we don't make the same demands of a chart or diagram that we would of a map. Only by insisting that charts and diagrams depict some reality—whether they illustrate population trends or profit-and-loss statements—will graphic designers get the message that significance, not style, should be a guiding principle.

The four most common chart forms used for communicating everyday statistics are: bar charts, pie charts, fever charts, and tables. Each lends itself to particular kinds of information. The selection of a particular form should be based on the kind of information to be mapped.

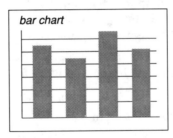

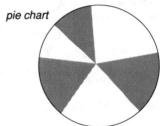

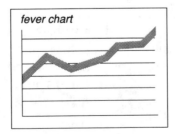

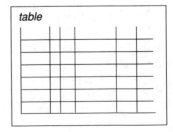

In *A Designer's Guide to Creating Charts and Diagrams*, Nigel Holmes discusses the kinds and uses of charts. He states, "Statistics may be presented graphically in many different ways, but there should always be a sound reason for choosing the particular form of presentation.

"By and large it is the material itself that will determine which kind is to be used, for it will naturally be visually clearer in that form than in any of the others. The purpose of a chart is to clarify or make visible the facts that otherwise would lie buried in a mass of written material, lists, balance sheets, or reports."

The diagrams below and on the following two pages are from the *Fluor Corporation 1976 Annual Report* designed by Jim Cross Design Office, Inc. The first diagram illustrates the assets and liabilities of Fluor Corporation. It gives stockholders a feel for where the value in the company lies as well as graphically illustrating a basic principle of accounting—the amount of money that comes in equals that which goes out.

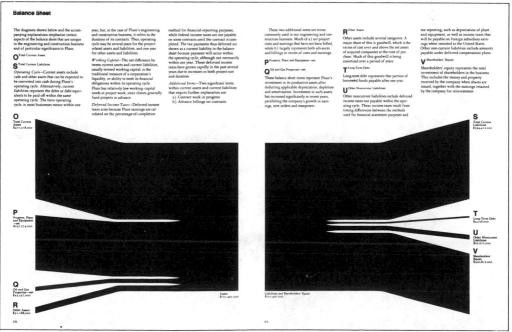

Bar Charts

Bar charts are good for comparing quantities. The height or length of the bar represents the quantity.

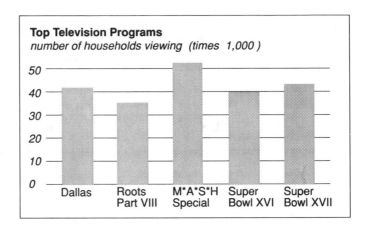

Top Television Programs
number of households viewing (times 1,000)

(Dallas, Roots Part VIII, M*A*S*H Special, Super Bowl XVI, Super Bowl XVII)

The lines represent the flow of money over a fiscal year in the diagram below.

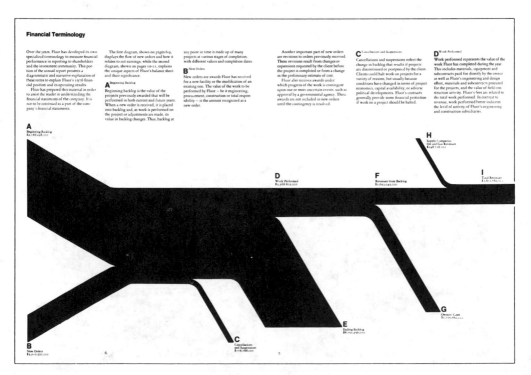

If you have a line, you can really see that one line is twice as long as the other line. Sometimes objects are used to represent the bar. This can be misleading because in reality both area and volume increase at a faster rate than height, and your mind senses this. Don't be fooled if you see an illustrated graph with a drawing of something huge next to something tiny. Usually the height is being compared, but the difference in apparent volume, while it can look dramatic, is incorrect.

Uneven scale increments can confuse the information. Not only should the scale be consistent for these types of charts, but also the location of the bases of the bars should be along the same horizontal or vertical axis. The bar chart on the next page, adapted from a popular weekly news magazine, is an example of a bar chart that is manipulated so as to support a certain editorial viewpoint. You may agree or disagree with the viewpoint

By varying the thicknesses of the lines, the reader gets a feel not only for the amount of money in each section but also for the relationship the amounts have to the total.

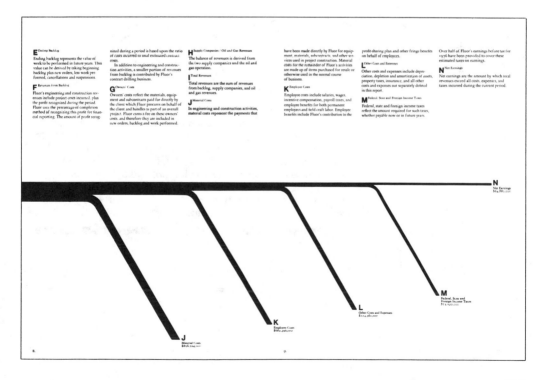

expressed (that the value of the dollar compared to the German mark at the time was dropping too far too fast), but in either case it is important to be able to see how the figures in the chart are graphically manipulated.

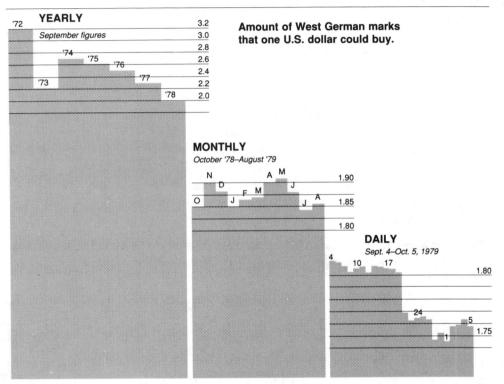

Amount of West German marks that one U.S. dollar could buy.

These graphs have been scaled and placed together in such a way that they seem to make one big graph, heading seriously downhill. The horizontal scale increment changes from graph to graph, representing, from left to right, seven years, two months, and four days, respectively. The vertical scale also changes with each graph, even though the line intervals remain constant. If you look closely at each part, the statistical case to back up an interpretation that the dollar is nose-diving compared with the German mark is there, but it's weak.

The two charts immediately below describe the same information. The height of the bars and the height of the oil barrels is the same, but the barrels look disproportionately larger because they suggest volume differences as well as height differences.

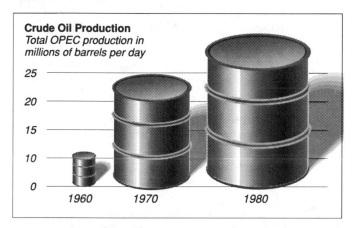

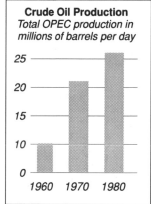

The chart below, adapted from a popular newspaper, is an example of the confusion which can arise when a bar chart uses inconsistent scales. Visually it appears as if Jackson has about as much support in the South as Bush does, yet the percentage figures supplied indicate that Bush has almost twice as much support among Republicans.

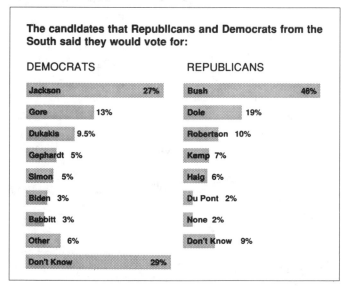

Pie charts

Another example of charts that often can lead to confusion instead of clarity are pie charts. Pie charts have been generally overused, partially because they are relatively easy to create using computers. We are flooded with them every day in the newspapers, annual reports, and even advertisements. The area of the circle is a poor way of comparing simple quantities because it is impossible for the eye to understand the relationship of the diameter of the circle to the area of the circle. They work only when the slices are substantial. Dividing pie charts into too many slices results in variations that are impossible to compare or even to detect.

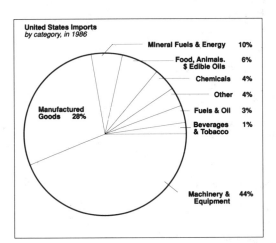

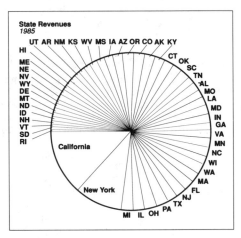

In making comparisons, lines, such as in a bar chart, are generally much easier to compare. If you have a line, you can really see that one line is twice as long as the other line. If you are comparing simple percentages, use a pie chart.

The two charts on the right describe the same information. The pie chart works better because you can sense the relationship of the parts to the whole.

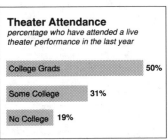

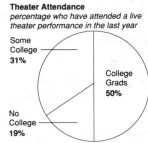

Fever Charts

"Fever charts" are great for showing trends. Lines that go up or down are so easy to understand that these kinds of "mountain graphs" are probably the most commonly used kind of chart.

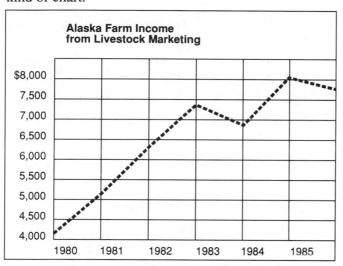

A chart like this is called a fever chart because doctors tradi- tionally used this form of map to record the changes in a patient's temperature during a fever.

The fever charts below show the increase in the number of components that could be placed on a computer chip between 1960 and 1980. The graph below on the left is exponential, that is, the scale changes by a factor of sixteen at each increment. For example, it would appear that the number of chips doubled in 1970 over 1965, but in fact it is over sixteen times as great. The graph below on the right shows the same information based on an arithmetic scale.

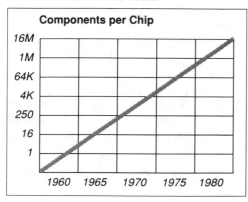

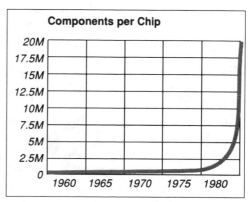

But just as for bar graphs, if the fever graph scale is not constant, or is not clearly annotated, then the information communicated is at best confusing, at worst misleading. Always ask of fever charts: "What's the scale?"

Tables

Tables make wonderful maps when it's desirable to know exact amounts. The tax tables we use to determine how much we owe Uncle Sam could be done as fever or bar charts, but it would be unrealistic to expect to be able to ascertain exact dollar figures from any kind of chart except a table.

Year End	All Countries	United States	Canada	Japan	West Germany
1976	1,014.23	274.68	21.62	21.11	117.61
1977	1,029.19	277.55	22.01	21.62	118.30
1978	1,036.82	276.41	22.13	23.97	118.64
1979	944.44	264.60	22.18	24.23	95.25
1980	952.99	264.32	20.98	24.23	95.18
1981	953.26	264.11	20.46	24.23	95.18
1982	948.69	264.03	20.26	24.23	95.18
1983	945.27	263.39	20.17	24.23	95.18
1984	946.09	262.79	20.14	24.23	95.18
1985	949.00	262.65	20.11	24.23	95.18
1986	948.80	262.04	19.72	24.23	95.18

Gold Reserves of Central Banks & Governments

NOWHERE MAPS

Because charts and diagrams have the patina of the scientific, we sometimes revere them without question. During the drought in the Midwest in 1988, *The New York Times* drew a map of the country which was shaded into three zones. They were labeled: "severely," "excessively," and "extremely" dry. I would bet that few people have the semantic subtlety to distinguish between these three words, which are virtually synonymous.

One kind of chart that is often deliberately misleading is the non-zero base graph. The newspapers were filled with them during the 1987 stock market crash. They start at some specified number and greatly exaggerate change. They are popular in annual reports because they can make it look as though a company's income went up by a third, when, in fact, it only went up a twentieth. It just depends on the point you choose to make your base. Equally misleading are non-zero based graphs which concentrate on specially selected portions of the scale in order to make a point, like the second one below. Either chart is technically correct but contrasting conclusions could be drawn from them. You have to be aware of the scale.

The Census Bureau and the United States Geological Survey have jointly developed the Topologically Integrated Geographic Encoding and Reference (TIGER) system producing for the first time a computerized data base of both socioeconomic and physical resources data for the forty-eight contiguous states. Use is limited to these government agencies right now, but entrepreneurs have been given the green light to find software applications that put this information to work for other users. Ideas such as an automated Yellow Pages and computerized road maps in cars are already being developed.

Martha Farnsworth Riche, "Tiger at the Frontier," *American Demographics* (3/87)

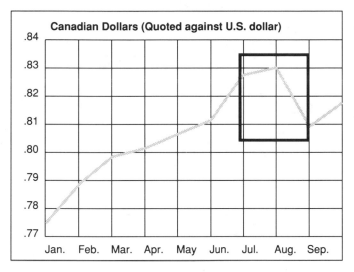

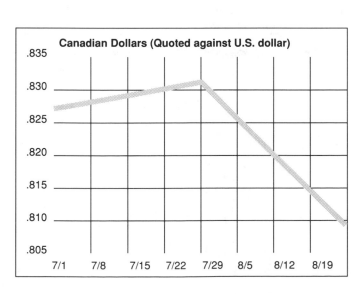

Mixed scales are something else to watch for in charts and diagrams. The fever chart below was adapted quite directly from a major daily newspaper. Unless you're statistically astute enough to notice that there are two different scales for the same chart space, you get the feeling that sales for the Cadillac Allanté exceeded total sales for all Cadillac models combined. Is that logical?

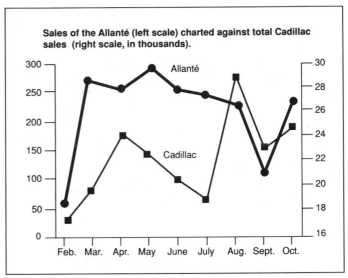

Sales of the Allanté (left scale) charted against total Cadillac sales (right scale, in thousands).

Not only does half of this chart use a non-zero baseline, but another graph with a completely different scale is placed in the graph area as if it were meant for direct comparison. It portrays an impossibility (that Cadillac's Allanté sales could be more than its car sales totals).

The capability of showing depth in charts creates more confusion when their depth has no numeric value. This is apparent in both pie and bar charts as well as in geographic maps. Are you supposed to look at length or depth? It serves only to cloud your perception of the information.

This map suffers from "Cliffitis," or the unnecessary depiction of depth. The illusion of dimension is busy and distracting.

Tour of the Americas

The first Pepsi Tour of the Americas bicycle race begins Friday. Here's a look at the riders' itinerary and map of the route:

Friday: Valencia, 2 1/2 mile time trial
Saturday: Valencia to Caracas, Venezula, 125 miles.
Sunday: Caracas circuit race, 85 miles
Monday: Travel day
Tuesday: Jacksonville 100-mile circuit race; bus to Orlando
Wednesday: Orlando 100-mile circuit race
Thursday: Orlando to Tampa 140-mile road race; bus to St. Petersburg
Feb. 26: St. Petersburg team time trial of 27.8 miles and 30-mile criterium(road race); bus to West Palm Beach

Feb. 27: West Palm Beach 100-mile circuit race

Feb. 28: West Palm Beach to Miami 85-mile circuit race

Total miles cycled: 795.3

Source: 1988 Pepsi Tour of The Americas

By Rod Little, USA TODAY

"Tour of the Americas," February 19, 1988. © 1988, USA TODAY. Reprinted with permission.

You can easily be misled by maps, whether intentionally or not.

The low premium on clarity is due in part to graphic designers who operate more as cosmeticians—putting mascara instead of meaning on information—instead of functioning as conscientious mapmakers.

But also at fault are those who employ the designers to create maps that are intentionally misleading or who want maps only for dazzling effect instead of for elucidation. Annual reports that impress but do not inform attest to this phenomenon. Executives encourage their designers to engage in electronic gymnastics with their computers for no other reason than to test the limits of the equipment, often at the expense of clarity.

It is incumbent upon the decision makers to learn a language of visual literacy with which to communicate and upon the map users to insist that they be able to draw meaning from the maps.

CONVERSATION WITH JOSH WURMAN

Josh Wurman is a meteorologist at the Massachusetts Institute of Technology in Cambridge, where he is completing his doctorate. He combines his curiosity about the world around him with his science background and a natural interest in communicating scientific information to others. Using the example of weather mapping, he points out how visual information can be made more meaningful. He also happens to be my son.

JW: I taught an introduction to meteorology course to first-year graduates in landscape architecture at the University of Pennsylvania. They had an assignment to present the meteorological conditions in some site near Philadelphia, where they were going to propose land-use changes. Seven groups got together to do the meteorology section; every single group made the same fatal flaw in their presentations. They presented gobs and gobs of statistics, all of which were meaningless to anyone who would want to know about the meteorology of the site. Somebody presented a graph of snowfall by the month, another person had wind speed per month and temperature per month and days of cloudiness per month, and days of frost and frost-free periods. During their presentations I would ask them, "So what?" "So what" that the frost-free season is 180 days; what does that mean? Does that mean I can grow tomatoes? What kind of place or region am I familiar with that has a 180-day frost-free season? And the students never thought to look up whether their statistics had any meaning. I wanted the impact of the statistics.

RSW: You call it impact and I call it understanding. I can't understand anything from that data. Did they ever understand what you were talking about?

JW: I don't think so and I guess I thought of that as a failure to communicate, lots of numbers without impact.

RSW: One of the most popular newspapers in the States today is *USA TODAY*. So we have to assume that one of the most popular weather maps is the *USA TODAY* weather map. It's prominent in the newspaper on the back of the A section and it is designed to be pretty, but I don't think it works as well as it could. It tells you only the weather, when it could tell you about comparative comfort, which is really what you want to know when you look at a weather map.

JW: For one thing, it doesn't tell you about the wind speed or humidity. You are going to be much colder if it's in a windy place; you are going to feel more uncomfortable if it is raining or snowing because you are going to get wet. If it is sunny in the South, you are going to be more uncomfortable there than if it is a cloudy day.

This map shows twenty-six bands of color representing temperature. Temperature alone does not tell you the degree of comfort. Temperature is an indication of when water freezes and when water boils.

RSW: Comfort is what the outdoors feels like relative to the human being. Comfort is a human condition. The *USA TODAY* weather map should show comparative comfort, because comfort is what relates to us. We decide what to wear each morning based on our desire to be comfortable in the environment.

Instead of indicating temperature, they could put a comfort index, similar to a windchill-factor chart. Varying degrees or lack of comfort could easily be shown using two color categories—one for temperature over comfort, the other for windchill below. Blue could be used for cold and red for warm. Gradations in these colors would show changes in magnitude, changes in the level of comfort.

The categories are warmer and more humid above comfort and colder and windier below comfort. The

---

MAP ILLITERATES GET HELP

The American Automobile Association has developed a series of maps for those who need a tour guide to find their way out of a broom closet. Called "Walks Through," the maps are printed with dots and arrows that trace the course that a person would walk in real life and include the locations of shops, cafés, telephones, public restrooms, and even benches.

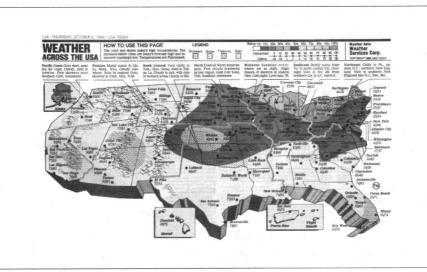

Drawn in a dramatic perspective, the *USA TODAY* weather map shows Maine smaller than Florida. Does this mean Maine has less weather? Or that Florida weather is more important? The "cliffs" would be approximately 150 miles high if they were in scale. It's exciting, but what's the point? This is an example of rainbow worship making the real information a little harder to understand.

MAP OF COMPARATIVE COMFORT
Comfort is human; temperature is for thermometers

In Washington, D.C., 90° with 90% humidity just doesn't feel the same as 90° in Flagstaff, Arizona, with 10% humidity. What a map like this should show is not temperature zones, but rather comfort zones that take into account humidity, elevation, and wind speed, as well as temperature—a comparative comfort map.

White would be the most comfortable, with tones getting more black or blue where it's less comfortable because it's colder. Tones could get gradually more red where it's less comfortable because it's warmer. And I wouldn't overdo the graphics—keep them simple, informative.

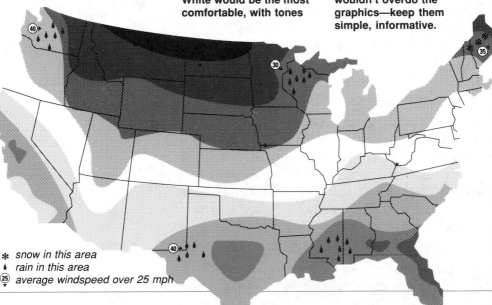

* snow in this area
♦ rain in this area
㉕ average windspeed over 25 mph

darker the red color, the warmer and more humid the environment above our standard of acceptable comfort. The darker the blue color, the colder and windier the environment above our standard of acceptable comfort. Now you could compare and understand the comfort level of 90 temperature/humidity index in New York and 90 temperature/humidity index in Phoenix.

Et voilà! A simpler map, fewer colors, and with human comfort as the normative reference.

USER-PARTICIPATION MAPS

Most of the maps of our lives come to us ready-made. The responsibility for clarity lies with the creator. But certain forms and applications serve as skeleton maps that demand our participation. Although most forms are not maps in the formal sense of the word, they can help us find our way through information. If the designers of forms regarded them as such, we could use them like maps to order information and outline the roads we must follow.

TAXING FORMS

Perhaps the most universal examples of forms gone awry are the United States income tax forms published by the Internal Revenue Service. There are few things we encounter that create as much anxiety. The only thing most people hate more than paying taxes is filling out the tax forms. They have come to symbolize the complexity and inscrutability of modern life.

Even the tax professionals are not exempt. Last year *Money* magazine sent out identical profiles of a hypothetical family to fifty tax preparers nationwide. They received fifty different answers varying from each other as much as $4,679. Some of the differences came from ignorance, bad judgment, or simply careless errors. If the professionals and experts cannot understand the tax code, how are we supposed to?

Tax forms are only one of the forms that make us shudder in exasperation—there are also loan applications, insurance forms, voting pamphlets, congressional bills, and purchase agreements. The whole purpose of various forms and documents is very often forgotten, lost in a quagmire of legalese and pomposity. The form of the document should follow the flow of the type of information within it and reflect how that information is used. The goal of a form should be to inform the consumer or client so that they understand what they are signing.

Many courts have ruled in favor of consumers in legal suits, even though they had signed away certain rights in a contract, because the documents were misleading or confusing. You might be surprised to find out the meaning of different paragraphs in contracts and documents. There might be items that you would never agree to if you understood them, but because they're not comprehendible, you don't realize their full meaning.

During his administration, President Jimmy Carter issued an executive order to simplify government documents. As a result, Alan Siegel of Siegel & Gale was hired to restructure the IRS tax forms. The first thing he found was that even though the complexity of the forms depended so much on the complexity of the tax code, the forms could be made significantly more informative and easier to use.

The forms Siegel & Gale developed were in "plain English," that is, in a common form of the language lay people use instead of the lingo used by lawyers, accountants, and politicians. They eliminated extraneous information and structured the forms into groups based on marital status (single, married, married with joint returns, etc.) and on filing status (itemized deductions, short form, etc.). This meant that there were more forms, but they contained only the information needed by that person and there were no tax tables. So, if you were a married woman filing separately from your husband, there would be a specific form for you.

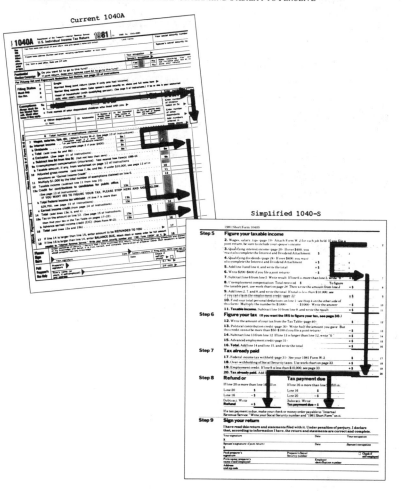

The form on the left above is the 1040A form from 1981 used by the IRS. Next to it is the simplified 1040S form that Siegel & Gale redesigned. Notice how much simpler the information flows on the redesigned form. Each step is explained clearly and in greater depth.

In test groups, people did surprisingly well. They found the forms easier to use, and they were more accurate with their figures. Also they were able to do complex calculations like income averaging that they could never do before.

Another great help in forms like these is to include examples (either verbal or visual) that are well explained and relevant, especially where complex figures and processes are involved.

Siegel & Gale were able to restructure the form system in such a way that roughly 80 percent of the taxpayers could use the simplest forms. So why weren't these forms used? The IRS resisted the whole project and canceled the project owing to lack of funds when the Reagan Administration took over. Now, the IRS is trying to implement those changes gradually by putting the new ideas into the old format, but the result has usually been worse than if they had done nothing at all.

Siegel & Gale has greatly improved other documents as well: insurance forms, contracts, loan applications, annual reports, technical manuals, training manuals, etc.

I think that charts, diagrams, and maps can be used in these documents to make understanding easier and greater. People can be taught about the process they are going through and educated about the subject while they are using these forms. For example, while using a tax form, a person could learn about the whole tax code and system (what taxes he or she is paying, why, how much, what is done with them), not just which box to write a particular sum in.

FORM AND DELIVERY

Maps aren't mirrors of reality; they are a means of understanding it. To accomplish this, mapmakers can reduce, distill, exaggerate, or abstract reality. Their mission is to capture the salient aspects of a particular reality that would enable someone to understand it—whether the reality is the State of Wisconsin or wine production in California.

Before

PBR 668 REV. 9-74

FIRST NATIONAL CITY BANK
PERSONAL FINANCE DEPARTMENT - NEW YORK
APPLICATION
NUMBER _____

**ANNUAL PER-
CENTAGE RATE** _____ %

$ _____

PROCEEDS TO BORROWER	(1) $ _____
PROPERTY INS. PREMIUM	(2) $ _____
FILING FEE	(3) $ _____
AMOUNT FINANCED (1) + (2) + (3)	(4) $ _____
PREPAID FINANCE CHARGE	(5) $ _____
GROUP CREDIT LIFE INS. PREMIUM	(6) $ _____
FINANCE CHARGE (5) + (6)	(7) $ _____

TOTAL OF PAYMENTS (4) + (7)
FOR VALUE RECEIVED, the undersigned (jointly and severally) hereby promise(s) to pay to FIRST NATIONAL CITY BANK (the "Bank")
at its office at 399 Park Avenue, New York, New York 10022 (i) THE SUM OF

_____ ($_____) (TOTAL OF PAYMENTS)
( ) IN _____ EQUAL CONSECUTIVE MONTHLY INSTALMENTS OF $ _____ EACH ON THE SAME DAY OF EACH MONTH, COM-
MENCING _____ DAYS FROM THE DATE THE LOAN IS MADE; OR ( ) IN _____ EQUAL CONSECUTIVE WEEKLY INSTALMENTS
OF $ _____ EACH ON THE SAME DAY OF EACH WEEK, COMMENCING NOT EARLIER THAN 5 DAYS NOR LATER THAN 45 DAYS FROM
THE DATE THE LOAN IS MADE; OR ( ) IN _____ EQUAL CONSECUTIVE BI-WEEKLY INSTALMENTS OF $ _____ EACH, COM-
MENCING NOT EARLIER THAN 10 DAYS NOR LATER THAN 45 DAYS FROM THE DATE THE LOAN IS MADE, AND ON THE SAME DAY
OF EACH SECOND WEEK THEREAFTER; OR ( ) IN _____ EQUAL CONSECUTIVE SEMI-MONTHLY INSTALMENTS OF $ _____
EACH, COMMENCING NOT EARLIER THAN 10 DAYS NOR LATER THAN 45 DAYS FROM THE DATE THE LOAN IS MADE, AND ON THE
SAME DAY OF EACH SEMI-MONTHLY PERIOD THEREAFTER, (ii) A FINE COMPUTED AT THE RATE OF 5¢ PER $1 ON ANY INSTALMENT
WHICH HAS BECOME DUE AND REMAINED UNPAID FOR A PERIOD IN EXCESS OF 10 DAYS, PROVIDED (A) IF THE PROCEEDS TO THE
BORROWER ARE $10,000 OR LESS, NO SUCH FINE SHALL EXCEED $5 AND THE AGGREGATE OF ALL SUCH FINES SHALL NOT EXCEED
THE LESSER OF 2% OF THE AMOUNT OF THIS NOTE OR $25, OR (B) IF THE ANNUAL PERCENTAGE RATE STATED ABOVE IS 7.50% OR
LESS, THE LIMITATIONS PROVIDED IN (A) SHALL NOT APPLY AND NO SUCH FINE SHALL EXCEED $25 AND THE AGGREGATE OF ALL
SUCH FINES SHALL NOT EXCEED 2% OF THE AMOUNT OF THIS NOTE, AND SUCH FINE(S) SHALL BE DEEMED LIQUIDATED DAM-
AGES OCCASIONED BY THE LATE PAYMENT(S); (iii) IN THE EVENT OF THIS NOTE MATURING, SUBJECT TO AN ALLOWANCE FOR
UNEARNED INTEREST ATTRIBUTABLE TO THE MATURED AMOUNT, INTEREST AT A RATE EQUAL TO 1% PER MONTH AND (iv) IF

This installment loan form was used by CitiBank several years ago. It's fairly typical of the traditional consumer contract. Written by lawyers, for lawyers, it's obviously not written to be read.

After

First National City Bank

Consumer Loan Note   Date _____, 19 ____

(In this note, the words **I, me, mine** and **my** mean each and all of those who signed it. The words **you, your** and **yours** mean First National City Bank.)

Terms of   To repay my loan, I promise to pay you _____ Dollars
Repayment   ($_____). I'll pay this sum at one of your branches in _____ uninterrupted _____
installments of $ _____ each. Payments will be due _____, starting
from the date the loan is made.

Here's the breakdown of my payments:

1. Amount of the Loan $_____
2. Property Insurance Premium $_____
3. Filing Fee for
   Security Interest $_____
4. Amount Financed (1+2+3) $_____
5. **Finance Charge** $_____
6. Total of Payments (4+5) $_____

Annual Percentage Rate _____ %

This form is a reorganized version of the one above it. It uses shorter headings, shorter sentences, active verbs, a personal tone, contractions, definitions, and a readable design to make a form that is really understandable.

Just how effectively maps can communicate information depends on their form as well as on the manner in which they are delivered. The way the information is delivered also influences the form of the map, which in turn alters the way it will be perceived. This holds true for geographic maps, charts, diagrams, and even language as the map by which we communicate.

A toaster delivered via a truck is no different from one delivered by parachute. But with information as a product, the delivery dramatically affects the form. Information that comes to you from the man next door will be perceived much differently than the same information found in a scientific journal.

Soft, or oral, information gets different consideration from hard, or printed, information. A conversation is more informal, less threatening than the printed page, and it is taken much less seriously. Yet it isn't inherently less accurate or useful. A service station attendant in the Mojave Desert pointing the way to the next hotel can be a more valuable reference tool than an intricate, four-color map of California.

Most people don't pay enough attention to just how their perceptions of information are altered by the manner in which it is delivered. This ignores the influence of technology, the delivery equipment in an information age, in producing and disseminating information and anxiety.

TECHNOMANIA: INFORMATION AS COMMODITY

The search for technological progress is no longer a
means, but has become an
end in itself, escaping from
human control and thus
dominating man, alienating
us from ourselves, our
society, and our environ-
ment.

Vartan Gregorian, President
of Brown University

*T**he information explosion didn't occur solely because of an increase in information. Advances in the technology of transmitting and storing it are as much a factor. We are affected as much by the flow as by the production of information.***

One of the great ironies of the information age is that as the technology of delivering information becomes more sophisticated, the possibility that we can process it all becomes more remote. It is as if we are at one tail end of an assembly line that is cranking out data at an alarming rate, and the machine has no off button.

Just keeping up with the flow of information in the workplace requires more of our attention and our time every year. The average American worked 40.6 hours a week in 1973. In 1985 the figure was 47.3, according to figures compiled in the *Harper's Index.*

The reverberations of this information explosion will dramatically change not only the lives of the individual, but of society at large.

Never has the cost of collecting, processing, and transmitting information been so low. Information equipment—telephones, facsimile machines, televisions, radios, video equipment, computers, and modems—are now well within the grasp of the majority of the American population. Computers have gone from the laboratory to the lap; what used to take up whole rooms in corporations and colleges now fits comfortably into briefcases and knapsacks. And the cost of computer power is now eight thousand times less than it was thirty years ago. If the price of a Cadillac had depreciated at the same rate, that car would cost $2.50 today.

There is now a computer-generated world, a hyper-world, that does not exist in the normal sense, but is challenging our definitions of *real* and *physical.* In this pseudo-world, ideas and products can be designed, developed, and displayed with photographic quality. The results obtained can be as accurate as if the products were actually built and tested, yet they have never *existed* anywhere except within the digital code of the computer. This begins to blur our distinctions between what is and isn't real.

Nathan Shedroff

"What we take for granted would have been a miracle to our grandparents," said Charles L. Brown, the CEO at AT&T addressing the Center for Strategic and International Studies. "The phone system, when coupled with computer technology, permits a person almost anywhere to plug into a world library of information. Those in rural areas now have access to information heretofore available only to those who lived in large cities. Business can operate and service equipment in distant places. Shopping, travel arrangements, banking, and other business transactions can be made by remote control.

"Just around the bend is an information network that would increase the range of perception of a single individual to include all of the information available anywhere in the network's universe," he said.

The developments in the field of information processing enable us to expect more of data, to ask more specific questions, and to demand more complex calculations. According to Jerome H. Friedman, a statistician at Stanford University, until recently the statistical packages we used were not developed for the computer age. The way we collect data, the reasons we collect it, and the things that we want it to communicate are just beginning to reflect the capabilities of the technology. Computers can now collect data automatically through point-of-purchase scanners, credit card transactions, and automated bank machines, to name but a few.

Martha Farnsworth Riche, a senior editor at *American Demographics*, said that "all these changes mean that we can move from analysis of the simple to the complex. But the real benefit of computers may be the analysis of the unknown by using techniques such as interactive computer graphics to explore data for the unexpected. New techniques allow us to take a large set of variables for every U.S. state and integrate them in such a way that they tell us a new story of state-to-state differences or similarities." For the first time the equipment exists to make the essential comparisons that give meaning to statistics.

U.S. businesses spend about $700 billion on communications, a tenth of which is spent on electronic communications . . . and about half the U.S. work force has jobs that are information-related.

Loy Singleton, *Telecommunications in the Information Age*

The dizzying options in office technology can obscure the critical component of information management—which is to serve the needs of the business. "Technology assessment departments" are all well and good, but before any decision is made, managers need to ask themselves: What will make our businesses successful? What are the upfront and the ongoing costs? And—most important—what do my employees need to know to make this technology useful to them in their jobs?

Brenton R. Schlender, "The Electronic Storm," *The Wall Street Journal* (6/12/87)

Computer systems have advanced from "back office" duties to the point where they provide the flow of information needed to make vital business decisions. Many executives, however, do not understand how spending more on information technology can change their business strategy. Nor do they yet know how to separate key information from the routine. Firms need to look at rebuilding existing systems and creating new ones to provide the quality data needed to make timely and responsible decisions.

Peter R. Scanlon, "View from the Front Line of the Information Systems Revolution," *Directors and Boards* (Summer 1987)

The linking of computers and telecommunications has made possible not only the large-scale processing of information, but its virtually instantaneous collection. In business, this has made possible a continuous dialogue between the buyer and the seller, the manufacturer and the dealer, the headquarters and the field offices.

Thousands of Benetton stores around the world are linked by computer. Every time an item is sold, its color is noted. The information collected is analyzed and used to determine the shade and amount of fabric to be dyed each day. This gives Benetton the instant ability to respond to color trends.

THE PROFIT POTENTIAL

Information technology is changing the way corporations compete in the marketplace, and industry leaders will likely be those companies that most productively employ its communication properties. Computer literacy has become *de rigueur* at higher and higher levels of management. Once the province of the enterprising typist, now it has become essential for even the president to have some familarity, if not with the operation of computers, at least with their capabilities. And more and more CEOs are finding themselves sitting in front of computer terminals. Once young management trainees who scoffed at the idea of typing, which they regarded as beneath them, are finding their less disparaging, more dextrous co-workers climbing faster up the corporate ladder because of keyboard proficiency.

According to William G. McGowan, chairman of MCI Communications, "Those already in business should learn to be computer literate . . . Individuals who possess both business and information technology skills could become invaluable to their companies, and highly prized candidates in the job market."

The computer has elevated the stature of equipment and of the equipment operator. Its capabilities have also raised the value of information. "Historically management has looked at information technology (data processing and telecommunications) as just another major expense that had to be monitored and controlled by budget. But now many executives have realized that they can use information not only to manage their company but also as a profit-making tool." McGowan cited the following examples: American Hospital Supply Corporation has set up terminals in client hospitals, allowing customers to send in orders directly; McKesson Drug Company has developed a new market by using information technology to process Medicaid bills for their customers; and the Tandy Corporation uses technology to keep track of daily sales at their stores, giving them instant information on customer response to their products.

Employing existing information technology enables companies to improve marketing efficiency, maintain smaller inventories, thus tying up less money, and comprehensively track resources—cash and otherwise.

At a symposium in Germany, "Global Information Society," West Berlin's senator for economics and labor credited the information industry for the vitality of the city's economy, citing the 35,000 new jobs related to information and communication that have been created in the last four years. Last year information products accounted for more than 22 percent of the city's production and employed 20 percent of the 1.9 million inhabitants.

Tom Wicker, "Information Revolution," *The New York Times* (9/22/87)

INFORMATION AS PRODUCT

As information technology matures, the focus will turn away from the machines themselves toward the information itself. The value of the technology lies only in its ability to manage and exploit the product—information.

According to Robert Waterman, a consultant and co-author of *In Search of Excellence,* successful businesses in the future will be those that can make the best use of information. Effective business strategies will be plotted by those who see information where others see data and who can react quickly to surprises, i.e. new information. This depends not so much on careful planning as on informed opportunism, with equal emphasis on both words. "It is my observation that the big strategic moves companies make are things that they never could have predicted or planned for, they just happen," said Waterman. "You have got to be both informed and opportunistic. If you are only opportunistic, you make dumb deals. If you only concentrate on information, you are not flexible. You study things to death. The question is what do you do about strategy if you assume (a) it is important to have some sense of direction and (b) the future is not predictable. My answer is you get very knowledgeable information about your business and your competitive environment. Information is the differential."

At present, efforts within the American business community both to gather and especially to disseminate information are often inefficient and misguided. Within a company, the dissemination of information is often handled by several different departments that operate independently of each other, often with little communication between them.

Traditionally the personnel department publishes house organs that chronicle the news of the staff. Company brochures and promotional material are handled by public relations, usually with a separate department or agency coordinating paid advertising. Then a department along the lines of corporate communications takes care of information that is sent to investors—potential and actual.

Even many midsize companies are structured in such a manner that information is disseminated by many different people, with different missions. Efforts are often redundant or even contradictory. Information dollars aren't always allocated commensurate with potential value.

Unsurprisingly, corporate communications departments often get the most generous budgets. Here the lavish, four-color annual reports are produced. The reports are sent to the brokerage houses, who employ people just to tear out the financial pages and throw out the rest. The only people who pay much attention to the annual reports are the proud spouses of the board of directors. Yet billions of dollars are spent in producing them every year.

In accordance with the initial computer architecture developed in the 1940s, nearly all computers until recently have been serial in that they did one thing at a time, however rapidly. Now, parallel-processing, where computers work on many aspects of a problem simultaneously, is evolving that will revolutionize computer capabilities. Not only will this potentially increase speed, but the process is more in line with how animals compute.

Compact-disc technology has advanced beyond the read-only stage to the point where users can interact with them to access and manipulate data as diverse as business statistics, first aid, educational curricula, and classical music. Through the compact discs, users will gain audio, graphic, and visual contact with information.

Bryan Brewer, president of Earth View Inc., a Seattle-based CD-ROM production company, writing in *CD-ROM Review*.

The increasing demands of information processing will cause companies to reassess how they dole out information dollars. To avoid the waste of duplication, companies will need more communications between departments involved in producing information—if not the merging of different divisions under the banner of information dissemination.

All these different departments labor under the common mission of communicating information about a company to a constituency, whether to secretaries or stockbrokers. By pooling efforts—one mission, one budget—companies can avoid fragmented information efforts, save time and money by encouraging cooperation between departments, and permit more informed decision making by allowing employees easier access to various information sources. By structuring an information program as one entity, employees will recognize the commonality of their endeavors and have a greater sense of how their efforts figure into the company as a whole.

The second wave of the information age is characterized by the general decentralization of computer intelligence and the networking of this intelligence, and is driven by the union of rapid technological progress and increasingly complex commercial and government demands. Information technology and networking have together become a strategic business weapon.

Ian M. Ross, "The Second Wave of the Information Age," *Chief Executive Magazine* (Summer 1987)

TAXING INFORMATION

The turning of more and more companies toward information as a profitable "product" will also have a monumental effect on the world economy. The ownership of information will be a key issue in the business community and will demand a rewriting of the principles of economics. The principles of economics were founded on principles of tangible goods. While a product is easy to trace and tax, to assign ownership, to store, to sell, to control information is not.

The balance of goods have heretofore been maintained on import and export tariffs under which the transportation and expediting industry have flourished. Information can be "shipped" at the touch of a button, beyond the control of customs departments, tax assessors, and even the original "owners" of the information themselves.

Never in history has distance meant less. Never has man's relationship with place been more numerous, fragile, and temporary . . . In 1914, according to Buckminster Fuller, the typical American averaged about 1,640 miles per year of total travel, counting some 1,300 miles of just plain everyday walking to and fro . . . Today, by contrast, the average American car owner drives 10,000 miles per year—and he lives longer than his father or grandfather. "At 69 years of age," wrote Fuller a few years ago, ". . . I am one of a class of several million human beings who, in their lifetimes, have each covered 3,000,000 miles or more."

Alvin Toffler, *Future Shock*

The traditional laws of copyright cannot begin to protect the ownership of information in a society where *Xerox* is listed in some dictionaries as a verb and information can be transmitted simultaneously around the world. You can no more track information than you can the path of an atom.

The omnipresence of information has created global anxieties on the part of both business communities and governments around the world. How will ownership be assigned and valued? How will tariffs be assessed? How will the potential for instantaneous transfer of products affect the world economy and international politics? How will it affect the dissemination of misinformation?

"With the accumulation of data and the relative ease of access to innumerable data bases, the confusion of information, often with dire consequences, has arisen," said Bob Davis in an article, "Abusive Computers," in *The Wall Street Journal* on August 20, 1987. "Ordinary citizens are identified as criminals; people are wrongly accused of bad credit; and medical records are mismatched. And consequently, mistakes are harder to correct, adding to the proliferation of misinformation."

In countries where political power depends on controlling information, governments are finding themselves unequal to the task. Control of information is directly at odds with technological modernization, an expressed aim of many of the same countries trying to limit access to information. According to an article, "Moscow Faces the New Age," in *Newsweek* (8/18/86):

"Suddenly, ideas are being shared in ways that commissars can't control, and people who want to beat the system are finding new tools.

. . . The Soviet system is secretive and highly centralized, and most of its citizens know little more than what their rulers want them to know—which is that they are surrounded by enemies and live in a superior society. Now, however, Mikhail Gorbachev and his colleagues face an agonizing dilemma: they want to modernize their economies, but they cannot hope to do so unless they adopt new technologies that could break their monopoly on information—and loosen their grip on political power. Gorbachev has said that he wants to be the "catalyst" of economic development, but it remains to be seen whether any Soviet leader can permit the free flow of information that computers need to work most effectively."

Computers and technology bring about the free flow of information. The instantaneous transmission of it via modems, satellites, fiber optics, etc. causes the boundaries to blur between countries. The pooling and exchanging of information will tend to homogenize different cultures. Where all countries have access to the same information, distinctions between cultures will diminish.

Those who understand the power and profitability potential of information will rule the business kingdom in the coming years, as more and more companies go into fields where the product is information. General Information is an example of such a company, which was founded by someone who understood the value of owning information a few years before the rest of us.

The information age has spawned its own executive, the Chief Information Officer. More than a glorified systems manager, the CIO is responsible for managing how information is distributed in an organization. The position usually reports to the president or CEO and carries the clout not only of technical expertise but often of sales, marketing, and administration experience.

Gordon Bok, Kimberly Carpenter, and Jo Ellen Davis, "Management's Newest Star," *Newsweek* **(10/13/86)**

CONVERSATION WITH DICK BRASS

When Dick Brass and I get together, we both talk at the same time, but invariably at some point, I realize that he is winning, or at least is talking louder and faster, so I listen. Brass is the president of General Information, Inc., a company in Kirkland, Washington, that publishes *The National Directory*—150,000 of the most important business listings in the country. Brass, who used to be the food editor for *Playboy* magazine, was also one of the first to realize the power of owning information through his acquisition of the electronic rights of several reference books. We had the following conversation in a car on the way to the Seattle airport.

Computer technology has created a global marketplace and will eliminate many layers of management.

Walter Wriston, the former CEO of Citicorp, "The Information Explosion and the Global Marketplace," *Computerworld* **(11/3/86)**

DB: I was a journalist and, like all journalists, I was using a reference book. One day I discovered someone had developed an electronic reference book of sorts, a spelling checker for microcomputers, back in 1981. There had been spelling checkers on larger machines, but they were usually used by programmers to look for bugs in their programs.

The idea that you could take a dictionary and automate it was relatively new. In 1981 a program called Spell Guard® came out which I began using on my personal computer as soon as I heard about it. I am a very poor speller, probably in retrospect owing to the fact that back in grade school one of the kids in my class died during a spelling test. The kid just keeled over and died. It was very traumatic for all of us. The kid had suffered a concussion; he banged his head on a bicycle earlier that day, and he just came to class and sat down at the spelling test. I believe he was spelling the word "autumn" as he rolled right over; it was awful.

RSW: It was his autumn.

DB: It sure was. The Spell Guard® program compared all the words you had written quickly in your document against an electronic dictionary, if you will, of about 14,000 words. The program part was terrific, but the dictionary had been put together by the programmer's wife from other dictionaries and a lot of the words were misspelled.

I went to Random House, and I said, "Do you have 50,000 words on magnetic media?" And they said, "What is magnetic media?" I said, "Do you have 50,000 words on tape that I could borrow or buy?"

Well, it turned out that they did not have magnetic media with words on it that I could use to teach my spelling checker how to spell and improve its dictionary. Although I had suspected that the electronic rights to the famous reference books of the world had long ago been spoken for, I discovered to my amazement that they hadn't. *The Random House Dictionary, Roget's Thesau-*

The success of a small firm's strategic plan is often contingent on the information used to create the plan. A firm that can scan and react to trends in its external environment is most likely to succeed. The information itself is often personal, or experience-based, rather than institutional, and this, too, appears to be significant in a changing, fluid business environment.

Pamela Hammers Specht, "Information Sources Used for Strategic Plannning Decisions in Small Firms," *American Journal of Small Business* (Spring 1987)

rus, and many other famous reference books were in play, if you will, and the publishers had no idea what the rights to their data were worth. They thought it was like movie rights. "You want the movie rights to *The Random House Dictionary*," they said to me, incredulous. They were dubious that there was any value to it. They warned me of it, but, if I was willing to pay them good money for the electronic rights, they wished me well.

RSW: What did you end up paying for it?

DB: *The Random House Dictionary* cost $10,000 down plus a minimum annual royalty that gradually accelerated up to $30,000 or $40,000 or the greater of that or the royalties on ten percent of the gross. In essence, I got *The Random House Dictionary* on consignment in perpetuity. I also picked up the electronic rights to *The Random House Thesaurus, Roget's International Thesaurus,* The Rodale *Word Finder,* the Rodale *Synonym Finder, The Chicago Manual of Style, Black's Law Dictionary, Stedman's Medical Dictionary, The Gazetteer, The Rand-McNally Atlas, The McGraw-Hill Dictionary of Scientific and Medical Terms*, certain Oxford Dictionaries in England, Douton in Germany, Robert in France, Van Dalla in Holland, and a lot of other reference books as well.

I had to develop electronic products in order to make use of my rights. We built the first spelling checkers with really good dictionaries and pretty well dominated the market in the early eighties. We invented the *Electronic Thesaurus*, which turned out to be a huge hit with well over a million copies of different kinds in use. In fact, it is very hard to find a decent word processor that doesn't come with an electronic synonym finder built in. We made grammar checkers and file checkers; we sold our products to Wang, Micropro, Microsoft, and Apple.

In 1983 Wang liked our product so much they bought our whole company, and I went to work there for a couple of years running Wang's electronic publishing division.

FLOPPY DISKS WITH BLUE-PENCIL POTENTIAL

Software now exists that can read through documents for split infinitives, passive voice, archaic or foreign words, improper punctuation, doubled words, clichés, hackneyed words, etc. The programs can then rate the document for reading levels and interest potential.

Information doesn't really change, in the sense that it is always valuable. Certain information is at different times more valuable than others, and the information itself changes but, as an abstract concept, information is always valuable—always has been and always will be.

Media change and sometimes a medium becomes very much less valuable and sometimes it disappears altogether. No one writes in cuneiform on clay anymore. It is a cinch that all of those reference books that we have been using next to our desks or on top of our desks or next to our computers are going to be electronified or computerized, and they will go right inside the computers themselves.

It will only happen in areas where some of the aspects of the book are not essential. For example, nearly everyone is very excited about computer maps. I am not. The finest monitor in the world costing thousands of dollars has only 25 percent of the potential display resolution of a reasonably printed paper map. Until the resolution is comparable to what can be done on paper, and as long as detail is one of the main important aspects of mapping, paper is going to remain an important medium for maps. Phone books are another matter, though. Phone books are not very finely printed to begin with and for the most part they are just text—which computers do very, very well. They are heavy, they are extremely expensive to distribute, and by putting them into the computer you gain all kinds of features like automation.

The basic idea is that when media change and data doesn't, it is possible to move in and buy the data for use in the new media at a tiny fraction of the cost of gaining control of the data for the existing media. It is not unlike the guy in Pennsylvania in the middle of the nineteenth century who went around buying rights to drill oil 1,000 feet deeper than any drill could reach. The price of the oil was very low, but the drill eventually got there, and when it did, his oil was just as valuable as anyone else's, more in some ways.

RSW: You mean the price of the rights was very low.

PC HOT LINE

Last year, [a computer software company] released a software program that can turn a personal computer into a national phone directory that will not only call up the names and addresses of 10,000 major businesses and organizations, and government agencies, but will dial the phone too. The program also permits the user to add numbers and code in frequently used numbers that will be automatically dialed at the touch of two keys.

Peter H. Lewis, "Phone Book for the PC," *The New York Times* (4/12/88)

DB: Right, the price of the rights was low; going for the oil was expensive. The same thing is true of data. Random House, in my case, would never have sold me *The Random House Dictionary*, certainly not for a price I would be willing to pay. But for $10,000 cash down, I was able to secure the rights to *The Random House Dictionary* in perpetuity. For all practical purposes, I had as much right to the data as Random House did. In the end, of course, it was a very successful venture and very successful for Random House; they ultimately made perhaps a million dollars in royalties.

The key for people who are making software products and reference books is to create reference books that don't require training. The information is immediately understandable.

Electronic media have a great deal of potential in eclipsing written media in a variety of ways. For one thing, they are obviously a lot more capacious. You can, on certain optical media like CD-ROM, have hundreds of volumes on a single accessible system. It can be sorted in different fields so that in an almanac, let's say, you can view a table of the worst earthquakes in chronological order and then push a button and view them instead in the order of the number of people who were killed, or alphabetically by the location of the earthquake, or by the Richter magnitude of the quake itself.

In a computer you don't need to have it sorted in different ways; by its nature, it can instantly be viewed in different ways.

When the media change and the data stays the same, the people who get into your new media are the newest group of millionaires. And the same thing is going to happen with reference books and newspapers. The media are going to change; they are changing now.

RSW: As the media change, how will this affect the issue of understandability? As data is transferred from one medium to another, should the presentation of it be altered?

Computer networks have grown so sophisticated as to stretch our conceptions of space and time. Getting credit approval to use your American Express card in Paris involves a 46,000-mile journey over phones and computers and can be completed in five seconds.

 Peter Large, *The Micro Revolution Revisited*

ENIAC, commonly thought to be the first modern computer, was built in 1944. It occupied 3,000 cubic feet of space, weighed 30 tons, and consumed 140 kilowatts of electricity. Today's microprocessor, the silicon chip, occupies 0.011 cubic feet of space, weighs approximately 1.5 grams, and uses less than 2.5 watts of electricity.

 Peter Large, *The Micro Revolution Revisited*

It's easy to understand the use of information when we have an end product in mind. But can we live only on sheer information, which flows readily and instantly around the world, and let the Japanese make the cars, the Hong Kong Chinese the textiles, and the Singapore Chinese the semiconductors? You can export all the manufacturing jobs and you can't eat the numbers.

Adam Smith, "And Now the Real News," *Esquire* (9/82)

DB: The computer data has to be presented in a manner that makes it more useful than it is in a book. If it is merely an on-screen presentation of the book, it is not enough.

When we did the *Electronic Thesaurus*, for example, we decided that to keep the data meaningful and to keep people from getting overly confused with what was popping up on the screen, we would follow the metaphor of the book itself. You would put your cursor on a synonym and hit a hot key. The key automatically pops up a window in which there are synonyms of the word highlighted. Put your cursor on a synonym in the box, hit a hot key, and the synonym replaces your word in the text. That is all there is to it.

This basic idea has been used by almost every manufacturer of an electronic thesaurus. In the beginning, the idea in terms of electronic presentation of data is to imitate existing data-presentation designs so that people won't become too confused. Reference books are among the easiest information [sources] to understand because people have been brought up with them for years, and they know how to use the data because they have been laboriously trained to do it in school. We know how to use a dictionary not because it is the easiest thing in the world to use or because the dictionary definitions are easy for nonexperts to read and understand quickly, but because we were taught how to use and navigate that kind of data system as kids in school.

The problem is that outside of school we don't have any particular training in how to access or utilize data. We know how to use the encyclopedia, we know how to use the telephone book, and none of these are really very easy things to use, to be honest. I would say the first three years of grade school are spent learning to read, and the second three years are spent learning how to read reference books.

In terms of assimilating information more generally—current events, stock prices, scientific developments, things that might indeed be very important—we have no training in that sort of thing at all. As a result most of us have no idea what is going on in the world at all. In a way, I think it contributes to our political freedom.

I think the reason why you can say anything in the United States is because there is so much noise, so much informational cacophony that no one is going to hear you, and the political leaders and businessmen know this. The key for making information understandable is to get it through the noise level.

INFORMATIONAL CACOPHONY

Getting through the noise level is not going to get any easier as both the amounts of available information and the media for delivering it expand.

Take advertising, for example. Nowhere is the problem of getting public attention more apparent than in advertising. Advertising agencies have declared war on our senses with a barrage of ads that demand to be looked at, heard, sniffed, and touched. Anyone who has tried to read a women's magazine nowadays knows what it's like to be fumigated with heavy-duty perfume ads that emit their conflicting scents long after you have forgotten what the articles were about.

Nasal warfare is only one attack. An article in *Business Week* (11/23/87) by Amy Dunkin, "Print Ads That Make You Stop, Look—and Listen," said that more advertisers are now using 3-D pop-up ads, musical microchips that play songs, and actual samples of products. But like the problem of too much noise, these ads lose their power to attract attention as more and more advertisers resort to special effects.

A dazzling array of information equipment is available to us at present, and we are on the verge of a new generation of technology. We are overwhelmed with special features. In much the same way that more information has

Everyone knows the frustration of buying a high-technology product and then not being able to make it work. Why? Because instruction manuals seem to be at the rock-bottom level of concern for product and marketing managers.

Help may be on the way with video instructions, if you can figure out how to work your VCR. Also, organizations such as the Communications and Design Center at Carnegie-Mellon University offer advanced degrees in functional writing.

Michael Schrage, "Struggling to Understand Manual-ese," *The Washington Post* (12/26/86)

become erroneously synonymous with more knowledge, more sophisticated technology is equated with an improved quality of life. However, the competition has become so intense in the field and the marketing of machines so creative that they are being sold on the basis of features that we lack the sense or senses to appreciate.

According to an article by Paul B. Carroll in *The Wall Street Journal* on April 27, 1988, Leonard Goldberg, president and chief operating officer of 20th Century Fox Film Corporation, does not know how to operate the various videocassette and stereo equipment that occupy his office. "It's my job security," says his assistant. "I actually know how to use the stuff."

Manufacturers of consumer goods, from cars to VCRs, continue to load their products with new electronic features, assuring us that "more is better." But even the most technically adept consumers frequently find themselves staring blankly at the sophisticated devices with which they have equipped their homes, offices, and automobiles in the name of convenience.

The article, "High-Tech Gear Draws Cries of 'Uncle': Electronic Goods Are Loaded with Extras Few Can Understand," cited BMW of North America, Inc., which "provides a 40-minute tape on how to use all of the electronics available on its top-of-the-line 735i-model cars. Instructions for locking and unlocking the car doors take three minutes of the tape."

Even the wizards get stumped by machinery. "When a dozen of the personal-computer industry's leading techno-nerds went bowling at a conference in February, none of them—not even Bill Joy, the technical wizard at Sun Microsystems, Inc., or Steve Ballmer, the Microsoft Corp. executive responsible for its complex operating-system software—could figure out how to use the automatic scoring system. The woman who ran the lanes had to show them how to program it," claimed the article.

Although we are led to believe that each new feature was designed only to make our lives easier, often they were designed to give the marketing department something to talk about.

This is a high-input society. It seems that not a minute may be wasted in consuming commodities and communicating with as many people as possible. But in a Babel of signals, we must listen to a great deal of chatter to hear one bit of information we really want.

Without significance, variety isn't the spice of life. It can be as dull as monotony when it has nothing to say . . . This is because to recognize a thing as new, one must be able to distinguish it from what is old . . . we can be surprised repeatedly only by contrast with that which is familiar . . . not by chaos.

Orrin Klapp, *Overload and Boredom: Essays on the Quality of Life in the Information Society*

MORE IS MORE EXPENSIVE

One has only to look at the front panel of some automobiles to see evidence of marketing gone wild. They are starting to rival DC-10s for instrument gauges and information provided. We have come to expect a level of comfort and control in our cars that would seem preposterous in our houses. You can set the temperature to a tenth of a degree, tilt your seat to infinite positions, calculate how much gas you would need to get to Amarillo, Texas, if you drove thirty, forty, or fifty miles an hour, and literally bombard yourself with information from readings on machinery you have probably never heard of before for the entire trip. But you will still have to stop for gasoline.

I would say any sound system that costs more than $2,000 is probably better than most people's ears. In other words, people often pay for mechanical and electronic nuances that their auditory systems lack the ability to distinguish. If you order $100 champagne, do you know or taste the difference from a $50 bottle? What is relative to our ability to use and judge?

I can't taste the difference. Similarly, I wouldn't be able to discriminate between the twenty-five best violinists in the world. The twenty-fifth would probably sound as flawless to me as the first. Some people could tell the difference, however. The importance is your own ability to distinguish; what are the variations that matter to you?

What you have to measure with technology as well as with information is your ability to use and measure it. What is accuracy? What is enough? How great is the need to know? Does it matter to me if they tell me that my flight time on the airplane is 4 hours 21 minutes and 13 seconds and 4 milliseconds or that we will be flying at an altitude of 31,331 feet?

What degree of accuracy do you need; what do you want to hear in terms of sound; what can you taste? Some people have trained themselves to be able to taste the dif-

The number of components that can be contained on a computer chip is doubling every eighteen months, according to a report of the Aspen Institute for Humanistic Studies.

The breakdown of human performance under heavy information loads may be related to psychopathology in ways we have not yet begun to explore. Yet, even without understanding its potential impact, we are accelerating the generalized rate of change in society. We are forcing people to adapt to a new life pace, to confront novel situations and master them in ever shorter intervals.

Alvin Toffler, *Future Shock*

ference between champagnes. There are certain areas in which my eye can see things and they really matter to me. And for those things I want that quality around me where my opinion and my ability to judge is finely tuned. But not in areas beyond my power to perceive.

Before the acquisition of any new equipment, you should recognize your own ability to utilize it. The equipment of our lives suggests questions that can be asked to make more intelligent decisions, questions that will help us answer what is the purpose.

- Is it necessary for my work, my life?
- How much of it will I be able to operate and enjoy?
- Of what possible benefit might this equipment be?
- How will it change the nature of information that is sent or received?

INFORMATION VULNERABILITY QUOTIENT

The ultra-sophistication and proliferation of the information delivery equipment has contributed to a strange phenomenon that is at the heart of *information anxiety:* we have lost the ability to control the flow of information. We used to have to make a conscious decision to go looking for information, to take action to find it. Now, the equipment of the information age permits the transmission of information without the desire, or even the permission of, the receiver. We are increasingly vulnerable to the invasion of information; it intrudes in our lives, often uninvited, at inopportune times.

The speed with which it is possible to collect information makes most endeavors out of date before they have even been completed. There is nothing more discouraging than working up a set of financial projections only to find that the figures upon which your projections were based have been "updated." This engenders a natural, but counterproductive defensive response, a feeling of being constantly vulnerable to the intrusion of information that will prevent you from ever finishing your job.

Look at the three means of information transmission that have become a staple of information exchange in the business community and increasingly in our personal lives: the telephone, the facsimile or fax machine, and various express mail services. By their nature, they take away our power of refusal. They keep us open twenty-four hours a day to new information.

The convenience of these three instruments of communication has guaranteed their widespread acceptance, but it has been at the expense of understanding how they change the information that is presented to us, without understanding what each form means to the nature of the information.

Phone conversations are inferior to talking to someone face-to-face. We are deprived of the nonverbal signals that add to the richness of communication—the eye contact, facial expressions, hand gestures, and body language.

But the speed, convenience, and low cost of it have made it the dominant form of communication in business and, increasingly, in our personal lives. I know many New Yorkers who conduct their whole social lives on the telephone and regard as friends people whom they haven't seen in years. Certainly businesses abound entirely dependent on telephones.

The fax machine is a further extension of the phone, and the recent drop in cost will ensure its greater proliferation in the future, as will the inevitable improvement in the reproduction quality. The fax does have its limitations. Unlike express mail, the range of delivery is limited to those who happen to own fax machines; documents often arrive blurred and illegible; and they are cumbersome for transmitting lengthy documents.

Research laboratories— once in the ivy towers of universities—are now influencing daily life, evidenced by a flurry of science-intensive patents. "The time between the creation of new knowledge and its incorporation into new products and processes is shortening very rapidly. To a certain extent, science is becoming technology," said John Irvine, a science policy analyst at the University of Sussex in England.

William Broad, "Science and Technology: The Gap is Shrinking Fast," *The New York Times* **(4/5/88)**

Looming on the horizon is the inevitable exploitation of their junk-mail potential. The machines now have the capability to transmit the same piece of paper simultaneously to several thousand numbers. It's only a matter of time before advertisers make use of this and turn the fax machine into another conduit for advertising. And unlike the postal delivery, the machine can only produce one piece of paper at a time, which means machines could theoretically be tied up for hours spitting out advertisements for office supplies and insurance programs—on paper paid for by the consumer/receiver.

While express mail permits the transmittal of the actual material, the cost of such service discourages the comprehensive exchange of information, and it induces a high level of anxiety because we must adhere to the strictures of the express mail companies—meeting their deadlines, package and weight requirements, drop-off times, etc. It adds the element of high drama to the exchange of information.

How many times have you said: It's hard to imagine life before the phone, Xerox, Federal Express, the fax machine? Yet how often do you consider just how each of these changes the shape of information?

THE REBOUND EFFECT

The channels by which we get information affect not only the form of the information, but our perception of its importance. Each channel carries its own sense of urgency. Packages that come by regular mail seem less pressing than those that come via express mail. Phone calls and fax messages seem more urgent than the mail. If I receive a letter in the mail, I will assume that my immediate attention isn't required. I automatically feel a sense of exigency about fax machines that I don't feel about the U.S. Postal Service.

We tend to respond in kind to the way information is sent. Yet the manner in which it is delivered is often determined more by the technology available than by the nature of the information being sent. We then let our response mirror the delivery instead of the merit of the information. I receive material all the time by Federal Express that hardly warrants my attention, immediate or otherwise. Yet I can't help feeling its urgency, not because of the subject matter, but because of the way it was sent.

We endow the information with an element of unnecessary panic. In our enthusiasm to exercise new machinery, we create unnecessary anxiety; the new toy syndrome operates with telecommunications equipment as much as with Tinkertoys.

And as with any new toy, once the thrill of its newness has worn off, our attitude toward it changes. Evidence of this can already be found in our usage of information technology. Where once we were excited by the prospect of new information and welcomed those devices, such as the telegraph, the telephone, and the radio, that brought us closer to the world, now we have begun to use technology to screen out communications. Many people now use answering machines, ostensibly marketed so people wouldn't miss calls when they were not at home, to screen their calls, waiting until callers identify themselves before picking up the phone. Phone services are now available in certain areas that identify the caller's number. Some phones can be programmed to respond with a preprogrammed message to calls from selected numbers. (Although this won't prevent unwelcome relatives from reaching you from pay phones.)

As with the maturing of any technology, we have begun to regard it in a different light. Whereas we once embraced wholeheartedly the ability to get in touch with more people in the fastest possible mode, we are now beginning to question the possible implications of that ability.

"Technological visionaries can never recognize the distinction between the feasible and the desirable. If a machine can be made to perform some dazzlingly complicated task, then the visionary assumes that the task is worth performing," wrote Edward Mendelson in a review of Michael Heim's *Electric Language: A Philosophical Study of Word Processing* in *the New Republic* (2/22/88).

"The computer has been endowed with features that diminish the quality of writing, causing writers to focus on lines and sentences and lose sight of their work as a whole. On paper you can glance at many pages at once. On a computer screen, you are confined to a matter of lines. The top and bottom of a sheet of paper are its unmistakable beginning and end, and you always know where you are. But when you work at a screen, you might as well be anywhere. You write on an imaginary surface with no beginning and no end."

Without technology, *information anxiety* would exist only on a minuscule level. It is the storage and transmission technology that has brought about the dramatic increase in information and permitted its instantaneous global dissemination. Efforts in these areas surpassed the support services, institutional policies, programs, and systems that would enable us to handle enormous quantities of information through understanding.

While in the early stages of information, the attention was on the technology of delivery, the focus is now shifting toward the "soft" support services. More sophisticated usage of information lies in data bases, personal newspapers, professional readers who sort through material for their employers, specialized news sources, digests and summaries, computer programs that speed the sorting and locating of information, such as HyperCard™ from Apple Computers, Inc., and businesses devoted to the understanding of information. As rules are rewritten to recognize information as a product, and as services evolve that make information perform, we will begin to exploit the full potential of a technology that provides us with access to an infinite pool of information.

15

PRESCRIPTION FOR ANXIETY

It is only when we forget all
our learning that we begin
to know.

Henry David Thoreau

*M*ost people regard information processing as a
specific job undertaken
by people who wear glasses on
chains and sit in vast open offices tinged with the greenish
cast of hanging fluorescent light
fixtures, caught in the glow of
the cathode ray as they stare
into computer screens.

In other words, information processing is something done by someone else, someone who can type.

In an information age, we must all come to regard ourselves as information processors. Every time we listen to a news report, talk to a coworker, read a magazine, look out over a crowd of faces at a convention, we are perceiving and processing information.

Once we have accepted this, then we can set about improving our skills as processors of information at all levels in our lives. This will demand:

● Changing our perceptions and attitudes and coming to a greater understanding of the society in which we live (*cultural information*)

● Improving our communication skills (*conversational information*)

● Learning how to find what we need from existing information and improve the quality of information that we generate (*reference information*)

● Getting more out of the media (*news information*)

FEWER, FEWER, FEWER

The secret to processing information is narrowing your field of information to that which is relevant to your life, i.e. making careful choices about what kind of information merits your time and attention. Decision making becomes more critical as the amount of information increases. Many approach decisions with apprehension because they involve eliminating possibilities.

I believe it is a myth that the more choices you have, the more appropriate actions you can take and the more freedom you will enjoy. Rather, more choices seem to produce more anxiety. If you can determine what is relevant to your interests and work, your choices will be fewer and easier to make. As you decrease the choices, you decrease the anxiety of having made a wrong choice.

Anyone who has ever panicked over the ten-page menus popular in Chinese restaurants will understand perfectly. Once you have decided that you would rather have chicken than beef or seafood, you are still faced with a host of decisions. Do you want it with vegetables or nuts? Okay, you decide to go for the nuts. Then you still have to decide whether you want walnuts, cashews, or peanuts. Then, you *still* have to decide whether you want a spicy or bland dish.

I have a theory that this is why Chinese food is always shared among the diners. To somewhat reduce the anxiety of having to make a decision from so many choices, diners have access to everyone else's selection, to make a poor choice less distasteful.

PAINLESS DECISIONS

Having to make a selection from too many choices isn't the only anxiety factor in decision making. Decisions have traditionally been viewed as the steps that lead to taking action. Thus wrong decisions are equated with wrong actions and are approached with trepidation. This doesn't have to be the case. Several sociologists working in the field of decision making have proposed that making a decision leads only to making more decisions. For example, I could decide to move. Then I would have to decide where to go. Do I move to another city? Do I move to the country? To a house or an apartment? How many bedrooms do I need? One decisions leads to countless others.

Instead of leading you closer to action, decisions can function as a stall tactic. Often, decisions serve little purpose other than to delay taking action, for often the decisions made before an action bear little relationship to the prior decisions. Let's say I decided that I wanted to move to Princeton into a newer home in mint condition. But I might actually buy an old saltbox home in Bridge-hampton because I happen to come across it at the right time in the right mood.

Accepting that decisions don't have to rationally lead up to or explain actions won't absolve you from having to make them, but it can further reduce the anxiety of having to make them.

Potentially infinite information coupled with finite capabilities will demand some decision making or sorting. Thus anything you can do to simplify and limit this process will make you less anxious.

SO MUCH INFORMATION, SO LITTLE TIME

This chapter outlines my own prescriptions for reducing anxiety, for making less painful and more sensible decisions about the information in your life, for developing practical defenses against the increasing onslaught of raw data. It includes the tactics I employ when the piles on my desk start to topple, my appointment schedule short-circuits, and my life seems ever more complex. My battle plan for conquering information and information anxiety is directed toward improving your attitude toward the subject, as well as the actual approach you take to information processing.

ROBUST ATTITUDES

● Accept that there is much that you won't understand. Let what you don't know spark your curiosity. Visualize the words "I don't know" as a bucket that can now be filled with the water of knowledge.

● As you learn about something, try to remember what it is like not to know. This will add immeasurably to your ability to explain things to other people.

● Reduce guilt feelings over the unread by recognizing that the quantity of information is such that you can't read everything.

● Every time you come across a new idea, try to relate it to something else. Find a connection from the new idea to other ideas.

● Think about opposites. When you have a problem, think of one solution, then of its opposite. When you choose a direction, think about what would happen if you went in an opposite direction.

ROBUST ACTIONS

● Become familiar with the traps and pitfalls of communicating information (addressed in Chapter 5). Determine whether you are a victim of:

The disease of familiarity

Thinking that looking good is being good

The uh-huh syndrome

Unhealthy comparisons

Discovery, whether by a schoolboy doing it on his own or by a scientist cultivating the growing edge of his field, is in its essence a matter of rearranging or transforming evidence in such a way that one is enabled to go beyond the evidence so reassembled to new insights.

Jerome Bruner, *On Knowing: Essays for the Left Hand*

IF SHAKESPEARE CAN, SO CAN YOU

"The fact that you can walk and talk means you can do 99 percent of what people such as Beethoven and Shakespeare did. If you can see something and describe it in a sentence, you're using 20 billion brain cells in a complicated way," said Marvin Minsky, Ph.D., author of *Society of Mind*. In an interview in *The Bottom Line/Personal* magazine, Minsky insisted that everyone is creative, but that some people don't let new ideas surface. If you want to be creative, you have to to able to suppress your internal critics for at least one minute.

Assuming that if something is accurate, it's informative
Unnecessary exactitude
Rainbow worship or adjectivitis
Chinese-dinner memory dysfunction
User-friendly intimidation
Some-assembly-required gambit
The expert-opinion syndrome
Don't tell me how it ends
Failing to recognize information imposters
Administrativitis
Edifitis

● Establish your own level of appropriateness when it comes to accuracy. Just because the information exists to take accuracy to the nth degree doesn't mean you have to use it. For example, when someone asks you the time, instead of faithfully recounting to the minute the time on your digital watch, try saying, "It's almost noon." The exact times are necessary for Olympic trials and air-traffic controllers.

● Make a list of the terms you use but don't really understand, e.g. the Dow-Jones Industrials or the M1, M2, M3, and make a point to learn what they mean—one at a time.

● Plan your information diet as you would plan a vacation. Outline a system for categorizing the information needs in your life based on your answers to the following questions:

What do you need for your job?
How much is essential?
How much is desirable?

What subjects pique your interest?
What do you like to talk about?
What do you spend time with that isn't really necessary?
How would the elimination of it change your life?

After you have established categories, develop a picture of your informational habits, i.e. the newspapers you read, the programs you watch, the books you consult, etc. How do they fit into the larger categories and subgroupings?

● Determine your preferred method of learning. Some people learn best by reading a book, taking a course, experimenting themselves, or asking someone else. Then, when you need to get information on a subject, try to find a way that will involve your preferred form. Personally, I learn more from talking to one other person.

● Isolate the informational areas in your life that give you the most anxiety. They could be:

Medical (talking to doctors)
Financial (banking, mortgages, insurance forms, loan applications)
Electronic (buying equipment and operating it)
Reference materials (reading train schedules or statistical abstracts)

FOREARM PLAY INCREASES MEMORY

A university study found that when students asked for information in a library, they were able to retain the information longer when the librarians made physical contact with them by lightly touching their arms while answering the student's questions.

● Just by the act of making a list, you will probably feel less anxious. You have a place to start reducing your anxiety. Rate the items from one to ten. Postulate what would have to happen to reduce your anxiety in each area. Would you have to take a course, study for two years, or could you call someone on the phone? Then you might decide what is worth conquering and what isn't. You might decide you would rather pay an accountant to figure out your taxes than overcome your form phobia. Once you admit that you can't know everything, you will be much more comfortable with the idea of not knowing something.

● Reduce your guilt pile of reading materials that seem to gaze disapprovingly at you from their high perch on your desk while they wait interminably to be read. I use the shard approach. First I let the stack of periodicals (piled on the floor next to my desk) get to a designated height (about two feet). Then I leaf through them and rip out any articles that interest me. This reduces my guilt pile to a small stack of articles that become my interest "shards."

COMMUNICATION SKILLS

● Try to explain something, like an article in *Time* or *Newsweek*, to your mother. Then try to explain it to a twelve-year-old. Each will teach you about how much you actually understood.

● Apply the same attention to listening that you do to talking.

● In appropriate situations, lightly touching someone's arm as you speak will improve the attention you get from the listener. Use this tactic with caution.

● Never nod your head at something you don't understand. Practice saying "Could you clarify that?" or "I'm not sure I understand what you are talking about" in front of your mirror. This can be a disarming tactic. It speaks of a childlike innocence.

● Ask a lot of questions that can't be answered yes or no.

● When you are talking to someone, imagine their environment, their home or office. Putting them into some physical context will help you remember what they are saying. If you have the chance, try to meet the people with whom you communicate professionally. Hold meetings in their offices instead of restaurants. Knowing from where they speak can be much more relaxing than listening to a disembodied voice over a telephone. Once you have the picture of their home or office, you can call it up when you must talk over the phone.

Meetings

Meetings are a peculiar form of communication that seem to continually inhibit the very things they seek to accomplish and bring out people's worst personality traits. I've seen more good ideas squashed, egos ruffled, danders raised, and time killed in meetings. Yet we spend such a sizable chunk of our lives in them that we ought to learn how to make them more productive.

Looking at the business community, let's say the average person spends 40 years working—10 years at the middle management level and 30 years at the senior management level. According to recent surveys, the average middle manager spends 11 hours a week in meetings. At the senior level, this figure is 23. That amounts to 41,510 meeting hours, or 5,188 eight-hour days, or about 21.6 years of your working life—certainly some justification for learning how to conduct them more productively.

The quality of meetings in your life would improve if:

● There were fewer of them, with fewer people. A meeting of two people is the ideal; three to five is manageable; six or more and you will probably have a show and not a meeting.

● There were fewer topics covered. Fewer topics will mean fewer decisions to be made and fewer minutes to read.

● No one ever called a meeting to prepare for another meeting.

MEETING COSTS

Companies may be under pressure to control costs, but the amount they are spending on meetings continues to rise. An estimated $41.2 billion will be spent on corporate and association conferences this year, up 15 percent from 1987, according to Bjorn Hanson, a hotel specialist for the accounting firm, Laventhol & Horwath.

Bruce Serlen, "Meetings With More Frills—and More Fun," *The New York Times* (9/18/88)

● The rules of each meeting were established at the start as to the length, purpose, agenda, and overall length of speeches permitted.

● The ultimate purpose of each meeting was clear in the minds of all attending, i.e. whether the meeting was being held to:

Determine job responsibilities
Brainstorm (which is invariably done best alone or with just one other person)
Share information
Plan education and training programs
Recognize achievements
Establish or reestablish the power structure or pecking order
Plot future actions

● Everyone present knew who was in charge. Often a clearly established and competent leader can make a meeting more effective. Democracy in meetings is not a value in itself.

● Latecomers were fined in proportion to how much time was wasted multiplied by the hourly salaries of the people involved. While it is the prerogative of presidents to show up late for meetings, they are the ones hurt the most by wasting the time of the staff whose salaries they must pay.

● No one was permitted to say anything negative about a new idea for a least five minutes after it was introduced. New ideas are fragile, no matter how brilliant or pro phetic they are. Like a good red wine, they need to breathe.

REFERENCE MATERIALS

Organizing Principles

Before you embark on any project, keep in mind that the ways of organizing are limited and manageable. The choices aren't overwhelming. You can organize by:

● *Category*. Category lends itself to the organization of goods. Category can mean different models, different types, or even different questions to be answered, such as in a brochure that is divided into questions about a company. This mode lends itself well to organizing items of similar importance.

● *Time*. Time works best as an organizing principle for events that happen over a fixed duration, such as con ventions. Time has also been used creatively to organize a place, such as in the Day in the Life book series. It works with exhibitions, museums, and histories, whether of countries or companies. Time is an easily understandable framework from which changes can be observed and comparisons made.

● *Location*. Location is the natural form to choose when you are trying to examine and compare information that comes from diverse sources or locales. If you were examining an industry, for example, you might want to know how it is distributed around the world. Locationcan work to organize books, such as my **ACCESS** city guides, but it doesn't always have to refer to a geographical site. Doctors use the different locations in the body as groupings to study medicine.

● *Alphabet*. This method lends itself to organizing extraordinarily large bodies of information, such as words in a dictionary or names in a telephone book.

● *Continuum*. This is the mode to use when you want to assign value or weight to the information, when you want to use it to study something like an industry or company. Which department had the highest rate of absenteeism? Which had the least? What is the smallest company engaged in a certain business? What is the largest?

Instruction Manuals

A successful manual should be written in simple language. It should include the time it takes to assemble the equipment, how to recognize when you have done something wrong, how to remedy the problem, and checkpoints along the way for assuring that you are following the instructions correctly.

Unfortunately few manuals meet these criteria. So don't blame yourself if you can't follow the instructions.

● Before you purchase any piece of equipment, make sure that you can operate or at least make arrangements to learn how to operate it. Salespeople trying to convince you to buy a computer will be much more concerned about whether or not you can operate it if they think the sale is contingent on your ability. Once the computer is sitting in a box in your house and the check has cleared, they will be much less sympathetic to your plight.

● Before attempting to assemble any piece of equipment, take a deep breath and try to imagine what it is like to be the thing itself.

● If a manual doesn't meet this criteria, don't blame yourself, blame Sears or Sony.

● See what happens if you leave a few blank spaces next time you fill out a form. If the sky falls, don't do it again. If it doesn't, you will have the tremendous sense of relief that comes from knowing that it doesn't matter.

Giving Instructions

Instruction manuals are only one aspect contained in the field of giving instructions. You could argue that the motivation of all communication is the giving or receiving of instructions. Certainly the sum total of activity in the workplace involves the giving and receiving of instructions. As parents we are synonymous with instructors.

And even in our social relations, we are communicating or "instructing" our friends and relatives as to our thoughts and concerns.

Therefore you would be wise to hone your skills in the art of giving instructions. A model for giving instructions is the directions you might give someone on how to find a restaurant in the country. They should include:

● **Time.** Directions should include the estimated time that the entire drive should take, as well as between points within the drive. *If you are driving in moderate traffic, you should be there in thirty minutes.*

● **Anticipation.** The sights you can expect to see along the way act as reassuring checkpoints that you are on the right path. *You should drive until you see the red brick church and take a right.*

● **Failure.** This is what is often missing from directions, yet is probably the most essential component. All directions should have in them the indications that you have gone too far, the warning lights to turn back. *In other words, if you see a second Mobil station, you have gone too far.*

MEDIA HABITS

● Examine your news habits. Minimize the time you spend reading or watching news that isn't germane to your work or your life. Many people feel compelled to watch the local news every night, when it is often just a listing of crime and catastrophe. If you aren't a criminologist or a fireman, this is probably superfluous information.

● As you watch or read the news, ask yourself the following litany of questions:

Why did the newscaster choose the particular details of the story?

What do the numbers mean?

To what other events does this incident relate?

What is the announcer not telling me?

Why is this story more important
than another?

And, the most crucial question,
how does this story apply to my life?

INFORMATION INVOLVEMENT INVENTORY

Fill out the following form about your news habits and compare the difference between the news you actually peruse and what you think would be desirable. The difference is your information anxiety quotient.

hours per day	**Daily Newspapers**
	Nationally distributed newspapers such as *The Boston Globe, The Chicago Sun-Times, The Wall Street Journal, USA TODAY, The Christian Science Monitor, The Los Angeles Times, The New York Times,* or *The Washington Post.*
	Local newspapers
	Other newspapers
	Total hours per day
	X 365 = hours per year

hours per week	**Weekly Publications,** including *Business Week, The New Yorker, Newsweek, Time, TV Guide,* or *U.S. News & World Report, or Sports Illustrated.*
	Other Weekly Publications
	Total hours per week
	X 52 = hours per year

Monthly or Bi-monthly Publications	*hours per month*
General Interest Magazines such as *American Legion, Changing Times, Family Circle, Harper's, Life, Modern Maturity, Reader's Digest, The Atlantic,* or *Premiere*	
Business Magazines such as *Business Month, Consumer Reports, Entrepreneur, Forbes, Fortune, Inc., Manhattan, inc.,* or *Money*	
Shelter or **Lifestyle Magazines** such as *Architectural Digest, Better Homes & Gardens, Bon Appetit, Good Housekeeping, Gourmet, House & Garden, House Beautiful, Metropolitan Home, Southern Living,* or *Sunset*	
Men's or **Women's Magazines** such as *Cosmopolitan, Elle, Esquire, GQ, Ladies' Home Journal, Lear's, M, McCall's, New Woman, Penthouse, Playboy, Redbook, Woman, Woman's Day,* or *Working Woman*	
Travel Magazines such as *National Geographic, Travel & Leisure,* or *Traveler*	
Science and **Technology Magazines** such as *Byte, Discover, Omni, Popular Science, Prevention, PC World, Science, Scientific American,* or *Smithsonian*	
Sports and **Auto Magazines** such as *Car & Driver, Field & Stream,* or *Road & Track.*	
Other Magazines	

Total hours per month

X 12 = hours per year

Television & Radio

	hours per week
News or news "magazines" such as "60 Minutes," "20/20," or "West 57th Street"	
TV Documentaries or PBS Specials	
Other programs	

Total hours per week

X 52 = hours per year

hours per week

	Books
	Fiction
	Nonfiction
	Biographies
	Miscellaneous Information
	Catalogs
	Atlases or maps
	Reference materials or instruction manuals
	Telephone book
	Other
	On the Job
	Attending meetings or presentations
	Writing or responding to letters, memos, or reports
	Reading trade publications
	Talking on the telephone
	Other
	Total hours per week
	X 52 = hours per year
	ADD UP THE TIME
	*hours per year **Newspapers***
	*hours per year **Weekly Publications***
	*hours per year **Monthly or Bi-monthly Publications***
	*hours per year **Television & Radio***
	*hours per year **Books***
	*hours per year **Miscellaneous Information***
	*hours per year **On the Job***
	Total hours per year involved with information
	Divided by 7 = working days per year

A STARTING POINT

With a map of your media habits, you have a starting point from which you can reduce some of your own information anxiety. You can begin to apply some of the prescriptions outlined in this chapter to your information habits.

● The list should reflect your interests, not your guilt.

● Try to isolate the material that best satisfies your curiosity about the world.

● Go through each listing and try to imagine how your life might be different if you didn't spend time on this item. Then consider eliminating some of the time spent on items that don't add to your life in some way.

● If you spend a considerable amount of time reading about subjects that have nothing to do with your life, but provide you with great satisfaction, try to incorporate these interests into your life or work in some way.

You don't need to fill out the form to recognize that a considerable portion of your life is spent processing information—whether reading, writing, talking, or even listening. Anything that you can do to streamline the amount of information you handle will reduce your anxiety.

Concepts leading us to make investigations are the expressions of our interest, and they direct our interests.

Ludwig Wittgenstein

EPILOGUE

"The most valuable commodity I know of is information. Wouldn't you agree?"

Gordon Gekko, the character played by Michael Douglas in the film *Wall Street*.

*I*nformation anxiety is the product of an information age that caught us ill prepared and anxious.

Perhaps this anxiety will inspire us to discover new ways of producing and understanding information that will reflect the expanding role it plays in our lives. Perhaps we will become accustomed to living in an information society. As the information age matures, so shall we, as information processors. For a long time, people didn't realize how much they didn't know—they didn't know what they didn't know. But now people know what they don't know, and that makes them anxious. Because of this, I think the stage of solutions is imminent and I'm prepared to make some predictions.

In the previous chapter, I have outlined some of the ways individuals can transcend anxiety and improve their information-processing skills. Inevitably, individual efforts will be manifest in the information society at large.

Some of the advancements we might expect are as follows:

● Corporations will turn their attention toward making information more understandable, which will result in a new generation of directories, forms, charts, diagrams, schedules, and handbooks. Particularly, income tax forms, loan and mortgage applications, and insurance forms will be revised.

● Information efforts within corporations will be consolidated with more cooperation between departments such as corporate communications, public relations, and personnel. Information activities will be paid for from single budgets instead of multiple budgets.

● Corporate directories and employee handbooks will become more accessible and pay for themselves by including advertising and through sponsorship. They will become increasingly effective at saving time and reducing confusion.

● The form of financial reports will be drastically altered, specifically annual reports. They will lose their glossy four-color glitz, the photos of plants, products, and members of the board, and will become meaningful documents of communication to underwriters and shareholders. Corporations will save millions of dollars. A major corporation will send its shareholders four extraordinary Xerox-copied pages instead of their usual shining tome.

● More directories to directories will appear. This will speed access to different information sources regarding services and products both in print and electronics.

● The organization of organizations—their implicit and explicit hierarchies, advancement procedures, and decision-making processes—will be demystified by a new series of visual reference books and a new form of dynamic chart.

● Major seminars, conventions, and workshops will be devoted to the topic of information understanding.

● A broad spectrum of the public will get increased exposure to the role that information plays in our lives. Stepped-up media coverage, museum exhibits dealing with information, and even a new phenomenon, an education-oriented entertainment industry that gives college credit, will underscore the importance of making information understandable.

● Realizing how important a sense of geography is to understanding the news, the major networks will amplify as well as simplify their map graphics. This will influence the print media as well. News communicators will embrace the concept that everything takes place some place.

● The U.S. 1990 Census will be completely transformed into visually understandable and entertaining documents, available in print and electronic form, and will be used

regularly by Americans to find out about
America.

● Less copy paper will be sold—not as a move toward the
paperless office, but in response to better judgments
about the information value of all communications, and
a resultant decrease in meaningless copies.

● Courses in conversation, meaning, and understanding
will be required in schools of business, journalism, and
graphic design.

● Art, design, language, and geography courses will be
restructured at the primary and secondary school level
to recognize their role in understanding information.
These courses will emerge as the framework around
which the entire curriculum is structured, providing a
path of wonder, delight, and culture for students.

● The President, in 1992, will create a new Cabinet
post: Secretary of Information or Secretary of Understanding.

● High-resolution color telefax machines will encourage
the development of personalized newspapers and magazines delivered to your home or office.

● Telefax junk mail will be banned by the FCC.

● The Smithsonian Institute will unveil a Museum of
Failure, featuring the extraordinary attempts of science
and industry that didn't work and why. It will become
a huge success overnight.

● Awards for making words and pictures understandable
will be established by the journalism and design fields;
the awards will have the prestige of Oscars.

● The universality of information will be recognized and
exploited.

The age of industry was fueled by the mining of finite
natural resources. Information is infinite and cannot be
treated as a tangible product. It is harder to define, to
control, to predict, but its potential is boundless.

We have only begun to tap the markets for information. It is capital in an unlimited supply. Information isn't just mathematical formulas or instructions for a computer. It is art, advice, technology, theory, and the motivation behind all communications.

Those who profit most from it will be those who recognize its universality and multiple applications. Those who tap into new sources of information with confidence and a sound sense of purpose will be the power brokers of tomorrow.

As the economy adapts to an unlimited supply of capital, we will come to view information in a different light and adjust our vision to accommodate it. And as we become more comfortable with living in an information age, we can shed some of our anxieties about it.

BIBLIOGRAPHY

Adams, James, *The Care and Feeding of Ideas: A Guide to Encouraging Creativity* (Reading, MA: Addison-Wesley Publishing Co., Inc., 1986).

Aynsley, Jeremy, "Graphic Design," *Design History: A Student's Handbook,* Hazel Conway, editor (London: Allen & Unwin, 1987).

Barthes, Roland, *The Grain of the Voice: Interviews 1962-1980*, translated by Linda Coverdale (New York: Hill & Wang, 1985).

Barthes, Roland, *S/Z*, translated by Richard Miller (New York: Hill & Wang, 1974).

Bateson, Gregory, *Steps to an Ecology of Mind* (San Francisco: Chandler Publishing Co., 1972).

Beniger, James R., *The Control Revolution: Technological and Economic Origins of the Information Society* (Cambridge, MA: Harvard University Press, 1986).

Bennis, Warren, *Thoughts from a Victim of Info-Overload Anxiety* (Yellow Springs, OH: Antioch Review, 1977).

Bennis, Warren, and Burt Nanus, *Leaders* (New York: Harper & Row, 1985).

Berger, John, *Ways of Seeing* (London: British Broadcasting Corp. and Penguin Books Ltd., 1972).

Bigge, Morris, *Learning Theories for Teachers* (New York: Harper & Row, 1981).

Blake, Reed, and Edwin Haroldsen, *A Taxonomy of Concepts in Communication* (New York: Hastings House Publishers, 1975).

Bodanis, David, *The Secret House* (New York: Simon & Schuster, 1987).

Boorstin, Daniel, *The Image: A Guide to Psuedo Events in America* (Magnolia, MA: Peter Smith Publishers, Inc., 1984).

Booth-Clibborn, Edward, and Daniel Baroni, *The Language of Graphics* (New York: Abrams Publishers, 1979).

Brand, Stewart, *The Media Lab* (New York: Viking Penguin, Inc., 1987).

Bruner, Jerome, *On Knowing: Essays for the Left Hand* (Cambridge, MA: Harvard University Press, 1966).

Campbell, Jeremy, *Grammatical Man: Information, Entropy, Language, and Life* (New York: Simon & Schuster, 1982).

Caplan, Ralph, *By Design: Why There Are No Locks on the Bathroom Doors in the Hotel Louis XIV and Other Object Lessons* (New York: St. Martin's Press, 1982).

Cherry, Colin, *On Human Communication: A Review, A Survey & A Criticism* , 3rd edition (Cambridge, MA: The MIT Press, 1978).

Clairborne, Robert, *Our Marvelous Native Tongue: The Life and Times of the English Language* (New York: Times Books, 1983).

Cott, Jonathan, *Visions and Voices* (Garden City, NY: Doubleday & Co., 1987).

Crichton, Michael, *Electronic Life: How to Think About Computers* (New York: Ballantine Books, 1983).

Davis, William and Allison McCormack, *The Information Age* (Reading, MA: Addison-Wesley, 1979).

Davison, W. Phillips, James Boylan and Frederic Yu, *Mass Media: Systems and Effects*, 2nd edition (New York: Holt, Rinehart & Winston, 1982).

de Derteau, Michael, "The Jabbering of Social Life," *On Signs*, Marshall Blonsky, editor (Baltimore: The Johns Hopkins University Press, 1985).

de Fleur, Melvin and Everette Dennis, *Understanding Mass Communication*, 2nd edition (Boston: Houghton Mifflin, 1985).

Delany, Samuel R., *Babel-17* (New York: Bantam Books, 1982).

Dexter, Lewis, "Introduction to 'Operation B.A.S.I.C.: The Retrieval of Wasted Knowledge,'" *People, Society and Mass Communications*, Lewis Dexter and David White, editors (New York: The Free Press, 1964).

Diebold, John, Making the Future Work: *Unleashing Our Powers of Innovation for the Decades Ahead* (New York: Simon & Schuster, 1984).

Donnelly, William, *The Confetti Generation: How the New Communications Technology Is Fragmenting America* (New York: Henry Holt, 1986).

Duncan, Hugh, *Communication and Social Order* (New Brunswick, NJ: Transaction Books, 1985).

Edwards, Betty, *Drawing on the Right Side of the Brain: A Course in Enhancing Creativity and Artistic Confidence* (Los Angeles: J.P. Tarcher, 1979).

Fuller, R. Buckminster, *R. Buckminster Fuller on Education*, Peter Wagschal and Robert Kahn, editors (Amherst: The University of Massachusetts Press, 1979).

Gardner, Martin, *Aha! Insight* (New York: Scientific American Inc., 1978).

Gordon, George, *The Communications Revolution: A History of Mass Media in the United States* (New York: Comunication Arts Books, 1977).

Greenberg, Bradley, "Mass Media in the United States in the 1980s," *The Media Revolution in America and* in *Western Europe*, Everett Rogers and Francis Balle, editors (New Jersey: Ablex Publishing, 1985).

The Grolier International Dictionary, Vol. 1 (Danbury, CT: Grolier Incorporated, 1981).

Hampden-Turner, Charles, *Maps of the Mind* (London: Mitchell Beazley Publishers, Ltd., 1981).

Heim, Michael, *Electric Language: A Philosophical Study of Word Processing* (New Haven, CT: Yale University Press, 1987).

Hertzberg, Hendrik, *One Million* (New York: Simon & Schuster, 1970).

Hirsch, E.D., Jr., *Cultural Literacy: What Every American Needs to Know* (Boston: Houghton Mifflin, 1987).

The History of Cartography. Harley, J. B. and David Woodward, editors, (Chicago: The University of Chicago Press, 1987).

Hofstadter, Douglas R., *Metamagical Themas* (New York: Basic Books, 1985).

Holmes, Nigel, *A Designer's Guide to Creating Charts & Diagrams* (New York: Watson-Guptill Publications, 1984).

Hunter, Carmen St. John, and David Harman, *Adult Illiteracy in the United States: A Report to the Ford Foundation* (New York: McGraw Hill Book Company, 1979).

Kahn, Louis, *What Will Be Has Always Been*, Richard Saul Wurman, editor (New York: Access Press and Rizzoli International, 1986).

Kirshenblatt-Gimblett, Barbara, editor, *Speech Play: Research and Resources for Studying Linguistic Creativity* (Harrisburg: The University of Pennsylvania Press, 1976).

Klapp, Orrin, *Overload and Boredom: Essays on the Quality of Life in the Information Society* (New York: Greenwood Press, 1986).

Klee, Paul, *Notebooks*, Volume 2: The Nature of Nature (London: Lund Humphries, 1973).

Koestler, Arthur, *The Act of Creation*, 2nd edition (London: Hutchinson & Co. Ltd., 1976).

Kozol, Jonathan, *Illiterate America* (Garden City, NY: Anchor Press/Doubleday & Co., 1985).

Kundera, Milan, *The Unbearable Lightness of Being*, translated by Michael Heim (New York: Harper & Row, 1984).

Landau, Sidney, *Dictionaries: The Art and Craft of Lexicography* (New York: Scribner, 1984).

Large, Peter, *The Micro Revolution Revisited* (New Jersey: Rowman & Allanheld Company, 1984).

Lederman, Linda Costigan, "Communication in the Workplace: The Impact of the Information Age and High Technology on Interpersonal Communication in Organizations," *Intermedia: Interpersonal Communication in a Media World*, 3rd edition, Gary Gumpert and Robert Cathcart, editors (New York: The Oxford University Press, 1986).

Markham, Beryl, *West with the Night* (Berkeley, CA: North Point Press, 1983).

Mayer, Richard, *Thinking, Problem Solving, Cognition* (New York: W.H. Freeman & Co., 1983).

Minsky, Marvin, *The Society of Mind* (New York: Simon &Schuster, 1985).

Musil, Robert, *The Man Without Qualities* (New York: G.P. Putnam's Sons, 1980).

Nadolny, Sten, *The Discovery of Slowness*, translated by Ralph Freedman (New York: Viking, 1987).

Naisbitt, John, *Megatrends* (New York: Warner Books, Inc., 1982).

Naisbitt, John, and Patricia Aburdene, *Re-inventing the Corporation: Transforming Your Job and Your Company* (New York: Warner Books, Inc., 1985).

The National Advisory Council on Adult Education Literacy Committee, *Illiteracy in America: Extent, Causes and Suggested Solutions* (Washington: U.S. Government Printing Office, 1986).

The National Directory of Addresses and Telephone Numbers (Kirkland, WA: General Information, Inc., 1987-88).

Nietzsche, Friedrich, *Ecce Homo* (London: Penguin Books, Ltd., 1979).

Nietzsche, Friedrich, *The Gay Science*, translated by Walter Kaufmann (New York: Random House, 1974).

Papert, Seymour, *Mindstorms: Children, Computers, and Powerful Ideas* (New York: Basic Books, Inc., 1982).

Phelan, John, Mediaworld: *Programming the Public* (New York: The Seabury Press, 1977).

The Random House Dictionary of the English Language, unabridged edition (New York: Random House, 1979).

Raskin, Eugene, *Architecturally Speaking* (New York: Bloch Publishing Co., 1970).

Reichman, Frieda Fromm, "Psychiatric Aspects of Anxiety," *Identity and Anxiety: Survival of the Person in Mass Society*, Maurice Stein, Arthur Vidich, and David White, editors (Glencoe: The Free Press, 1960).

Rifkin, Jeremy, *Entropy* (New York: Bantam Books, Inc., 1981).

Robbins, Tom, *Even Cowgirls Get the Blues* (New York: Bantam Books, 1976).

Rogers, Carl R., *Freedom to Learn for the Eighties* (Columbus, OH: Merrill Publishing Co., 1983).

Rosenberg, Richard, *Computers and the Information Society* (New York: John Wiley & Sons, 1986).

Roszak, Theodore, *The Cult of Information: The Folklore of Computers and the True Art of Thinking* (New York: Pantheon Books, 1986).

Salk, Jonas, *The Survival of the Wisest* (New York: Harper & Row, 1973).

Schramm, Wilbur and William Porter, *Men, Women, Messages and Media: Understanding Human Communication, 2nd edition* (New York: Harper & Row Publishers, 1982).

Schwartz, Barry, "Video Tape and the Communications Revolution," *Human Connection and the New Media*, Barry Schwartz, editor (Englewood Cliffs, NJ: Prentice-Hall, Inc., 1973).

Severin, Werner and James Tankard, Jr., *Communication Theories: Origins, Methods, Uses*, 2nd edition (New York: Pitman, 1987).

Shallis, Michael, *The Silicon Idol: The Micro Revolution and its Social Implications* (New York: Schocken Books, 1984).

Shannon, Claude and Warren Weaver, *The Mathematical Theory of Communication* (Champaign-Urbana: The University of Illinois Press, 1949).

Shipley, Joseph T., *In Praise of English: The Growth and Use of Language* (New York: Times Books, 1977).

Simons, Geoff, *Silicon Shock: The Menace of the Computer Invasion* (New York: Basil Blackwell Inc., 1985).

Singleton, Loy, *Telecommunications in the Information Age* (New York: Ballinger, 1984).

Solomon, William, "The Newspaper Business," *Mass Media and Society*, Allan Wells, editor (Massachusetts: Lexington Books, 1987).

Sparke, Penny, *An Introduction to Design and Culture in the Twentieth Century* (London: Allen & Unwin, 1986).

Stanley, Robert, *Mediavisions: The Art and Industry of Mass Communication* (New York: Praeger, 1987).

Sterne, Laurence, *The Life and Opinions of Tristram Shandy, Gentleman* (New York: The Odyssey Press, Inc., 1940)

Stillman, Stanley, editor, *The Information Industry: Structure, Characteristics and Trends* (New York: Access Publishing Company, 1987).

Stone, Lawrence, "Literacy and Education in England 1640-1900," *The Past and the Present* (Boston: Routledge & K. Paul, 1981).

Toffler, Alvin, *Future Shock* (New York: Random House, 1970).

Tufte, Edward, *Envisioning Information* (Cheshire, CT: Graphics Press, 1989).

Tufte, Edward, *The Visual Display of Quantitative Information* (Cheshire, CT: Graphics Press, 1983).

Waterman, Robert, *The Renewal Factor* (New York: Bantam Books, 1987).

Webster's New World Dictionary of the American Language, David Guralnik, editor (New York: Simon & Schuster, 1982).

Wenk, Edward, Jr., *Tradeoffs: Imperatives of Choice* in *a High-Tech World* (Baltimore: The Johns Hopkins University Press, 1986).

Whorf, Benjamin, *Language, Thought, and Reality* (Cambridge, MA: The MIT Press, 1956).

Widmer, Kingsley, "Sensibility Under Technocracy," *Human Connection and the New Media*, Barry Schwartz, editor (Englewood Cliffs, NJ: Prentice-Hall, Inc., 1973).

Wurman, Richard Saul, **ACCESS** Guide Series (20 vols.) (New York: Access Press).

Wurman, Richard Saul, *Cities: Comparisons of Form and Scale* (Philadelphia: Joshua Press, 1974).

Wurman, Richard Saul, *Yellow Pages of Learning Resources*, written by George Borowsky et al. (Cambridge, MA: The MIT Press, 1972).

Zinsser, William, *On Writing Well* (New York: Harper & Row, 1976).

ACKNOWLEDGEMENTS

I clearly recognize that I couldn't have produced this project without the efforts of the extraordinary team of people who contributed to this book.

My translator **Loring Leifer** turned Wurmanspeak into English. She knows how to ask good questions and she isn't afraid to yell back.

Michael Everitt, my left hand (I am left-handed) and design associate, turned my rough sketches and scribbles into real pages, something he has been doing for the last eight years. He also oversaw the computer formatting and typography of the entire manuscript.

Boy wonder **Nathan Shedroff,** an industrial design student on leave from the Art Center in Pasadena, filled in gaps with fresh ideas for the text and graphics.

Loretta Barrett, an executive vice-president and my editor at Doubleday, had the foresight to see a book in what started as hundreds of pages of conversation transcripts and the fortitude to stick around until they were turned into one.

My patron saint **Nancy Evans,** president of Doubleday, gave the manuscript her close personal attention and on-the-mark suggestions for improving it. Then she helped to tell the world about it.

So did **Jackie Deval** in the promotions department at Doubleday.

Maura Carey Damacion took on the task of copy-editing, compiling a bibliography, abstracting marginalia, and then asked if there was anything else she could do.

My research associate **Lonnie Browning** put her critical eye toward assembling relevant marginalia.

Sally Sisson, Sarah Riegelman, Ruth Kedar, Loretta Staples, Jerry Stanton, Richard Scheve, Denia Kirwan, Lisa Stage, Henia Miedzinski, Nancy Campana, Rob Healy, Heidi Thompson, Kristina Clarke and Francesca Vass helped with the nitty-gritty details of the production of the book.

The manuscript for *Information Anxiety* was produced electronically, using using Aldus' *PageMaker*™ software, in conjunction with graphic software tools including Aldus' *Freehand*™, Adobe's *Illustrator*™, Silicon Beach's *SuperPaint*™, DataCopy's *MacImage*™, and Think Technology's *MORE*™. The text for the book was set in 11 point Times and the marginalia in 8 point Helvetica Bold, both by Adobe Systems, Inc.

A very special thanks to **Mark Johnson** who is the minder of my maze and who helps me find the path through it.

Many people contributed their time and ideas toward the realization of this book—talking with me about their thoughts regarding the problem of *information anxiety*, allowing me to reprint portions of their own work, or suggesting new directions for the manuscript. Their contributions have given a special depth of texture to this book.

I am indebted to the following people who spoke with me about their ideas on the problem of *information anxiety*: **Peter Bradford** (who also allowed me to reprint photos from his book, *Chairs*), **Tom Brokaw, Dick Brass, Vartan Gregorian, Nigel Holmes, Joel Katz, Paul Kaufman, Alan Kay, Ed Schlossberg, John Sculley, Robert Waterman,** and **Josh Wurman**.

The following people made other contributions to the book: **Jim Cross** for graphics of Fluor Corporation, **Rudy De Harak** for the Communicard, **John Naisbitt** for the introduction, **Sally O'Malley** and **Loring Leifer** for their résumés, **Nathan Felde** and **Lance Shaw** for Fat- Free Daily Reading Diet, **Siegel & Gale** for graphics, **Frank Stanton** for marginalia, **Edward Tufte** for contributing camera-ready art for graphics and allowing me to reprint passages from his book, and **William Zinsser** for his wisdom on writing well.

And finally, there are the people who were involved at the early but essential stage of fits, starts, and stalls that got the book moving: **Eric Baker, Debra Gailin,** and **Tom Wood**.

THANK YOU

For permission to reprint excerpts from copyrighted material, the author is indebted to the following authors and publishers:

THE ANTIOCH REVIEW for *Thoughts from a Victim of Info-Overload Anxiety* by Warren Bennis. Copyright 1974 by The Antioch Review, Inc.

BANTAM BOOKS for *Even Cowgirls Get the Blues* by Tom Robbins. Copyright 1976 by Thomas Robbins.

PAULA BERN PH.D. for "The Art of Listening," published in the May 1988 issue of *New Woman*.

BLOCH PUBLISHING CO., INC., for *Architecturally Speaking* by Eugene Raskin. Copyright 1970 by Eugene Raskin.

THE BODLEY HEAD for *Future Shock* by Alvin Toffler, for sale in the British Commonwealth excluding Canada.

GEMINI SMITH, INC. for *One Million* by Hendrik Hertzberg. Copyright 1970 by Hendrick Hertzberg.

GRAPHICS PRESS for *The Visual Display of Quantitative Information* by Edward Tufte. Copyright 1983 by Edward Tufte.

JEFF GREENWALD for "On Maps," published in the March 15, 1987 issue of *The San Francisco Examiner*.

GREENWOOD PRESS for *Overload and Boredom: Essays on the Quality of Life in the Information Age* by Orrin Klapp. (Contributions in Sociology, No. 57) Copyright 1986 by Orrin Klapp.

HARPER & ROW, PUBLISHERS, INC. for *The Survival of the Wisest* by Jonas Salk. Copyright 1973 by Jonas Salk.

RICHARD SAUL WURMAN

With the publication of his first book in 1962 at the age of 26, Richard Saul Wurman began the singular passion of his life: that of making information understandable. In his 45th book, *Information Anxiety*, he has developed an overview of the motivating principles found in his previous work. Each project has focused on some subject or idea that he personally had difficulty understanding. His work stems from his desire to know, rather than from his already knowing—from his ignorance rather than his intelligence, from his inability rather than his ability.

Along the way, Richard Saul Wurman has received both master's and bachelor's degrees in architecture from the University of Pennsylvania, where in 1959 he was graduated with highest honors and where he established a deep personal and professional relationship with the architect Louis I. Kahn. He is a fellow of the American Institute of Architects, a vice-president of the American Institute of Graphic Arts, and a member of the Alliance Graphique Internationale. He has been awarded several grants from the National Endowment for the Arts, a Guggenheim Fellowship, two Graham Fellowships, and two Chandler Fellowships.

A parallel channel for his ideas about communication has been his involvement with a number of conferences. He chaired the International Design Conference in Aspen in 1972, co-chaired the First Federal Design assembly in 1973, chaired the American Institute of Architects convention in 1976, and co-chaired the Technology Entertainment Design (TED) conference in 1984.

His career has spanned a 13-year architectural partnership to teaching (Cambridge University, England; City College, New York; University of Southern California; University of California, Los Angeles; Washington University, St. Louis; Princeton University; North Carolina State University, Raleigh; and serving as dean at California State Polytechnic University, Pomona) to city government as deputy director of Housing and Community Development in Philadelphia to consultant to the Jerde Partnership and Charles Eames.

He is currently co-owner of **ACCESS**Press Ltd. (with Frank Stanton, president emeritus of CBS, Inc.), and president of The Understanding Business (TUB). A major recent project has been the annual restructuring and design of the 33,000,000 Yellow Pages directories distributed in California by Pacific Bell Directory. In addition to his **ACCESS** travel guides to London, Paris, Rome, Tokyo and major U.S. cities, his latest publications are *Wall Street Journal ACCESS*, *MoMA ACCESS*, *What Will Be Has Always Been: the Words of Louis I. Kahn,* and the development of a new road atlas of the U.S. He is a regular consultant to major corporations in matters relating to the design and understanding of information and communications.

Richard Saul Wurman is married to novelist Gloria Nagy, has four children, and lives in Manhattan and Bridgehampton, New York.